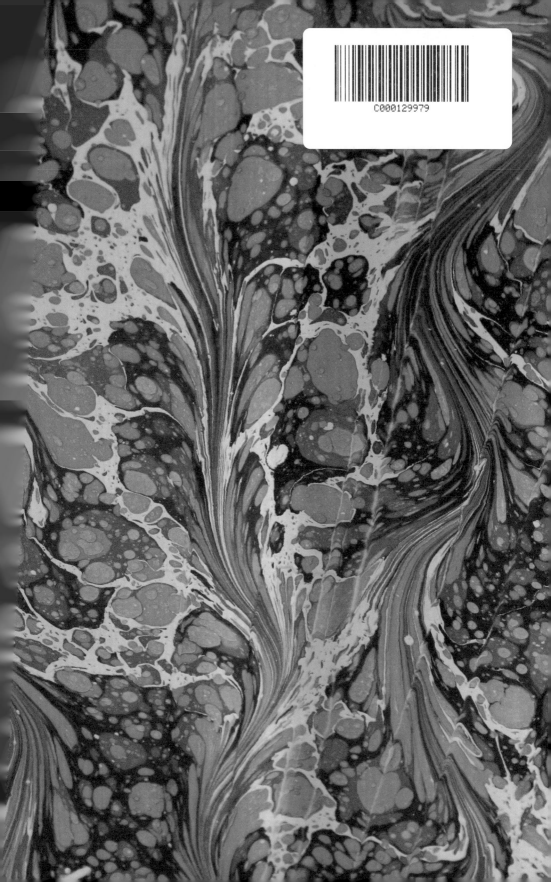

EX LIBRIS

P. G. WODEHOUSE

ABOVE AVERAGE AT ≡GAMES≡

EDITED BY

Richard T. Kelly

HUTCHINSON
LONDON

1 3 5 7 9 10 8 6 4 2

Hutchinson
20 Vauxhall Bridge Road
London SW1V 2SA

Hutchinson is part of the Penguin Random House group of companies
whose addresses can be found at global.penguinrandomhouse.com

www.penguin.co.uk

A CIP catalogue record for this book is available from the British Library

ISBN 9781786332004

Typeset in 11.75/16 pt Adobe Caslon Pro
by Integra Software Services Pvt. Ltd, Pondicherry

Printed and bound in Great Britain by Clays Ltd, Elcograf S.p.A.

Penguin Random House is committed to a sustainable future for
our business, our readers and our planet. This book is made from
Forest Stewardship Council® certified paper.

CONTENTS

Foreword by Henry Blofeld   1

Introduction by Richard T. Kelly   7

'Some Aspects of Game-Captaincy' (1900)   13

'Now, Talking About Cricket' (1901)   17

'Football, My Dear Sir, Why?' (1901)   26

'The Sports': from *The Pothunters* (1902)   32

New York Baseball: Reportage for *Vanity Fair* (1904)   37

Sheen's Shot at Redemption: from *The White Feather* (1907)   46

'The Rout at Ripton': Rugby in *The White Feather* (1907)   72

'A cricket genius': Various Innings by *Mike* (1907)   81

Mike and Psmith (1908)   115

From *Psmith in the City* (1910)   132

'Reginald's Record Knock' (1909)   148

Cricket, Baseball, and 'Rounders': from *Piccadilly Jim* (1917)   166

'A Plea for Indoor Golf' (1919)   174

'A Woman Is Only A Woman' (1919)   181

'Ordeal By Golf' (1919)   203

'Sundered Hearts' (1920)   225

'The Salvation of George Mackintosh' (1921)   246

'The Clicking of Cuthbert' (1921)   264

'The Magic Plus Fours' (1922)   282

'The Awakening of Rollo Podmarsh' (1923)   304

CONTENTS

'The Heart of a Goof' (1923)   324

The Pride of Bermondsey: 'The Exit of Battling
Billson' (1923)   350

'Prospects for Wambledon' (1932)   374

Wodehouse & Cricket: Interregnum Years   385

'How's That, Umpire?' (1950)   388

Preface to *The Golf Omnibus* (1973)   405

FOREWORD

By Henry Blofeld

There is nothing more wonderful in life than to be asked to write a foreword to a collection of writings by P.G. Wodehouse. The problem is how to do it. For me, Wodehouse is synonymous with perfection. All I can do is bask in a reflected glory and hope no literary suntan lotion would ever be able to shield me from the fun, the joy, the characters, the charming and gentle irreverence and, above all, those unforgettable, apt and original similes which every time hit the nail squarely on the head, or *rem acu tetigisti* as Jeeves would have put it.

First things first: the editor, Richard T. Kelly, has been brilliant. He has picked out a fantastic selection of PGW's sporting output. Easy, perhaps, to pick out some plums (pun intended), but they are all plums, and the difficult bit is what on earth to leave out. All of us impassioned Wodehouse disciples are honorary Clever Dicks and have our own pieces which surely no one in their senses could leave out. If Richard had gone that way, we would have had just about the entire works of Wodehouse, for they are all stuffed full with envious and glorious sporting allusions and metaphors.

Of course the cricket stories, which the great man wrote at the start of his unique literary adventure, have grabbed me the most among the sporting stories. If I have a complaint about Wodehouse, and perish the thought, it is that his decision to make so much of his life in America meant the inevitable and, I have to say, extremely comfortable, switch from cricket to baseball. Fuller Pilch and Alfred Mynn gave way to Babe Ruth and the pitcher. At Lord's Cricket Ground, Mike Jackson's peerless cover drive is greeted with contained applause; across the pond a home run is greeted by an hysterical ululating of noise inspired and directed by the 'Rooter-in-Chief', who is employed as a cheerleader and is positioned, as you would expect, 'back of first base'. Richard has included a wonderful story from *Piccadilly Jim*. An American actor, Bingley Crocker, has hit lucky marrying into a rich English family and is in tolerable exile in Grosvenor Square, London, SW1. At breakfast, the butler, Bayliss, also happily the name of England cricket's current Australian coach, tries to explain events at the Oval after watching Surrey and Kent do battle on a sticky wicket. A scene not to be missed.

I get very excited about the Jackson saga. Mike Jackson, a highly talented young batsman from a well-to-do cricketing family, has an entertaining upbringing at two public schools, Wrykyn and then Sedleigh. At the latter, he meets up with Psmith, one of PGW's greatest inventions – the P is, of course, silent – and their adventures in three books are about as good as it gets. I identify with the Mike and Psmith saga because when Mike's father fell on hard times, he found himself thrust into the City of London as a trainee banker. The same fate befell me when, after two years, my academic prowess failed to measure up to the requirements of King's College, Cambridge. Wodehouse, personified by Mike, enjoyed this scintillating experience about as much as I did. Mike's relationship with Mr Bickersdyke, who became his boss at the New Asiatic

Bank, was a little bit like mine with a Mr Paine – although at least Mr Paine did not walk in front of the sight screen when I had scored 98.

Wodehouse hugely enjoyed his years at boarding school and he was a notable games player, always a useful path to popularity. He was at Dulwich, where he played cricket and football, which was of course Rugby and not Association, a game which at his time would have been frowned upon. All through his life, which was lived out in America after the Second World War, the results of Dulwich's matches against other schools were of extraordinary importance to him. On his occasional visits to England in the twenties and thirties, he would time his visits to coincide with their big matches. The school Dulwich feared most in rugby was Bedford. On one occasion he watched a match when they beat Bedford and, such was his delirious happiness, that he walked all the way from Dulwich to his house in Davies Street, W1.

Part of Pelham (Plum) Grenville Wodehouse never grew up, and certainly no part of him appeared to take any account of a fast-changing world. This was his charm and the schoolboy within him is still present in everything he wrote. There is a wonderful childlike enthusiasm which shines through especially in his descriptions of action in the sporting stories within this book. When I read them, I feel I can picture in my mind exactly how events unfolded, be it Jackson batting or Psmith bowling his off breaks. Psmith was based on Rupert d'Oyley Carte, but I wonder if his off spin was a product of his friendship with Sir Aubrey 'Round-The-Corner' Smith. He captained England in the only Test Match in which he played (in South Africa in 1888/89); became a famous film actor; and started the Hollywood Cricket Club for which Wodehouse was vice-president during his years in the west as a screenwriter.

For a short time while he was at a Dulwich, Wodehouse was a boxer until his bad eyesight put a stop to it. The story of Sheen boxing himself to glory for Wrykyn in the competition at Aldershot is terrifically exciting and could only have been written by someone who had himself been in the ring. There are also four stories about an unlikely pugilist, Wilberforce 'Battling' Billson, who was picked by Stanley Featherstonehaugh Ukridge, PGW's entertaining main chancer, who always imagined he was on the threshold of riches. At one point, he thought managing a boxer was the answer; the red-haired Battler showed him it was not. Wodehouse was also involved in athletics at Dulwich and there is a stirring account of Drake (no first name) beating a Jim Thomson in the mile, winning by no more than a foot in just about the last stride on the School Sports Day of St Austin's College. Wodehouse was never a wet bob and rowing never came his way, but he knew the breed. One of Bertie Wooster's friends was G. 'Stilton' Cheesewright, who was Captain of Boats at Eton, in the Oxford boat for four years, and had 'a head like a solid concrete pumpkin'.

The last sport to grab Wodehouse was golf – and grab him it did. He wrote some wonderful (and wonderfully self-deprecating) pieces about his own golf, which for one brief, heady moment actually embraced an eighteen handicap. He once won a striped umbrella in a tournament at Aiken in South Carolina. 'I went through a field of some of the fattest retired businessmen in America like a devouring flame,' was how he put it. His golf stories were brilliantly done and produced some unforgettable characters. The Oldest Member, who told so many of these stories, was always excellent and never the bore that, by rights, he should have been. There was Mitchell Holmes who 'missed short putts because he was put off by the uproar of the butterflies in the adjoining meadow'. The meeting of the famous Russian novelist, Vladimir Brusiloff with Cuthbert (called 'Cootaboot' by the Russian) is a highlight. There is often romance on the horizon too, with many a captivating lady around to either hinder or help with the game at hand.

I could go on for ever. This is a supreme collection of Wodehouse's sporting stories and it is a book I shall take with me wherever I go. I shall not read it too fast for then it would be over all too soon. It will ensure I go to sleep with a smile on my face for some time to come. Thank you, Richard T. Kelly, and eternal applause, of course, to the Great Man himself.

INTRODUCTION

By Richard T. Kelly

Sports fans who seek to find their love of the game reflected on a printed page don't always get the greatest pickings from the fictional canon. While the pleasures of great sports reporting are amply on offer – see Norman Mailer, George Plimpton, Michael Lewis, Hugh McIlvanney et al. – fewer imaginative storytellers seem to possess the true knack for making the game come alive in words. I expect, reader, that you are a sports fan yourself, and you might well hold a few sporting novels in high esteem. But just a handful, perhaps?*

I'd venture this is because sports have their own special drama: an inherent rise-and-fall of action in their real-life narratives of success or failure that engage our giddiest emotions – excitement, wonder, commingled joy and sorrow. When we watch sport we see great dramatic archetypes appear before our eyes – the consummate artist, the flat-track bully, the dogged underdog, the comeback kid;

---

* This fan's top picks, in case you don't know them, would include *Playing Days* by Benjamin Markovits, *Chinaman* by Shehan Karunalitaka, *The Rider* by Tim Krabbé and *This Sporting Life* by David Storey.

and an accomplished sportswriter knows how to use those inches on the back pages to remind us of what we saw. But for us scribes who look to make things up for our living? The suspicion persists that sport contains its very own artistic perfection, which the storyteller envies and labours to imitate.

It's a factor also that a lot of very fine and artful sports fiction tends towards studies in failure, and can be gloomy on that score. So it helps if the writer brings a sense of irony, an appreciation that the obsessiveness of games has its comical side, approximate to the follies of humankind. And it goes a long way, too, if the writer has actually played, and played well.

P.G. Wodehouse was an ardent, lifelong sports fan who wrote with distinction on a rich range of games: boxing, rugby, athletics were all grist to his mill. He pitched in and played up, and always saw the funny side. He wrote about cricket and golf, in particular, about as well as anyone ever has. And Wodehouse was, for sure, a proper player, a true baller. As a cricketer, he made runs and took wickets at Lord's. (Even 'Plum', the fond family diminutive that he embraced, had a cricketing dimension – young Wodehouse having been pleased to learn that Middlesex batsman Pelham Warner enjoyed the same nickname.) As a golfer, well ... Wodehouse was more of an 18-handicap man, beginning rather too late to get very much better; and yet, as his biographer Frances Donaldson notes, the golfing stories bear witness that 'his theoretical knowledge is immense'.

This anthology is a selective tour through the sporting side of Wodehouse's oeuvre, beginning with early school sports journalism, taking in extended extracts from certain novels, and noteworthy short stories in their entirety. The intention has been to do justice to the breadth and delights of his storytelling on this subject. The fare is arranged more or less chronologically, in order of composition, introduced and linked here and there so as to give the lay reader some attendant understanding of the course of the author's remarkable writing life.

Wodehouse's school years at Dulwich College from 1894 to 1900 were more meaningful to him than to most, perhaps. He enjoyed them hugely, for one, which is rare in itself; but they also proved the womb of his future literary production. At Dulwich he was, as his friend William Townend testified, 'a noted athlete, a fine footballer and cricketer, a boxer'. And his experiences, and his enjoyment, gave him his debut in print by way of *Public School Magazine*, as well as the inspiration for his earliest fictions. As Frances Donaldson observed:

> 'No boy who is good at games ever has a bad time at school. He is assured of the admiration of his fellows ... It was important to Plum's later career that he was above average at games. In the school stories both games and boxing are described with a practical knowledge, and an enthusiasm which only personal participation and enjoyment could give.'*

The school stories set Wodehouse's fiction off on a firmly sporting foot, with cricket leading the pack, but with boxing, athletics and rugby bunched close behind. The reader will see an intriguing shift of focus circa 1904, as Wodehouse developed an interest in baseball during his first trip to New York (a *Hey, Manhattan!* encounter with the exuberant promise of that city, which endured and changed him majorly). His principal cricket writing was still to come, in the sequence of fictions from 1907 to 1910 that starred batting prodigy Mike Jackson; and those works are generously represented here. George Orwell and Evelyn Waugh, the best English writers

---

* p.49

of their era, are there to vouch for the standard that Wodehouse achieved with *Mike*.

Wodehouse's romance with America, though, would only deepen; he married in New York in October 1914 and settled thereafter in Long Island, whereupon the chief concentration of his sports fiction changed utterly. The Sound View Golf Club was his new stomping ground, and, from 1919 especially, golf was his game, as Wodehouse increasingly performed for a US audience more or less impervious to the smack of willow on leather. He missed the cricket, no doubt; but Wodehouse was nothing if not a professional, with a perennially keen eye on the marketplace. As Benny Green puts it, 'In changing from an English readership and scene to meet his American public, in kissing cricket goodbye, Wodehouse did so only in fiction, not in life; passionately though he loved the game, he knew it must be expelled from his work.'

This is not for one moment to suggest the merest slip in the quality of the product. Wodehouse's golfing tales are a rightly revered strand of his productions, and their advocates are just as blue-chip as for the cricket. Take John Updike, a keen Wodehousian from his teens and similarly the curator of 'a hard-won and precarious handicap of eighteen'. For Updike, Wodehouse's golf stories are 'just as wonderful as the rest, and to this day they seem the best fiction ever done about the sport'.

The organising principle of this volume next to chronology is variety; but one hopes the reader will find the whole thing both relishable and properly representative, with a good number of match-winning innings set next to some lesser-appreciated knocks; not to mention a few early juvenile medal-winning efforts that the author put on the clubhouse board before his great run of major titles began.

P. G. Wodehouse

P. G. Wodehouse in cricket whites in front of Dulwich College.
Reproduced by kind permission of the Governors of Dulwich College.

The Dulwich Classical VI Cricket XI, 1899. Wodehouse is seated to the left of the captain. Reproduced by kind permission of the Governors of Dulwich College.

'SOME ASPECTS OF
GAME-CAPTAINCY'

*We begin where Wodehouse began as a published writer: in his school
years and the years straight after, during which he put into print occasional short humorous pieces reporting or reflecting on sport. Here we
find him limbering up and trying out his muscles as a humorist, working
towards 'the voice' that will see him durably through a seventy-year
writing career.*

*He was nineteen, still at Dulwich in February 1900, when he enjoyed
his first paid publication. An essay entitled 'Some Aspects of Game-
Captaincy' appeared as a prize-winning contribution to* Public School
Magazine, *for which effort he received ten shillings and sixpence.*

*This little essay might (at a squint) be granted a modest place in the
literature regarding leadership on the sports field, which is an acknowledged art (or science.) You can make out here key elements of later
Wodehouse style – the internal rhythms of his sentences, the blithe allusions to the ancients and the Bible ('changed withal'), and the wry view
of human foibles – as evidenced in school sports by those who prefer not
to play up but, rather, to find out what is the very least they might get
away with.*

*

To the Game-Captain (of the football variety) the world is peopled by three classes, firstly the keen and regular player, next the partial slacker, thirdly, and lastly, the entire, abject and absolute slacker.

Of the first class, the keen and regular player, little need be said. A keen player is a gem of purest rays serene, and when to his keenness he adds regularity and punctuality, life ceases to become the mere hollow blank that it would otherwise become, and joy reigns supreme.

The absolute slacker (to take the worst at once, and have done with it) needs the pen of a Swift before adequate justice can be done to his enormities. He is a blot, an excrescence. All those moments which are not spent in avoiding games (by means of that leave which is unanimously considered the peculiar property of the French nation) he uses in concocting ingenious excuses. Armed with these, he faces with calmness the disgusting curiosity of the Game-Captain, who officiously desires to know the reason of his non-appearance on the preceding day. These excuses are of the 'had-to-go-and-see-a-man-about-a-dog' type, and rarely meet with that success for which their author hopes. In the end he discovers that his chest is weak, or his heart is subject to palpitations, and he forthwith produces a document to this effect, signed by a doctor. This has the desirable result of muzzling the tyrannical Game-Captain, whose sole solace is a look of intense and withering scorn. But this is seldom fatal, and generally, we rejoice to say, ineffectual.

The next type is the partial slacker. He differs from the absolute slacker in that at rare intervals he actually turns up, changed withal into the garb of the game, and thirsting for the fray. At this point begins the time of trouble for the Game-Captain. To begin with, he is forced by stress of ignorance to ask the newcomer his name. This is, of course, an insult of the worst kind. 'A being who does not know my name,' argues the partial slacker, 'must be something not far from a criminal lunatic.' The name is, however, extracted, and the partial slacker strides to the arena. Now arises insult No. 2. He is wearing his cap. A hint as to the advisability of removing this piece de resistance not being taken, he is ordered to assume a capless state, and by these means a coolness springs up between him and the G.-C. Of this the Game-Captain is made aware when the game commences. The partial slacker, scorning to insert his head in the scrum, assumes a commanding position outside and from this point criticises the Game-Captain's decisions with severity and pith. The last end of the partial slacker is generally a sad one. Stung by some pungent home-thrust, the Game-Captain is fain to try chastisement, and by these means silences the enemy's battery.

Sometimes the classes overlap. As for instance, a keen and regular player may, by some more than usually gross bit of bungling on the part of the G.-C., be moved to a fervour and eloquence worthy of Juvenal. Or, again, even the absolute slacker may for a time emulate the keen player, provided an opponent plant a shrewd kick on a tender spot. But, broadly speaking, there are only three classes.

Authors v. Publishers.

TUESDAY, AUGUST 22.

PUBLISHERS.	First Innings.	Second Innings.
1 W. Cutbush	c Croome, b Doyle 0	
2 W. Farquharson	c Selincourt, b Doyle ... 0	
3 R. Truslove	b Wodehouse 27	
4 A. G. Agnew	b Wodehouse 82	
5 A. C. Dene	b Thurston................... 60	
6 L. E. G. Abney	b Wodehouse 19	
7 W. Longman	b Wodehouse 5	
8 S. S. Pawling	run out 0	
9 E. Fagg	c Croome, b Thurston ... 8	
10 F. J. Harvey Darton	st Croome, b Thurston... 24	
11 H. H. Thomas	not out 5	
	B 4, l-b 2, w 4, n-b , 10	B , l-b , w , n-b ,
	Total 240	Total ....

BOWLING ANALYSIS.

Name.	O.	1st Innings. M. R. W. Wds. N-b.	2nd Innings. O. M. R. W. Wds. N-b.
Doyle	13	4 38 2	.. ..
Selincourt	7	1 23 0	.. ..
Irwin	7	1 37 0 1 ..	.. ..
Croome	9	1 23 0 2 ..	.. ..
Wodehouse	20	3 75 4	.. ..
Thurston	4.3	0 16 3	.. ..
Scott	2	0 13 0 1 ..	.. ..

AUTHORS.	First Innings.	Second Innings.
1 R. B. J. Scott	b Thomas 24	
2 A. Worsley	c Pawling, b Cutbush ... 75	
3 A. C. M. Croome	c and b Thomas 0	
4 P. G. Wodehouse	c Pawling, b Cutbush ... 60	
5 Sir A. Conan Doyle	b Pawling 14	
6 W. Livingstone Irwin	c Cutbush, b Pawling ... 6	
7 E. Temple Thurston	c Dene, b Longman 10	
8 Hugh de Selincourt	c and b Longman 7	
9 Gunby Hadath	not out 5	
10 G. C. Ives	not out 1	
11 John Barnett		
	B 11, l-b 5, w , n-b , 16	B , l-b , w , n-b ,
	Total 218	Total ....

BOWLING ANALYSIS.

Name.	O.	1st Innings. M. R. W. Wds. N-b.	2nd Innings. O. M. R. W. Wds. N-b.
Longman	19	4 63 2	.. ..
Cutbush	10	2 39 2	.. ..
Abney	3	0 17 0	.. ..
Pawling	11	1 40 2	.. ..
Thomas	9	1 29 2 .. .	.. ..
Farquharson	4	1 14 0	.. ..

Umpires—Atfield and Whiteside.　　　　Scorers—Storer and Attewell.

Drawn.

Lord's 1905. Reproduced by kind permission of MCC.

'NOW, TALKING ABOUT CRICKET'

After Dulwich, Wodehouse might have gone on to Oxford and won a Blue if his father's business hadn't collapsed, compelling him instead to seek gainful employment at the Hong Kong and Shanghai Bank, a shift that lasted from September 1900 to September 1902. If the work was a bore, he gained some satisfaction in turning out for the bank's rugby and cricket teams, and often returned to Dulwich to cheer on the school XIs. And, of course, he wrote: in his 'spare' time, avidly, and with growing assurance.

The final verdict on his cricketing accomplishment at Dulwich had been delivered in the July 1900 edition of the college magazine, The Alleynian*: 'P.G. Wodehouse – A fast right-hand bowler with a good swing, though he does not use his head enough. As a bat he has very much improved, and he gets extraordinarily well to the pitch of the ball. Has wonderfully improved in the field, though rather hampered by his sight.'*

The following piece, again for Public School Magazine*, was written when Wodehouse was merely twenty, and yet he adopts the voice of a seasoned old buffer, a little akin to The Oldest Member of his later golfing stories, if lacking the Member's gimlet-eyed powers of analysis. In* *other words, the style is done in jest: this narrator 'couldn't play cricket for nuts', but Wodehouse surely could.*

(Indeed, come 1903 he would make his debut for the Authors cricket team founded by J.M. Barrie and known as 'The Allahakbarries', who played annual fixtures at Lord's against XIs made up of Actors, Publishers, etc. Wodehouse's teammates included Arthur Conan Doyle, whom he revered, and E.W. Hornung, Conan Doyle's brother-in-law and the creator of the 'gentleman thief' Arthur J. Raffles.)

In the days of yore, when these white hairs were brown – or was it black? At any rate, they were not white – and I was at school, it was always my custom, when Fate obliged me to walk to school with a casual acquaintance, to whom I could not unburden my soul of those profound thoughts which even then occupied my mind, to turn the struggling conversation to the relative merits of cricket and football.

'Do you like cricket better than footer?' was my formula. Now, though at the time, in order to save fruitless argument, I always agreed with my companion, and praised the game he praised, in the innermost depths of my sub-consciousness, cricket ranked a long way in front of all other forms of sport. I may be wrong. More than once in my career it has been represented to me that I couldn't play cricket for nuts. My captain said as much when I ran him out in *the* match of the season after he had made forty-nine and looked like stopping. A bowling acquaintance heartily endorsed his opinion on the occasion of my missing three catches off him in one over. This, however, I attribute to prejudice, for the man I missed ultimately reached his century, mainly off the deliveries of my bowling acquaintance. I pointed out to him that, had I accepted any one of the three chances, we should have missed seeing the prettiest century made on the ground that season; but he was one of those bowlers who sacrifice all that is beautiful in the game to mere wickets. A sordid practice.

Later on, the persistence with which my county ignored my claims to inclusion in the team, convinced me that I must leave cricket fame to others. True, I did figure, rather prominently, too, in one county match. It was at the Oval, Surrey *v.* Middlesex. How well I remember that occasion! Albert Trott was bowling (Bertie we used to call him); I forget who was batting. Suddenly the ball came soaring in my direction. I was not nervous. I put down the sandwich I was eating, rose from my seat, picked the ball up neatly, and returned it with unerring aim to a fieldsman who was waiting for it with becoming deference. Thunders of applause went up from the crowded ring.

That was the highest point I ever reached in practical cricket. But, as the historian says of Mr Winkle, a man may be an excellent sportsman in theory, even if he fail in practice. That's me. Reader (if any), have you ever played cricket in the passage outside your study with a walking-stick and a ball of paper? That's the game, my boy, for testing your skill of wrist and eye. A century *v.* the M.C.C. is well enough in its way, but give me the man who can watch 'em in a narrow passage, lit only by a flickering gas-jet – one for every hit, four if it reaches the end, and six if it goes downstairs full-pitch, any pace bowling allowed. To make double figures in such a match is to taste life. Only you had better do your tasting when the Housemaster is out for the evening.

I like to watch the young cricket idea shooting. I refer to the lower games, where 'next man in' umpires with his pads on, his loins girt, and a bat in his hand. Many people have wondered why it is that no budding umpire can officiate unless he holds a bat. For my part, I think there is little foundation for the theory that it is part of a semi-religious rite, on the analogy of the Freemasons' special handshake and the like. Nor do I altogether agree with the authorities who allege that man, when standing up, needs something as a prop or support. There is a shadow of reason, I grant, in this supposition, but after years of keen observation I am inclined to think that the umpire keeps his bat by him, firstly, in order that no unlicensed hand shall commandeer it unbeknownst, and secondly, so that he shall be ready to go in directly his predecessor is out. There is an ill-concealed restiveness about his movements, as he watches the batsmen getting set, that betrays an overwrought spirit. Then of a sudden one of them plays a ball on to his pad. ''s *that*?' asks the bowler, with an overdone carelessness. 'Clean out. Now *I'm* in,' and already he is rushing up the middle of the pitch to take possession. When he gets to the wicket a short argument ensues. 'Look here, you idiot, I hit it hard.' 'Rot, man, out of the way.' '!!??!' 'Look here, Smith, *are* you going to dispute the umpire's decision?' Chorus of fieldsmen: 'Get out, Smith, you ass. You've been given out years ago.' Overwhelmed by popular execration, Smith reluctantly departs, registering in the black depths of his soul a resolution to take on the umpireship at once, with a view to gaining an artistic revenge by giving his enemy run out on the earliest possible occasion. There is a primeval *insouciance* about this sort of thing which is as refreshing to a mind jaded with the stiff formality of professional umpires as a cold shower-bath.

I have made a special study of last-wicket men; they are divided into two classes, the deplorably nervous, or the outrageously confident. The nervous largely outnumber the confident. The launching of a last-wicket man, when there are ten to make to win, or five minutes left to make a draw of a losing game, is fully as impressive a ceremony as the launching of the latest battleship. An interested crowd harasses the poor victim as he is putting on his pads. 'Feel in a funk?' asks some tactless friend. 'N-n-no, norrabit.' 'That's right,' says the captain encouragingly, 'bowling's as easy as anything.'

This cheers the wretch up a little, until he remembers suddenly that the captain himself was distinctly at sea with the despised trundling, and succumbed to his second ball, about which he obviously had no idea whatever. At this he breaks down utterly, and, if emotional, will sob into his batting glove. He is assisted down the pavilion steps, and reaches the wickets in a state of collapse. Here, very probably, a reaction will set in. The sight of the crease often comes as a positive relief after the vague terrors experienced in the pavilion.

The confident last-wicket man, on the other hand, goes forth to battle with a light quip upon his lips. The lot of a last-wicket batsman, with a good eye and a sense of humour, is a very enviable one. The incredulous disgust of the fast bowler, who thinks that at last he may safely try that slow head-ball of his, and finds it lifted genially over the leg-boundary, is well worth seeing. I remember in one school match, the last man, unfortunately on the opposite side, did this three times in one over, ultimately retiring to a fluky catch in the slips with forty-one to his name. Nervousness at cricket is a curious thing. As the author of *Willow the King*, himself a county cricketer, has said, it is not the fear of getting out that causes funk. It is a sort of intangible *je ne sais quoi*. I trust I make myself clear. Some batsmen are nervous all through a long innings. With others the feeling disappears with the first boundary.

A young lady – it is, of course, not polite to mention her age to the minute, but it ranged somewhere between eight and ten – was taken to see a cricket match once. After watching the game with interest for some time, she gave out this profound truth: 'They all attend specially to one man.' It would be difficult to sum up the causes of funk more lucidly and concisely. To be an object of interest is sometimes pleasant, but when ten fieldsmen, a bowler, two umpires, and countless spectators are eagerly watching your every movement, the thing becomes embarrassing.

That is why it is, on the whole, preferable to be a cricket spectator rather than a cricket player. No game affords the spectator such unique opportunities of exerting his critical talents. You may have noticed that it is always the reporter who knows most about the game. Everyone, moreover, is at heart a critic, whether he represent the majesty of the Press or not. From the lady of Hoxton, who crushes her friend's latest confection with the words, 'My, wot an 'at!' down to that lowest class of all, the persons who call your attention (in print) to the sinister meaning of everything Clytemnestra says in *The Agamemnon*, the whole world enjoys expressing an opinion of its own about something.

In football you are vouchsafed fewer chances. Practically all you can do is to shout 'off-side' whenever an opponent scores, which affords but meagre employment for a really critical mind. In cricket, however, nothing can escape you. Everything must be done in full sight of everybody. There the players stand, without refuge, simply inviting criticism.

It is best, however, not to make one's remarks too loud. If you do, you call down upon yourself the attention of others, and are yourself criticised. I remember once, when I was of tender years, watching a school match, and one of the batsmen lifted a ball clean over the pavilion. This was too much for my sensitive and critical young mind. 'On the carpet, sir,' I shouted sternly, well up in the treble clef, 'keep 'em on the carpet.' I will draw a veil. Suffice it to say that I became a sport and derision, and was careful for the future to criticise in a whisper. But the reverse by no means crushed me. Even now I take a melancholy pleasure in watching school matches, and saying So-and-So will make quite a fair *school-boy* bat in time, but he must get rid of that stroke of his on the off, and that shocking leg-hit, and a few of those *awful* strokes in the slips, but that on the whole, he is by no means lacking in promise. I find it refreshing. If, however, you feel compelled not merely to look on, but to play, as one often does at schools where cricket is compulsory, it is impossible to exaggerate the importance of white boots. The game you play before you get white boots is not cricket, but a weak imitation. The process of initiation is generally this. One plays in shoes for a few years with the most dire result, running away to square leg from fast balls, and so on, till despair seizes the soul. Then an angel in human form, in the very effective disguise of the man at the school boot-shop, hints that, for an absurdly small sum in cash, you may become the sole managing director of a pair of *white buckskin* boots with real spikes. You try them on. They fit, and the initiation is complete. You no longer run away from fast balls. You turn them neatly off to the boundary. In a word, you begin for the first time to play the game, the whole game, and nothing but the game.

There are misguided people who complain that cricket is becoming a business more than a game, as if that were not the most fortunate thing that could happen. When it ceases to be a mere business and becomes a religious ceremony, it will be a sign that the millennium is at hand. The person who regards cricket as anything less than a business is no fit companion, gentle reader, for the likes of you and me. As long as the game goes in his favour the cloven hoof may not show itself. But give him a good steady spell of leather-hunting, and you will know him for what he is, a mere *dilettante*, a dabbler, in a word, a worm, who ought never to be allowed to play at all. The worst of this species will sometimes take advantage of the fact that the game in which they happen to be playing is only a scratch game, upon the result of which no very great issues hang, to pollute the air they breathe with verbal, and the ground they stand on with physical, buffooneries. Many a time have I, and many a time have you, if you are what I take you for, shed tears of blood, at the sight of such. Careless returns, overthrows – but enough of a painful subject. Let us pass on.

I have always thought it a better fate for a man to be born a bowler than a bat. A batsman certainly gets a considerable amount of innocent fun by snicking good fast balls just off his wicket to the ropes, and standing stolidly in front against slow leg-breaks. These things are good, and help one to sleep peacefully o' nights, and enjoy one's meals. But no batsman can experience that supreme emotion of 'something attempted, something done', which comes to a bowler when a ball pitches in a hole near point's feet, and whips into the leg stump. It is one crowded second of glorious life. Again, the words 'retired hurt' on the score-sheet are far more pleasant to the bowler than the batsman. The groan of a batsman when a loose ball hits him full pitch in the ribs is genuine. But the 'Awfully-sorry-old-chap-it-slipped' of the bowler is not. Half a loaf is better than no bread, as Mr Chamberlain might say, and if he cannot hit the wicket, he is perfectly contented with hitting the man. In my opinion, therefore, the bowler's lot, in spite of billiard table wickets, red marl, and such like inventions of a degenerate age, is the happier one.

And here, glowing with pride of originality at the thought that I have written of cricket without mentioning Alfred Mynn or Fuller Pilch, I heave a reminiscent sigh, blot my MS., and thrust my pen back into its sheath.

Actors v. Authors.

THURSDAY, JUNE 29.

AUTHORS.	First Innings.		Second Innings.
1 Sir A. Conan Doyle	b Warner	2	
2 P. G. Wodehouse, Esq...	b Smith	0	
3 Cecil Headlam, Esq......	b Smith	9	
4 J. C. Snaith, Esq.........	c Denbigh, b O'Connor ..	17	
5 A. Kinross, Esq.	b Smith	5	
6 Horace Bleakley, Esq. ..	not out	54	
7 C. C. Hoyer Millar, Esq.	b Denbigh	3	
8 Major Philip Trevor......	b Warner	44	
9 Leo Trevor, Esq.	b Warner	4	
10 E. W. Hornung, Esq. ...			
11 P. Graves, Esq.............			
12 F. Stayton, Esq.			

[Innings closed.]

B 5, l-b 3, w 2, n-b 1, 11   B , l-b , w , n-b ,
Total 149   Total ....

BOWLING ANALYSIS.

Name.	O.	1st Innings.					2nd Innings.				
		M.	R.	W.	Wds.	N-b.	O.	M.	R.	W.	Wds.	N-b.
O'Connor	10	5	28	1	..	..	..	..	..	..	..	..
Smith........................	11	1	39	3	...	..	..	..	..	..	..	..
Warner	9	0	24	3	2	..	..	..	..	..	..	..
Denbigh....................	7	0	23	1	..	..	..	..	..	..	..	..
Evett	3	0	10	0	..	..	.	..	..	..	..	..
Asche	4	1	14	0	..	1	..	..	..	..	..	..

ACTORS.	First Innings.		Second Innings.
1 V. O'Connor, Esq.........	not out 100		
2 H. B. Warner, Esq	b Wodehouse..............	6	
3 Reeve Denbigh, Esq......	b Millar	21	
4 C. Aubrey Smith, Esq...	c Wodehouse, b Millar...	9	
5 Gerald Du Maurier, Esq.	not out	13	
6 A. S. Homewood, Esq...			
7 Oscar Asche, Esq.........			
8 Robert Evett, Esq.			
9 P. F. Knox, Esq.			
10 H. Nye Chart, Esq.			
11 Kenneth Douglas, Esq...			
12 C. Hayden Coffin, Esq...			

B 3, l-b 3, w , n-b 1, 7   B , l-b , w , n-b ,
Total 156   Total ....

BOWLING ANALYSIS.

Name.	O.	1st Innings.					2nd Innings.				
		M.	R.	W.	Wds.	N-b.	O.	M.	R.	W.	Wds.	N-b.
Snaith	4	1	16	0	..	..	..	..	..	..	..	..
Doyle	8	1	45	0	..	1	..	..	..	..	..	..
Wodehouse	10	0	58	1	..	..	..	..	..	..	..	..
Millar......................	6	0	30	2	..	..	..	..	..	..	..	..

Umpires—Pougher and Brown.   Scorers—Martin and Atfield.

Actors won by 7 wickets and 7 runs.

Lord's 1911. Reproduced by kind permission of MCC.

'FOOTBALL, MY DEAR SIR, WHY?'

The game here is rugby, of course, and not the Association football which was at the time a mere upstart in the English sporting scene. Wodehouse undoubtedly enjoyed his rugby while in the heat of the contest; but in this piece, as in his later evocations of rugger on the page, we can feel a tendency to focus on certain more forbidding aspects of the sport: the commonplace discomfort of spectating conditions, the haunting psychology of goal-kicking, and the oft-demoralising mire of the rugby pitch in midwinter.

I think I may claim the distinction of being the only male adult in the United Kingdom (exclusive of those who are unable to write) who has never written a song about football, rhyming 'leather' with 'weather' and placing the adjectives 'glorious' and 'wintry' before the latter word. At one time there were three of us, myself, a Mr Williams of Upper Tooting, and a Mr Smythe of South Penge. That was early in the eighties. Since then Mr Smythe has died, while Mr Williams took to drink in the summer of 1890, and now writes odes to prominent players for the football edition of the *Upper Tooting Sporting Lynx*. I am, therefore, the only claimant to the title, and under the circumstances it is only fitting that I should express myself on the subject in prose.

Football is essentially an undignified game, and can never be to the artist soul quite what cricket is. The best part of cricket is, undoubtedly, sitting in the pavilion and watching the game. In football you miss this. The football spectator is a wretched being, lashed by the rain and the sport of the wind, and frozen into one solid mass from the feet upwards. He cannot take that calm, restful interest in the play which makes the lot of the cricket spectator so pleasant. He is given to understand that the only way in which he may help his side to victory is by shouting, and without a stop at that. Often after a school match the actual players are as fresh as paint compared to the spectators, who go home feeling that any remarks they may wish to make for the next week or so must be made in guttural croaks eked out with dumb show. [...]

The fly in the ointment of the Rugby footballer is in the matter of dropped goals. No soccer player can experience that supremest and divinest of ecstasies. The nearest he gets to it, I suppose, is when his hot shot gets past into the net. But really the two things are not to be compared. The chief charm of an attempt at a dropped goal lies in its uncertainty. There is literally nothing on this earth so gloriously uncertain. Cricket? Bah. Roulette? Pooh. The breakfast egg? Tush. They are not to be mentioned in the same breath as a drop at goal. Suppose, for the sake of argument, that you have the ball and that you have for the moment sufficiently mastered your conscience to enable you to make the attempt. Why, anything may happen then. The ball may touch the side of your foot and trickle off towards the spectators, an offence to gods and men, or you may kick it perpendicularly into the air, which is worse, or you may fail to kick it altogether, which is worst of all. Juvenal talks about the utter pettiness of life and the hollowness of all things human. What did *he* know about it? He had never been collared from behind at the exact moment when he ought to have kicked the ball but didn't. Most footballers have experienced the mental and physical anguish of kicking nothing exceedingly hard. Let them speak of the woes of life.

Never to have dropped a goal poisons the most successful football existence. An international of my acquaintance met me one evening after a club match in which he had scored five times. I congratulated him. To my surprise he sighed heavily. 'Cheer up,' I said, 'surely five tries are enough to go on with?' 'It isn't that,' he replied, dashing away a tear from his left eye, 'I was thinking that in all my life I have never dropped a goal. Look here, if I can find time I shall get up a team consisting entirely of English internationals, and take them to play some small private school. Then I may get a chance.' 'Do,' I said, 'it ought to be a magnificent game, judging from England's form of late. Rather a sell for you, though, if their masters play for them. Better start with the kindergartens and work slowly upwards. Good-night.' We parted.

The dangers of football are, in my opinion, over-rated. Accidents will happen in every game, witness the melancholy case of the man who played at pretending that his gun was not loaded, or the unfortunate gentleman who was struck by lightning during a game of Spillikins. Nobody calls Spillikins a dangerous game. Yet the fact remains that the man was killed. Why then has football such a bad name? Simply because the comic papers have formed a secret society, one of the rules of which is that no mention of football be made unless, at the same time, the poor dear old jest is allowed to totter out. With the exception of those games, which in England take the place of the old code of the duello, football is almost painfully safe. Accidents, of course, sometimes occur. I can remember the case of a friend of my own, a man noted for the crispness and despatch of his tackling. He invited an aunt, whose heir he was, to see him play in a college match. After the game she refused to speak to him, and when the will came to be read it was found that the bulk of her money had been left to the Society for Supplying Square Meals to Orphan Cats, while my friend came off with fourpence in coppers and a bound volume of tracts on the subject of ruling the temper. All this because one of the players whom he had happened to tackle in his own bold style had fallen on his aunt instead of on the ground. And my friend was a man who had never killed a fly, though this, I am bound in honesty to admit, was not for want of trying. A counter instance, which goes to prove that football is after all not so very rough, is the case of another friend, who bought a couple of eggs on his way to a football match, thrust them carelessly into his pocket and forgot all about them. As he was leaving the ground at the end of the game he suddenly remembered them, and felt in his pocket, expecting, as was only natural, to find them mainly pulp. They were absolutely intact!! (Note. I ought perhaps to mention that it was in the pocket of his great-coat that he had placed the eggs, though this does not affect the main point, that they were unbroken at the end of a long game.)

Football is at its pleasantest in early autumn or early spring. In winter the only game that ought to be played is chestnut roasting. There is a special variety of wind which never comes out except during a football match, that takes away in two minutes the pent-up enthusiasm of months. 'Blow, blow, thou winter wind,' wrote Shakespeare, probably at a time when he was joining Ben Jonson at the latter's expense in sixpenn'orth of something warm at the fireside of the Mermaid tavern, and listening to the blasts roaring in the chimney, 'Thou art not so unkind as man's ingratitude.' Now, without wishing to injure William's well-earned reputation in any way, I should like to remark that this is purely a matter of opinion. A jury of footballers would, I am inclined to think, have a good many words to say in favour of the opposite view. And when wind and rain and cold combine, one feels that life was made for sterner, higher things than football. I asked a footballer, once noted for his keenness for the game, why he had given it up while his strength and wind were yet unimpaired. It was as I had guessed. One bitter day in December he was playing on a wet ground. He was a wing three-quarter of extraordinary pace, and when he got hold of the ball thought of nothing else except how to get past the opponent's full-back. On this particular day he was skimming down the touch-line, when he trod with inconceivable violence in the very centre of a deep puddle. The result may be easily imagined. Football knickers (as the advertisements call them) are built with an eye to these special cases. Not a drop of that puddle was wasted. 'Until that moment,' he told me, with a shiver at the recollection, 'I had not believed that anything on earth could be so fearfully cold and yet remain liquid. They asked me to play for England that year. I said that I should be charmed to oblige them if they would only consent to play the game in a well-warmed room. The secretary replied that he had laid my request before the authorities, but was afraid that it was not feasible. So I wired my refusal, and gave up the game for good. I go in for incubating chickens now.'

With all these objections to the game, it may be wondered why football is ever played at all. The reason probably is that by no other means can one obtain that feeling of absolute peace and bodily comfort which comes to the footballer, when, his battles o'er, he boils himself at full length in a bath, and remembers how desperately cold it was out in the field. Omar Khayyam – I think I recollect rightly – says on the subject:

> *'I often think that ne'er was bath so warm*
> *As that in which reclines the tired form*
> *Of him who played some twenty minutes since*
> *Two weary 'thirty-fives' of wind and storm.'*

*

It is the thought of this that nerves him throughout the fray. It shines before him like a beacon. It consoles him for the dropped goals and the shots that did not come off. To quote Omar once more:

'Some
Sigh for the Prophets' Paradise to come.'

I cannot help thinking that he had the aftermath of football in his mind when he wrote those lines. They express the yearning so exactly.

'THE SPORTS':
FROM *THE POTHUNTERS*

Wodehouse's incarceration at the bank ended in 1902 thanks to an offer of work at London's Globe *evening newspaper – a helping hand at which he snapped. Already he had made himself a prodigious freelancer, contributing to multiple magazines, but perhaps more significantly he had taught himself to write serialised fiction, in particular for* Public School Magazine *and the* Captain. *He wrote public school stories – 'because that was the only atmosphere I knew at all' – and it was sport, above all, that provided him with his dramatic predicaments. The Pot-hunters, one such serial, became Wodehouse's first book proper, published in September 1902.*

This little extract concerns athletics, in the context of School Sports Day, a pulse-racing rite through which surely every schoolchild passes. Amid a large cast, the main character to step forward is Jim Thomson, who for various reasons finds himself out of pocket and in need of funds – a crisis that will be resolved if he can just win the mile race on Sports Day. But to do so he must outpace his principal rival, Drake – the Steve Ovett, if you like, to Jim's Sebastian Coe.

*

Sports weather at St Austin's was as a rule a quaint but unpleasant solution of mud, hail, and iced rain. These were taken as a matter of course, and the school counted it as something gained when they were spared the usual cutting east wind.

This year, however, occurred that invaluable exception which is so useful in proving rules. There was no gale, only a gentle breeze. The sun was positively shining, and there was a general freshness in the air which would have made a cripple cast away his crutches, and, after backing himself heavily both ways, enter for the Strangers' Hundred Yards. [...]

The Sports were to begin at two o'clock with a series of hundred-yards races, which commenced with the 'under twelve' (Cameron of Prater's a warm man for this, said those who had means of knowing), and culminated at about a quarter past with the open event, for which Welch was a certainty. By a quarter to the hour the places round the ropes were filled, and more visitors were constantly streaming in at the two entrances to the school grounds, while in the centre of the ring the band of the local police force – the military being unavailable owing to exigencies of distance – were seating themselves with the grim determination of those who know that they are going to play the soldiers' chorus out of *Faust*. The band at the Sports had played the soldiers' chorus out of *Faust* every year for decades past, and will in all probability play it for decades to come.

The Sports at St Austin's were always looked forward to by everyone with the keenest interest, and when the day arrived, were as regularly voted slow. In all school sports there are too many foregone conclusions. In the present instance everybody knew, and none better than the competitors themselves, that Welch would win the quarter and hundred. The high jump was an equal certainty for a boy named Reece in Halliday's House. Jackson, unless he were quite out of form, would win the long jump, and the majority of the other events had already been decided. The gem of the afternoon would be the mile, for not even the shrewdest judge of form could say whether Jim would beat Drake, or Drake Jim. Both had done equally good times in practice, and both were known to be in the best of training. The adherents of Jim pointed to the fact that he had won the half off Drake – by a narrow margin, true, but still he had won it. The other side argued that a half-mile is no criterion for a mile, and that if Drake had timed his sprint better he would probably have won, for he had finished up far more strongly than his opponent. And so on the subject of the mile, public opinion was for once divided. [...]

The afternoon wore on. Welch won the hundred by two yards and the quarter by twenty, and the other events fell in nearly every case to the favourite. The hurdles created something of a surprise – Jackson, who ought to have won, coming down over the last hurdle but two, thereby enabling Dallas to pull off an unexpected victory by a couple of yards. Vaughan's enthusiastic watch made the time a little under sixteen seconds, but the official timekeeper had other views. There were no instances of the timid new boy, at whom previously the world had scoffed, walking away with the most important race of the day.

And then the spectators were roused from a state of coma by the sound of the bell ringing for the mile. Old Austinian number one gratefully seized the opportunity to escape from Old Austinian number two, and lose himself in the crowd. Young Pounceby-Green with equal gratitude left his father talking to the Head, and shot off without ceremony to get a good place at the ropes. In fact, there was a general stir of anticipation, and all round the ring paterfamilias was asking his son and heir which was Drake and which Thomson, and settling his glasses more firmly on the bridge of his nose. [...]

There were six competitors in all, each of whom owned a name ranking alphabetically higher than Thomson. Jim, therefore, had the outside berth. Drake had the one next to the inside, which fell to Adamson, the victim of the lost two pounds episode.

Both Drake and Jim got off well at the sound of the pistol, and the pace was warm from the start. Jim evidently had his eye on the inside berth, and, after half a lap had been completed, he got it, Drake falling back. Jim continued to make the running, and led at the end of the first lap by about five yards. Then came Adamson, followed by a batch of three, and finally Drake, taking things exceedingly coolly, a couple of yards behind them. The distance separating him from Jim was little over a dozen yards. A roar of applause greeted the runners as they started on the second lap, and it was significant that while Jim's supporters shouted, 'Well run,' those of Drake were fain to substitute advice for approval, and cry 'Go it'. Drake, however, had not the least intention of 'going it' in the generally accepted meaning of the phrase. A yard or two to the rear meant nothing in the first lap, and he was running quite well enough to satisfy himself, with a nice, springy stride, which he hoped would begin to tell soon.

With the end of the second lap the real business of the race began, for the survival of the fittest had resulted in eliminations and changes of order. Jim still led, but now by only eight or nine yards. Drake had come up to second, and Adamson had dropped to a bad third. Two of the runners had given the race up, and retired, and the last man was a long way behind, and, to all practical purposes, out of the running. There were only three laps, and, as the last lap began, the pace quickened, fast as it had been before. Jim was exerting every particle of his strength. He was not a runner who depended overmuch on his final dash. He hoped to gain so much ground before Drake made his sprint as to neutralise it when it came. Adamson he did not fear.

And now they were in the last two hundred yards, Jim by this time some thirty yards ahead, but in great straits. Drake had quickened his pace, and gained slowly on him. As they rounded the corner and came into the straight, the cheers were redoubled. It was a great race. Then, fifty yards from the tape, Drake began his final sprint. If he had saved himself before, he made up for it now. The gap dwindled and dwindled. Neither could improve his pace. It was a question whether there was enough of the race left for Drake to catch his man, or whether he had once more left his sprint till too late. Jim could hear the roars of the spectators, and the frenzied appeals of Merevale's House to him to sprint, but he was already doing his utmost. Everything seemed black to him, a black, surging mist, and in its centre a thin white line, the tape. Could he reach it before Drake? Or would he collapse before he reached it? There were only five more yards to go now, and still he led. Four. Three. Two. Then something white swept past him on the right, the white line quivered, snapped, and vanished, and he pitched blindly forward on to the turf at the track-side. Drake had won by a foot.

NEW YORK BASEBALL:
REPORTAGE
FOR *VANITY FAIR*

Wodehouse's interest in baseball begins (aged twenty-two) with his April 1904 visit to New York – an excursion for which he had long and devoutly wished. By now a columnist on the Globe, *he took a five-week break and blew his savings to travel steerage ('second class with three other men in the cabin') on the* SS St Louis. *As he later recorded, 'To say that New York came up to its advance billing would be the baldest of understatements. Being there was like being in heaven, without going to all the bother and expense of dying.'*

In time, Wodehouse would suggest that a purpose of the visit had been to school himself in the American boxing circuit. In the memoir Over Seventy *he writes: 'I was an enthusiastic boxer in those days and had a boyish reverence for America's pugilists – James J. Corbett, James J. Jeffries, Tom Sharkey, Kid McCoy and the rest of them. I particularly wanted to meet Corbett and shake the hand that had kay-oed John L. Sullivan.'*

But in New York, Wodehouse picked up a new bug in baseball, its appeal to him perhaps as much to do with the exuberance of the game's following, and its distinctive idiom, as any of the action on and around the diamond. That vernacular is what Wodehouse focuses on in the following piece: a droll deconstruction of a newspaper write-up on a game between the Boston Americans and the New York Highlanders. The intention is to explain baseball to a sceptical UK readership while at the same time, of course, having some sport with it.

'Baseball' (*Vanity Fair* UK, 25 August 1904)

Next to divorce, baseball is New York's favourite pastime. What Americans, as a nation, think of cricket I do not know. One gentleman from way back informed me that in his opinion the only merit of the game was the constant opportunity it provided of taking in a long drink. In the same way the English mind has never been able to get that strange hold on the beauties of baseball which is so noticeable on the other side. What is there in the game to send a crowd of forty thousands frantic with excitement? To the uninitiated, it is simply 'rounders', played, to judge by appearances, by picked teams from the local lunatic asylums. Indeed, the eccentricity is not confined to the players. The crowd has its share. Also the reporter in next morning's paper. In the early days of the season New York beat Boston. That is the theme. Here is the theme with variations as recorded by the ball expert of the *New York Journal*. We will start with a few headlines, if you please:

YANKEES BAT TO VICTORY IN BOSTON.

GRIFFITH'S MEN SWAT DINEEN FOR FIVE TALLIES IN ONE INNING.

Then the reporter gets off from the mark in his breezy, 'git-thar' style:

'Wow! Whoop! Fine! Oh, fine! Any number of cheers. Here, quick, dear friend, take this highball of happiness – just a-brimmin' over, just a-brimmin' over.' (He spells it with one 'm'; but what of spelling when it covers a warm heart?) 'Listen to James, will you? Nice man to have, James, who isn't supposed ever to show his feelings on any occasion, and Nowke's running around like a Comanche, yelling: "'Ip! 'Ip! 'Ooooorye!" Say, maybe you heard it, maybe you didn't that whooping joy cry uttered in Boston at about half-past three this afternoon. Well it was we. It was we. Whee!'

This is the right stuff. It stirs. It invigorates. It would thrill a pew-opener. You feel that you want to read on and find out what it is all about.

'Why did we cheer, dear friend?' proceeds the scribe. 'Only too happy to explain, only too happy. Half-mast for the two pennants that fly at the Beanville American Grounds yesterday, thank you.' (Beanville is Boston, where the baked beans come from.) 'Half-mast for pennant of American League Championship – half-mast for the one that declares they are champions of the world, no less. Champeens, hey? Champeens? Huh! Bet when we got through with them they felt like running home and sobbing out the sad story at mother's knee. Champeens, hey? Chanpeens? It seems very hard to believe it tonight, dear friend. Why, sized beside a Yankee, a champeen didn't look any bigger than a freckle on a frog's leg yesterday, and there's an affidavit to go with that statement, if necessary.'

'Nobody, Champeens or Griffith's gay boys, had trod the rosy pathway to the score-board for the first two innings. Up steps McGuire. (This is New York batting now.) He stepped down again in a hurry. A little bulb that scuttled to third found first base long before McGuire.'

Now, the facts in the case of McGuire, translated into English, are thus: He opened the batting in New York's third inning. He was armed with a weapon which was a blend of policeman's truncheon and Indian club. Behind him stood the catcher, wearing on one hand a huge padded glove. Behind the catcher stood the umpire. Facing

McGuire was the 'pitcher'. The rules of the game enact that the batsman shall be at liberty to refuse to play any of the pitcher's deliveries that may not be to his taste, and to wait until he happens on a congenial one before smiting. But to prevent this happening too often, the ingenious persons who look after the game have arranged that the batsman shall stand on a tin plate of moderate size. If the pitcher pitches a ball that passes over this plate at a height that is not above the batsman's shoulder or below his waist, and the batsman fails to hit it the umpire calls 'Strike one.' The batsman is allowed three balls of this kind, that are officially considered playable, and if he misses all three he is out, and retires to the bench till the next inning.

We left Mister McGuire grasping his club and facing the pitcher. The pitcher, who, like the batsman, is restricted as to the space in which he may move, began to prance down the field in a menacing manner. At last, being then some fifteen yards from the batsman, he twisted his body in a sort of spasm, brought his left knee sharply across until it nearly touched his face, then suddenly uncoiled and delivered the ball like a shot from a rifle. Whether it was the first ball or the second or third we do not know, but Mr McGuire smote out at one of the three and sent the ball flying in the direction of third field. Then he flew himself for first base. But the ball arrived first, and he was out. At the first base a fieldsman had been posted. When third field got to the ball, he flung it to the man at the first base, and the latter, standing on the plate which marks the base, touched it with the ball before Mr McGuire could get there. It is to avoid being out in this way that causes the player, to hurl themselves along the ground at a base instead of running – a process which adds to the game that suggestion of insanity beforementioned. As the Girton Girl wrote after seeing a match:

I feel that I could watch baseball
With interest and even passion,

If but the players wouldn't fall
In that extraordinary fashion.

So Mr McGuire is out. But there are others.

'Next Fultz. Flashed out to little Parent at third. Parent gathered it all right, but then he tried to bring Keeler's young hairs in sorrow to the grave at the home plate. Where the deuce was that ball he threw going? Well, dear friend, it wasn't going anywhere near the catcher at the home plate.' So Keeler got home, or, as the writer puts it, 'copped off his little rim,' and Fultz meanwhile 'flipflapped to second under the circumstances'. Boston never recovered the lost ground. The report concludes with the words: 'Score – Griffith's grand little men 6; pennant possessions 3.'

The reader may be wondering who this Griffith is. He is evidently somebody of importance. Who is it has his name mentioned in the papers as if the game had been played under his patronage, and nobody else's? Griffith. When there are hot batteries of goo-goo eyes being handed about by pink-cheeked Boston girls, who is it that gets them? The man Griffith. Then who is he, and what has he done? We do not read of him as beating the home rubber. We hear nothing of his flipflapping to second. All he does is to strut back from the coaching-box. Who is this man? Griffith is the manager of the team, and if I were asked to select what they call, in New York, a real lead-pipe cinch – in other words, a walk in life of the pleasantest and most lucrative kind – I should choose the managership of a crack baseball team.

The duties are strenuous, but interesting. And the pay is quite good. Two thousand pounds a year is what the average manager gets. So does the pitcher. A first-class pitcher can command his own terms. He generally commands ten thousand dollars per annum. Taking into consideration the fact that the ball season only lasts six months of the year, this pay may be called adequate. But a pitcher's post is not a sinecure. A pitcher must not be merely good, he must be very, very good. He must be able to throw the ball at lightning speed, and yet control it so wonderfully that he can make it swerve from left to right, from right to left, upwards or downwards at will. There are many men earning two thousand pounds a year at banking, acting, company-promoting, and in other spheres of action, who could not make it swerve an inch in any direction. So let us not grudge the pitcher his pittance. [...]

*

Wodehouse actually attended his first professional baseball game at the home of the New York Giants: the Polo Grounds, on Manhattan's Upper West Side. The experience begat the following short portrait of the culture of the bleachers.

'New York Crowds' (*Vanity Fair* UK, 24 November 1904)

If the visitor to New York chances to possess a dollar-bill for which he has no particular use at the moment, he should certainly spend it on a ticket for a ball-game, if only to see the crowd. In his ignorance of its subtleties he may find the game itself dull; but he cannot fail to be interested by the spectators. A baseball crowd is like no other. I do not refer to the elect, who watch the game from the aristocratic seclusion of the Grand Stand, but to the 'shilling public' who fill the 'bleachers', the cheap wooden seats at the opposite side of the ground behind the first base. These are the true followers of the game, keen critics to a man, with eagle eyes and no mercy for a weak piece of batting or a bungled catch. There is an atmosphere of joyous rowdyism, toned down somewhat by a certain respect for authorities constituted by themselves and elected from their own number, which is refreshing – at a distance.

How the players enjoy it one cannot say. The home team possibly find a pleasure in the shout of welcome which they meet as they walk to the batting-plate. But when the enemy's turn at the bat comes round, the note is changed. Barracking reigns supreme, and barracking of a peculiarly aggressive and systematic type withal. For a baseball crowd is not a collection of individuals who cheer and hoot as the spirit moves them. It is an organised mass, and it gives tongue just when it is directed so to do by its leader, the officially-appointed 'Rooter-in-chief'. They leave nothing to chance, a baseball crowd. Left to themselves, they might cheer at moments when they should be silent, or be silent when it was necessary for the welfare of the New York nine that they should cheer.

To prevent this a leader is appointed, and his powers are autocratic. He is, to quote an evening paper, President, King, Kaiser, Tsar, Mikado, Pooh-Bah, Mandarin, Sultan, and Emperor of all the 'Rooters'. He it is who 'bosses things back of first base, and rules trained "fans" with a hand of iron'. 'Fans' are those who sit on the bleachers, and stay there in scorching sun or driving rain until the ninth inning of each team is an accomplished fact. The Rooter-in-chief has lungs of brass, and a spirit that no reverse can subdue. So the barracking proceeds merrily, and the visitors bat in an atmosphere of contemptuous hostility. But only collectively. As individuals they receive the applause that is due to them for any clever piece of play. Not such a spontaneous ring about the cheers when one of the Brooklyn nine puts a New York batsman out with a clever throw, as when a New Yorker performs a similar feat at the expense of a Brooklynite. But still cheers there are, and no man can complain that he has played well without recognition.

But as a team the enemy are anathema.

'Well, who ever heard of Brooklyn?' shrills the Rooter-in-chief, just now a gentleman of the name of Dillon.

Nobody ever heard of it. Suppose it's in America or Europe or somewhere. Remember seeing the name in a paper once. But never really *heard* of it. Certainly not as a rival to New York at the ball-game.

'Where *is* Brooklyn?' enquires the 'fans'. Personalities follow.

'Say, Hanlon, what do you get that ten thousand dollars for?'

'Are those fellows ball-players or cinder-pickers?'

Now and then 'fandom' becomes lyrical.

> *'Give 'em the axe! Give 'em the axe!*
> *The axe! the axe! the axe!*
> *Where?*
> *In the neck! In the neck! In the neck!*
> *In the neck!*
> *There!'*

Nothing special, considered purely as a poem, but distinctly effective when shouted in unison by thousands of cast-iron throats.

But it is in the encouragement of their own side that the 'bleachers' come out strongest.

We will suppose Mertes, left fielder of New York, to have made one of his best catches. The dialogue proceeds on the lines of the illustrious Messieurs Bones and Johnsing, thus:

Dillon (enquiringly): 'What's the matter with Mertes?'

The Crowd (all together): 'What's the matter with Mertes?'

Dillon (patiently): 'Well, *what's* the matter with Mertes?'

The Crowd (reassuringly): '*He's* all right!'

Dillon: 'What?'

The Crowd: 'He's all right.'

Dillon: 'Who?'

The Crowd: 'Mertes.'

Dillon: '*Who?*'

The Crowd: '*Mer*-tes.'

Dillon: 'WHO?'

The Crowd (with a glad bellow that nearly brings down the neighbouring skyscrapers with a run): 'MERTES. HE'S ALL RIGHT!!!!!'

SHEEN'S SHOT AT
REDEMPTION:
FROM *THE WHITE FEATHER*

Wodehouse published The White Feather *first as a serial in the* Captain *and then between covers in 1907. Its setting is the fictional Wrykyn public school, originally invented by Wodehouse for* The Gold Bat *(1904), and soon to play host to* Mike.

The theme here is boxing, in which Wodehouse excelled at Dulwich. The image of Plum as stripped-to-the-waist pugilist might not fit with some readers' preconceptions of the creator of Jeeves and Wooster; but by all accounts Wodehouse fought gamely and ably. As he recalled for an interviewer in 1955, 'I never got exhausted in the ring. After three rounds I was always willing and anxious to go on and could never understand why the decision went against me, as I couldn't remember the other fellow hitting me at all. This although I was streaming with blood.'

The White Feather *is the story of a reserved, bookish boy named Sheen, who disdains all sports apart from the school game of 'fives' (like squash played with hands rather than racquets.) Sheen's main competitive drive in life is to win an in-school scholarship known as 'the Gotford'. But at the start of a Wrykyn term Sheen finds himself faced with a town-and-gown street tussle between Wrykyn boys and local youths,*

and elects to run rather than risk trouble – in other words, he 'funks it'.
This leads to social ostracism: he is 'cut' by those who stayed and fought,
who call him coward for 'letting the house down'. Sheen feels a sore need
to 'do something to put things right again' – and boxing will be his shot
at redemption. He resolves against the odds to win the house boxing
championship.

And so Sheen must apprentice himself to a master – Joe Bevan, a
former lightweight champ turned trainer, who leavens his advice with
lines from Shakespeare ('Beware of entrance to a quarrel; but, being in,
bear't that th' opposed may beware of thee.') One fine day Sheen heads
to the Blue Boar, 'a picturesque inn, standing on the bank of the river
Severn', to begin his tutelage at Bevan's upstairs gym.

From the other side of the gymnasium door came an unceasing
and mysterious shuffling sound.

Sheen tapped at the door, and went in.

He found himself in a large, airy room, lit by two windows and
a broad skylight. The floor was covered with linoleum. But it was
the furniture that first attracted his attention. In a farther corner
of the room was a circular wooden ceiling, supported by four narrow
pillars. From the centre of this hung a ball, about the size of an
ordinary football. To the left, suspended from a beam, was an
enormous leather bolster. On the floor, underneath a table bearing
several pairs of boxing-gloves, a skipping-rope, and some wooden
dumb-bells, was something that looked like a dozen Association
footballs rolled into one. All the rest of the room, a space some
few yards square, was bare of furniture. In this space a small sweater-
clad youth, with a head of light hair cropped very short, was darting
about and ducking and hitting out with both hands at nothing,
with such a serious, earnest expression on his face that Sheen could
not help smiling. On a chair by one of the windows Mr Joe Bevan
was sitting, with a watch in his hand.

As Sheen entered the room the earnest young man made a sudden dash at him. The next moment he seemed to be in a sort of heavy shower of fists. They whizzed past his ear, flashed up from below within an inch of his nose, and tapped him caressingly on the waistcoat. Just as the shower was at its heaviest his assailant darted away again, side-stepped an imaginary blow, ducked another, and came at him once more. None of the blows struck him, but it was with more than a little pleasure that he heard Joe Bevan call 'Time!' and saw the active young gentleman sink panting into a seat.

'You and your games, Francis!' said Joe Bevan, reproachfully. 'This is a young gentleman from the college come for tuition.'

'Gentleman—won't mind—little joke—take it in spirit which is—meant,' said Francis, jerkily.

Sheen hastened to assure him that he had not been offended.

'You take your two minutes, Francis,' said Mr Bevan, 'and then have a turn with the ball. Come this way, Mr—'

'Sheen.'

'Come this way, Mr Sheen, and I'll show you where to put on your things.'

Sheen had brought his football clothes with him. He had not put them on for a year. [...]

The art of teaching boxing really well is a gift, and it is given to but a few. It is largely a matter of personal magnetism, and, above all, sympathy. A man may be a fine boxer himself, up to every move of the game, and a champion of champions, but for all that he may not be a good teacher. If he has not the sympathy necessary for the appreciation of the difficulties experienced by the beginner, he cannot produce good results. A boxing instructor needs three qualities, skill, sympathy, and enthusiasm. Joe Bevan had all three, particularly enthusiasm. His heart was in his work, and he carried

Sheen with him. 'Beautiful, sir, beautiful,' he kept saying, as he guarded the blows; and Sheen, though too clever to be wholly deceived by the praise, for he knew perfectly well that his efforts up to the present had been anything but beautiful, was nevertheless encouraged, and put all he knew into his hits. Occasionally Joe Bevan would push out his left glove. Then, if Sheen's guard was in the proper place and the push did not reach its destination, Joe would mutter a word of praise. If Sheen dropped his right hand, so that he failed to stop the blow, Bevan would observe, 'Keep that guard up, sir!' with almost a pained intonation, as if he had been disappointed in a friend.

The constant repetition of this maxim gradually drove it into Sheen's head, so that towards the end of the lesson he no longer lowered his right hand when he led with his left; and he felt the gentle pressure of Joe Bevan's glove less frequently. At no stage of a pupil's education did Joe Bevan hit him really hard, and in the first few lessons he could scarcely be said to hit him at all. He merely rested his glove against the pupil's face. On the other hand, he was urgent in imploring the pupil to hit *him* as hard as he could.

'Don't be too kind, sir,' he would chant, '*I* don't mind being hit. Let me have it. Don't flap. Put it in with some weight behind it.' He was also fond of mentioning that extract from Polonius' speech to Laertes, which he had quoted to Sheen on their first meeting.

Sheen finished his first lesson feeling hotter than he had ever felt in his life.

'Hullo, sir, you're out of condition,' commented Mr Bevan. 'Have a bit of a rest.'

Once more Sheen had learnt the lesson of his weakness. He could hardly realise that he had only begun to despise himself in the last fortnight. Before then, he had been, on the whole, satisfied with himself. He was brilliant at work, and would certainly get a scholarship at Oxford or Cambridge when the time came; and he had specialised in work to the exclusion of games. It is bad to specialise in games to the exclusion of work, but of the two courses the latter is probably the less injurious. One gains at least health by it.

But Sheen now understood thoroughly, what he ought to have learned from his study of the Classics, that the happy mean was the thing at which to strive. And for the future he meant to aim at it. He would get the Gotford, if he could, but also would he win the house boxing at his weight.

After he had rested he discovered the use of the big ball beneath the table. It was soft, but solid and heavy. By throwing this – the medicine-ball, as they call it in the profession – at Joe Bevan, and catching it, Sheen made himself very hot again, and did the muscles of his shoulders a great deal of good.

'That'll do for today, then, sir,' said Joe Bevan. 'Have a good rub down tonight, or you'll find yourself very stiff in the morning.'

'Well, do you think I shall be any good?' asked Sheen.

'You'll do fine, sir. But remember what Shakespeare says.'

'About vaulting ambition?'

'No, sir, no. I meant what Hamlet says to the players. "Nor do not saw the air too much, with your hand, thus, but use all gently." That's what you've got to remember in boxing, sir. Take it easy. Easy and cool does it, and the straight left beats the world.'

Sheen paddled quietly back to the town with the stream, pondering over this advice. He felt that he had advanced another step. He was not foolish enough to believe that he knew anything about boxing as yet, but he felt that it would not be long before he did.

Sheen improved. He took to boxing as he had taken to fives. He found that his fives helped him. He could get about on his feet quickly, and his eye was trained to rapid work.

His second lesson was not encouraging. He found that he had learned just enough to make him stiff and awkward, and no more.

But he kept on, and by the end of the first week Joe Bevan declared definitely that he would do, that he had the root of the matter in him, and now required only practice.

'I wish you could see like I can how you're improving,' he said at the end of the sixth lesson, as they were resting after five minutes' exercise with the medicine-ball. 'I get four blows in on some of the gentlemen I teach to one what I get in on you. But it's like riding. When you can trot, you look forward to when you can gallop. And when you can gallop, you can't see yourself getting on any further. But you're improving all the time.'

'But I can't gallop yet?' said Sheen.

'Well, no, not gallop exactly, but you've only had six lessons. Why, in another six weeks, if you come regular, you won't know yourself. You'll be making some of the young gentlemen at the college wish they had never been born. You'll make babies of them, that's what you'll do.'

'I'll bet I couldn't, if I'd learnt with someone else,' said Sheen, sincerely. 'I don't believe I should have learnt a thing if I'd gone to the school instructor.'

'Who is your school instructor, sir?'

'A man named Jenkins. He used to be in the army.'

'Well, there, you see, that's what it is. I know old George Jenkins. He used to be a pretty good boxer in his time, but, there! boxing's a thing, like everything else, that moves with the times. We used to go about in iron trucks. Now we go in motor-cars. Just the same with boxing. What you're learning now is the sort of boxing that wins championship fights nowadays. Old George, well, he teaches you how to put your left out, but, my golly, he doesn't know any tricks. He hasn't studied it same as I have. It's the ring-craft that wins battles. Now, sir, if you're ready.'

They put on the gloves again. When the round was over, Mr Bevan had further comments to make.

'You don't hit hard enough, sir,' he said. 'Don't flap. Let it come straight out with some weight behind it. You want to be earnest in the ring. The other man's going to do his best to hurt you, and you've got to stop him. One good punch is worth twenty taps. You hit him. And when you've hit him, don't you go back; you hit him again. They'll only give you three rounds in any competition you go in for, so you want to do the work you can while you're at it.'

As the days went by, Sheen began to imbibe some of Joe Bevan's rugged philosophy of life. He began to understand that the world is a place where every man has to look after himself, and that it is the stronger hand that wins. That sentence from Hamlet which Joe Bevan was so fond of quoting practically summed up the whole duty of man – and boy too. One should not seek quarrels, but, 'being in', one should do one's best to ensure that one's opponent thought twice in future before seeking them. These afternoons at the Blue Boar were gradually giving Sheen what he had never before possessed – self-confidence. He was beginning to find that he was capable of something after all, that in an emergency he would be able to keep his end up. The feeling added a zest to all that he did. His work in school improved. He looked at the Gotford no longer as a prize which he would have to struggle to win. He felt that his rivals would have to struggle to win it from him.

After his twelfth lesson, when he had learned the ground work of the art, and had begun to develop a style of his own, like some nervous batsman at cricket who does not show his true form till he has been at the wickets for several overs, the dog-loving Francis gave him a trial. This was a very different affair from his spars with Joe Bevan. Frank Hunt was one of the cleverest boxers at his weight in England, but he had not Joe Bevan's gift of hitting gently. He probably imagined that he was merely tapping, and certainly his blows were not to be compared with those he delivered in the exercise of his professional duties; but, nevertheless, Sheen had never felt anything so painful before, not even in his passage of arms with Albert. He came out of the encounter with a swollen lip and a feeling that one of his ribs was broken, and he had not had the pleasure of landing a single blow upon his slippery antagonist, who flowed about the room like quicksilver. But he had not flinched, and the statement of Francis, as they shook hands, that he had 'done varry well', was as balm. Boxing is one of the few sports where the loser can feel the same thrill of triumph as the winner. There is no satisfaction equal to that which comes when one has forced oneself to go through an ordeal from which one would have liked to have escaped.

'Capital, sir, capital,' said Joe Bevan. 'I wanted to see whether you would lay down or not when you began to get a few punches. You did capitally, Mr Sheen.'

'I didn't hit him much,' said Sheen with a laugh.

'Never mind, sir, you got hit, which was just as good. Some of the gentlemen I've taught wouldn't have taken half that. They're all right when they're on top and winning, and to see them shape you'd say to yourself, By George, here's a champion. But let 'em get a punch or two, and hullo! says you, what's this? They don't like it. They lay down. But you kept on. There's one thing, though, you want to keep that guard up when you duck. You slip him that way once. Very well. Next time he's waiting for you. He doesn't hit straight. He hooks you, and you don't want many of those.' [...]

Sheen paid his daily visits to the Blue Boar, losing flesh and gaining toughness with every lesson. The more he saw of Joe Bevan the more he liked him, and appreciated his strong, simple outlook on life. Shakespeare was a great bond between them. Sheen had always been a student of the Bard, and he and Joe would sit on the little verandah of the inn, looking over the river, until it was time for him to row back to the town, quoting passages at one another. Joe Bevan's knowledge, of the plays, especially the tragedies, was wide, and at first inexplicable to Sheen. It was strange to hear him declaiming long speeches from *Macbeth* or *Hamlet* and to think that he was by profession a pugilist. One evening he explained his curious erudition. In his youth, before he took to the ring in earnest, he had travelled with a Shakespearean repertory company. 'I never played a star part,' he confessed, 'but I used to come on in the Battle of Bosworth and in Macbeth's castle and what not. I've been First Citizen sometimes. I was the carpenter in *Julius Caesar*. That was my biggest part. "Truly sir, in respect of a fine workman, I am but, as you would say, a cobbler." But somehow the stage – well … *you* know what it is, sir. Leeds one week, Manchester the next, Brighton the week after, and travelling all Sunday. It wasn't quiet enough for me.'

The idea of becoming a professional pugilist for the sake of peace and quiet tickled Sheen. 'But I've always read Shakespeare ever since then,' continued Mr Bevan, 'and I always shall read him.'

It was on the next day that Mr Bevan made a suggestion which drew confidences from Sheen, in his turn.

'What you want now, sir,' he said, 'is to practise on someone of about your own form, as the saying is. Isn't there some gentleman friend of yours at the college who would come here with you?'

They were sitting on the verandah when he asked this question. It was growing dusk, and the evening seemed to invite confidences. Sheen, looking out across the river and avoiding his friend's glance, explained just what it was that made it so difficult for him to produce a gentleman friend at that particular time. He could feel Mr Bevan's eye upon him, but he went through with it till the thing was told – boldly, and with no attempt to smooth over any of the unpleasant points.

'Never you mind, sir,' said Mr Bevan consolingly, as he finished. 'We all lose our heads sometimes. I've seen the way you stand up to Francis, and I'll eat— I'll eat the medicine-ball if you're not as plucky as anyone. It's simply a question of keeping your head. You wouldn't do a thing like that again, not you. Don't you worry yourself, sir. We're all alike when we get bustled. We don't know what we're doing, and by the time we've put our hands up and got into shape, why, it's all over, and there you are. Don't you worry yourself, sir.'

'You're an awfully good sort, Joe,' said Sheen gratefully.

Failing a gentleman friend, Mr Bevan was obliged to do what he could by means of local talent. On Sheen's next visit he was introduced to a burly youth of his own age, very taciturn and apparently ferocious. He, it seemed, was the knife and boot boy at the Blue Boar, 'did a bit' with the gloves, and was willing to spar with Sheen provided Mr Bevan made it all right with the guv'nor; saw, that is to say, that he did not get into trouble for passing in unprofessional frivolity moments which should have been sacred to knives and boots. These terms having been agreed to, he put on the gloves.

For the first time since he had begun his lessons, Sheen experienced an attack of his old shyness and dislike of hurting other people's feelings. He could not resist the thought that he had no grudge against the warden of the knives and boots. He hardly liked to hit him.

The other, however, did not share this prejudice. He rushed at Sheen with such determination that almost the first warning the latter had that the contest had begun was the collision of the back of his head with the wall. Out in the middle of the room he did better, and was beginning to hold his own, in spite of a rousing thump on his left eye, when Joe Bevan called 'Time!' A second round went off in much the same way. His guard was more often in the right place, and his leads less wild. At the conclusion of the round, pressure of business forced his opponent to depart, and

Sheen wound up his lesson with a couple of minutes at the punching-ball. On the whole, he was pleased with his first spar with someone who was really doing his best and trying to hurt him. With Joe Bevan and Francis there was always the feeling that they were playing down to him. Joe Bevan's gentle taps, in particular, were a little humiliating. But with his late opponent all had been serious. It had been a real test, and he had come through it very fairly. On the whole, he had taken more than he had given – his eye would look curious tomorrow – but already he had thought out a way of foiling the burly youth's rushes. Next time he would really show his true form.

*

Though Sheen's developing prowess in the ring is clear, he runs into an obstacle: his standing round school remains so low that he cannot get himself picked to fight in the inter-house boxing competition. And so, with Bevan's encouragement, he aims higher – the annual competition at Aldershot military centre, where he would face 'the best boxers of all the public schools'. To obtain this shot, Sheen must appeal to a schoolmaster, Mr Spence, who boxed for Cambridge, and is impressed by Bevan's reference, but retains his doubts nonetheless.

'My position is this, you see, Sheen. There is nothing I should like more than to see the school represented at Aldershot. But I cannot let anyone go down, irrespective of his abilities. Aldershot is not child's play. And in the Light-weights you get the hardest fighting of all. It wouldn't do for me to let you go down if you are not up to the proper form. You would be half killed.'

'I should like to have a shot, sir,' said Sheen.

'Then this year, as you probably know, Ripton are sending down Peteiro for the Light-weights. He was the fellow whom

Drummond only just beat last year. And you saw the state in which Drummond came back. If Drummond could hardly hold him, what would you do?'

'I believe I could beat Drummond, sir,' said Sheen.

Mr Spence's eyes opened wider. Here were brave words. This youth evidently meant business. The thing puzzled him. On the one hand, Sheen had been cut by his house for cowardice. On the other, Joe Bevan, who of all men was best able to judge, had told him that he was good enough to box at Aldershot.

'Let me think it over, Sheen,' he said. 'This is a matter which I cannot decide in a moment. I will tell you tomorrow what I think about it.'

'I hope you will let me go down, sir,' said Sheen. 'It's my one chance.'

'Yes, yes, I see that, I see that,' said Mr Spence, 'but all the same – well, I will think it over.'

All the rest of that evening he pondered over the matter, deeply perplexed. It would be nothing less than cruel to let Sheen enter the ring at Aldershot if he were incompetent. Boxing in the Public Schools Boxing Competition is not a pastime for the incompetent. But he wished very much that Wrykyn should be represented, and also he sympathised with Sheen's eagerness to wipe out the stain on his honour, and the honour of the house. But, like Drummond, he could not help harbouring a suspicion that this was a pose. He felt that Sheen was intoxicated by his imagination. Everyone likes to picture himself doing dashing things in the limelight, with an appreciative multitude to applaud. Would this mood stand the test of action?

Against this there was the evidence of Joe Bevan. Joe had said that Sheen was worthy to fight for his school, and Joe knew. Mr Spence went to bed still in a state of doubt.

Next morning he hit upon a solution of the difficulty. Wandering in the grounds before school, he came upon O'Hara, who had won the Light-weights at Aldershot in the previous year. He had come to Wrykyn for the Sports. Here was the man to help him. O'Hara should put on the gloves with Sheen and report.

'I'm in rather a difficulty, O'Hara,' he said, 'and you can help me.'

'What's that?' inquired O'Hara.

'You know both our light-weights are on the sick list? I had just resigned myself to going down to Aldershot without anyone to box, when a boy in Seymour's volunteered for the vacant place. I don't know if you knew him at school? Sheen. Do you remember him?'

'Sheen?' cried O'Hara in amazement. 'Not *Sheen!*'

His recollections of Sheen were not conducive to a picture of him as a public-school boxer.

'Yes. I had never heard of him as a boxer. Still, he seems very anxious to go down, and he certainly has one remarkable testimonial, and as there's no one else—'

'And what shall I do?' asked O'Hara.

'I want you, if you will, to give him a trial in the dinner-hour. Just see if he's any good at all. If he isn't, of course, don't hit him about a great deal. But if he shows signs of being a useful man, extend him. See what he can do.'

'Very well, sir,' said O'Hara.

'And you might look in at my house at tea-time, if you have nothing better to do, and tell me what you think of him.'

At five o'clock, when he entered Mr Spence's study, O'Hara's face wore the awe-struck look of one who had seen visions.

'Well?' said Mr Spence. 'Did you find him any good?'

'Good?' said O'Hara. 'He'll beat them all. He's a champion. There's no stopping him.'

'What an extraordinary thing!' said Mr Spence.

*

At Sheen's request Mr Spence made no announcement of the fact that Wrykyn would be represented in the Light-weights. It would be time enough, Sheen felt, for the school to know that he was a boxer when he had been down and shown what he could do. His appearance in his new *rôle* would be the most surprising thing that had happened in the place for years, and it would be a painful anti-climax if, after all the excitement which would be caused by the discovery that he could use his hands, he were to be defeated in his first bout. Whereas, if he happened to win, the announcement of his victory would be all the more impressive, coming unexpectedly. To himself he did not admit the possibility of defeat. He had braced himself up for the ordeal, and he refused to acknowledge to himself that he might not come out of it well. Besides, Joe Bevan continued to express hopeful opinions.

'Just you keep your head, sir,' he said, 'and you'll win. Lots of these gentlemen, they're champions when they're practising, and you'd think nothing wouldn't stop them when they get into the ring. But they get wild directly they begin, and forget everything they've been taught, and where are they then? Why, on the floor, waiting for the referee to count them out.'

This picture might have encouraged Sheen more if he had not reflected that he was just as likely to fall into this error as were his opponents.

'What you want to remember is to keep that guard up. Nothing can beat that. And push out your left straight. The straight left rules the boxing world. And be earnest about it. Be as friendly as you like afterwards, but while you're in the ring say to yourself, "Well, it's you or me," and don't be too kind.'

'I wish you could come down to second me, Joe,' said Sheen.

'I'll have a jolly good try, sir,' said Joe Bevan. 'Let me see. You'll be going down the night before – I can't come down then, but I'll try and manage it by an early train on the day.'

'How about Francis?'

'Oh, Francis can look after himself for one day. He's not the sort of boy to run wild if he's left alone for a few hours.'

'Then you think you can manage it?'

'Yes, sir. If I'm not there for your first fight, I shall come in time to second you in the final.'

'If I get there,' said Sheen.

'Good seconding's half the battle. These soldiers they give you at Aldershot – well, they don't know the business, as the saying is. They don't look after their man, not like I could. I saw young what's-his-name, of Rugby – Stevens: he was beaten in the final by a gentleman from Harrow – I saw him fight there a couple of years ago. After the first round he was leading – not by much, but still, he was a point or two ahead. Well! He went to his corner and his seconds sent him up for the next round in the same state he'd got there in. They hadn't done a thing to him. Why, if I'd been in his corner I'd have taken him and sponged him and sent him up again as fresh as he could be. You must have a good second if you're to win. When you're all on top of your man, I don't say. But you get a young gentleman of your own class, just about as quick and strong as you are, and then you'll know where the seconding comes in.'

'Then, for goodness' sake, don't make any mistake about coming down,' said Sheen.

'I'll be there, sir,' said Joe Bevan.

*

The Queen's Avenue Gymnasium at Aldershot is a roomy place, but it is always crowded on the public schools' day. Sisters and cousins and aunts of competitors flock there to see Tommy or Bobby perform, under the impression, it is to be supposed, that he is about to take part in a pleasant frolic, a sort of merry parlour game. What their opinion is after he emerges from a warm three rounds is not known. Then there are soldiers in scores. Their views on boxing as a sport are crisp and easily defined. What they want is Gore. Others of the spectators are Old Boys, come to see how the school can behave in an emergency, and to find out whether there are still experts like Jones, who won the Middles in '96, or Robinson, who was runner-up in the Feathers in the same year; or whether, as they have darkly suspected for some time, the school has Gone To The Dogs Since They Left.

The usual crowd was gathered in the seats round the ring when Sheen came out of the dressing-room and sat down in an obscure corner at the end of the barrier which divides the gymnasium into two parts on these occasions. He felt very lonely. Mr Spence and the school instructor were watching the gymnastics, which had just started upon their lengthy course. The Wrykyn pair were not expected to figure high on the list this year. He could have joined Mr Spence, but, at the moment, he felt disinclined for conversation. If he had been a more enthusiastic cricketer, he would have recognised the feeling as that which attacks a batsman before he goes to the wicket. It is not precisely funk. It is rather a desire to accelerate the flight of Time, and get to business quickly. All things come to him who waits, and among them is that unpleasant sensation of a cold hand upon the portion of the body which lies behind the third waistcoat button.

The boxing had begun with a bout between two feather-weights, both obviously suffering from stage-fright. They were fighting in a scrambling and unscientific manner, which bore out Mr Bevan's statements on the subject of losing one's head. Sheen felt that both were capable of better things. In the second and third rounds this proved to be the case and the contest came to an end amidst applause.

The next pair were light-weights, and Sheen settled himself to watch more attentively. From these he would gather some indication of what he might expect to find when he entered the ring. He would not have to fight for some time yet. In the drawing for numbers, which had taken place in the dressing-room, he had picked a three. There would be another Light-weight battle before he was called upon. His opponent was a Tonbridgian, who, from the glimpse Sheen caught of him, seemed muscular. But he (Sheen) had the advantage in reach, and built on that.

After opening tamely, the Light-weight bout had become vigorous in the second round, and both men had apparently forgotten that their right arms had been given them by Nature for the purpose of guarding. They were going at it in hurricane fashion all over the ring. Sheen was horrified to feel symptoms of a return of that old sensation of panic which had caused him, on that dark day early in the term, to flee Albert and his wicked works. He set his teeth, and fought it down. And after a bad minute he was able to argue himself into a proper frame of mind again. After all, that sort of thing looked much worse than it really was. Half those blows, which seemed as if they must do tremendous damage, were probably hardly felt by their recipient. He told himself that Francis, and even the knife-and-boot boy, hit fully as hard, or harder, and he had never minded them. At the end of the contest he was once more looking forward to his entrance to the ring with proper fortitude.

The fighting was going briskly forward now, sometimes good, sometimes moderate, but always earnest, and he found himself contemplating, without undue excitement, the fact that at the end of the bout which had just begun, between middle-weights from St. Paul's and Wellington, it would be his turn to perform. As luck would have it, he had not so long to wait as he had expected, for the Pauline, taking the lead after the first few exchanges, out-fought his man so completely that the referee stopped the contest in the second round. Sheen got up from his corner and went to the dressing-room. The Tonbridgian was already there. He took off his coat. Somebody crammed his hands into the gloves, and from that moment the last trace of nervousness left him. He trembled with the excitement of the thing, and hoped sincerely that no one would notice it, and think that he was afraid.

Then, amidst a clapping of hands which sounded faint and far-off, he followed his opponent to the ring, and ducked under the ropes.

The referee consulted a paper which he held, and announced the names.

'R. D. Sheen, Wrykyn College.'

Sheen wriggled his fingers right into the gloves, and thought of Joe Bevan. What had Joe said? Keep that guard up. The straight left. Keep that guard – the straight left. Keep that –

'A. W. Bird, Tonbridge School.'

There was a fresh outburst of applause. The Tonbridgian had shown up well in the competition of the previous year, and the crowd welcomed him as an old friend.

Keep that guard up – straight left. Straight left – guard up.

'Seconds out of the ring.'

Guard up. Not too high. Straight left. It beats the world. What an age that man was calling Time. Guard up. Straight –

'Time,' said the referee.

Sheen, filled with a great calm, walked out of his corner and shook hands with his opponent.

It was all over in half a minute.

The Tonbridgian was a two-handed fighter of the rushing type, and almost immediately after he had shaken hands, Sheen found himself against the ropes, blinking from a heavy hit between the eyes. Through the mist he saw his opponent sparring up to him, and as he hit he side-stepped. The next moment he was out in the middle again, with his man pressing him hard. There was a quick rally, and then Sheen swung his right at a venture. The blow had no conscious aim. It was purely speculative. But it succeeded. The Tonbridgian fell with a thud.

Sheen drew back. The thing seemed pathetic. He had braced himself up for a long fight, and it had ended in half a minute. His sensations were mixed. The fighting half of him was praying that his man would get up and start again. The prudent half realised that it was best that he should stay down. He had other fights before him before he could call that silver medal his own, and this would give him an invaluable start in the race. His rivals had all had to battle hard in their opening bouts.

The Tonbridgian's rigidity had given place to spasmodic efforts to rise. He got on one knee, and his gloved hand roamed feebly about in search of a hold. It was plain that he had shot his bolt. The referee signed to his seconds, who ducked into the ring and carried him to his corner. Sheen walked back to his own corner, and sat down. Presently the referee called out his name as the winner, and he went across the ring and shook hands with his opponent, who was now himself again.

He overheard snatches of conversation as he made his way through the crowd to the dressing-room.

'Useful boxer, that Wrykyn boy.'

'Shortest fight I've seen here since Hopley won the heavy-weights.'

'Fluke, do you think?'

'Don't know. Came to the same thing in the end, anyhow. Caught him fair.'

'Hard luck on that Tonbridge man. He's a good boxer, really. Did well here last year.'

Then an outburst of hand-claps drowned the speakers' voices. A swarthy youth with the Ripton pink and green on his vest had pushed past him and was entering the ring. As he entered the dressing-room he heard the referee announcing the names. So that was the famous Peteiro! Sheen admitted to himself that he looked tough, and hurried into his coat and out of the dressing-room again so as to be in time to see how the Ripton terror shaped.

It was plainly not a one-sided encounter. Peteiro's opponent hailed from St. Paul's, a school that has a habit of turning out boxers. At the end of the first round it seemed to Sheen that honours were even. The great Peteiro had taken as much as he had given, and once had been uncompromisingly floored by the Pauline's left. But in the second round he began to gain points. For a boy of his weight he had a terrific hit with the right, and three applications of this to the ribs early in the round took much of the sting out of the Pauline's blows. He fought on with undiminished pluck, but the Riptonian was too strong for him, and the third round was a rout. To quote the *Sportsman* of the following day, 'Peteiro crowded in a lot of work with both hands, and scored a popular victory.'

Sheen looked thoughtful at the conclusion of the fight. There was no doubt that Drummond's antagonist of the previous year was formidable. Yet Sheen believed himself to be the cleverer of the two. At any rate, Peteiro had given no signs of possessing much cunning. To all appearances he was a tough, go-ahead fighter, with a right which would drill a hole in a steel plate. Had he sufficient skill to baffle his (Sheen's) strong tactics? If only Joe Bevan would come! With Joe in his corner to direct him, he would feel safe. But of Joe up to the present there were no signs.

Mr Spence came and sat down beside him.

'Well, Sheen,' he said, 'so you won your first fight. Keep it up.'

'I'll try, sir,' said Sheen.

'What do you think of Peteiro?'

'I was just wondering, sir. He hits very hard.'

'Very hard indeed.'

'But he doesn't look as if he was very clever.'

'Not a bit. Just a plain slogger. That's all. That's why Drummond beat him last year in the feather-weights. In strength there was no comparison, but Drummond was just too clever for him. You will be the same, Sheen.'

'I hope so, sir,' said Sheen.

After lunch the second act of the performance began. Sheen had to meet a boxer from Harrow who had drawn a bye in the first round of the competition. This proved a harder fight than his first encounter, but by virtue of a stout heart and a straight left he came through it successfully, and there was no doubt as to what the decision would be. Both judges voted for him.

Peteiro demolished a Radleian in his next fight.

There were now three light-weights in the running – Sheen, Peteiro, and a boy from Clifton. Sheen drew the bye, and sparred in an outer room with a soldier, who was inclined to take the thing easily. Sheen, with the thought of the final in his mind, was only too ready to oblige him. They sparred an innocuous three rounds, and the man of war was kind enough to whisper in his ear as they left the room that he hoped he would win the final, and that he himself had a matter of one-and-sixpence with Old Spud Smith on his success.

'For I'm a man,' said the amiable warrior confidentially, 'as knows Class when he sees it. You're Class, sir, that's what you are.'

This, taken in conjunction with the fact that if the worst came to the worst he had, at any rate, won a bronze medal by getting into the final, cheered Sheen. If only Joe Bevan had appeared he would have been perfectly contented.

But there were no signs of Joe.

'Final, Light-Weights,' shouted the referee.

A murmur of interest from the ring-side chairs.

'R. D. Sheen, Wrykyn College.'

Sheen got his full measure of applause this time. His victories in the preliminary bouts had won him favour with the spectators.

'J. Peteiro, Ripton School.'

'Go it, Ripton!' cried a voice from near the door. The referee frowned in the direction of this audacious partisan, and expressed a hope that the audience would kindly refrain from comment during the rounds.

Then he turned to the ring again, and announced the names a second time.

'Sheen – Peteiro.'

The Ripton man was sitting with a hand on each knee, listening to the advice of his school instructor, who had thrust head and shoulders through the ropes, and was busy impressing some point upon him. Sheen found himself noticing the most trivial things with extraordinary clearness. In the front row of the spectators sat a man with a parti-coloured tie. He wondered idly what tie it was. It was rather like one worn by members of Templar's house at Wrykyn. Why were the ropes of the ring red? He rather liked the colour. There was a man lighting a pipe. Would he blow out the match or extinguish it with a wave of the hand? What a beast Peteiro looked. He must look out for that right of his. The straight left. Push it out. Straight left ruled the boxing world. Where was Joe? He must have missed the train. Or perhaps he hadn't been able to get away. Why did he want to yawn, he wondered.

'Time!'

The Ripton man became suddenly active. He almost ran across the ring. A brief handshake, and he had penned Sheen up in his corner before he had time to leave it. It was evident what advice his instructor had been giving him. He meant to force the pace from the start.

The suddenness of it threw Sheen momentarily off his balance. He seemed to be in a whirl of blows. A sharp shock from behind. He had run up against the post. Despite everything, he remembered to keep his guard up, and stopped a lashing hit from his antagonist's left. But he was too late to keep out his right. In it came, full on the weakest spot on his left side. The pain of it caused him to double up for an instant, and as he did so his opponent uppercut him. There was no rest for him. Nothing that he had ever experienced with the gloves on approached this. If only he could get out of this corner.

Then, almost unconsciously, he recalled Joe Bevan's advice.

'If a man's got you in a corner,' Joe had said, 'fall on him.'

Peteiro made another savage swing. Sheen dodged it and hurled himself forward.

'Break away,' said a dispassionate official voice.

Sheen broke away, but now he was out of the corner with the whole good, open ring to manoeuvre in.

He could just see the Ripton instructor signalling violently to his opponent, and, in reply to the signals, Peteiro came on again with another fierce rush.

But Sheen in the open was a different person from Sheen cooped up in a corner. Francis Hunt had taught him to use his feet. He side-stepped, and, turning quickly, found his man staggering past him, overbalanced by the force of his wasted blow. And now it was Sheen who attacked, and Peteiro who tried to escape. Two swift hits he got in before his opponent could face round, and another as he turned and rushed. Then for a while the battle raged without science all over the ring. Gradually, with a cold feeling of dismay, Sheen realised that his strength was going. The pace was too hot. He could not keep it up. His left counters were losing their force.

Now he was merely pushing his glove into the Ripton man's face. It was not enough. The other was getting to close quarters, and that right of his seemed stronger than ever.

He was against the ropes now, gasping for breath, and Peteiro's right was thudding against his ribs. It could not last. He gathered all his strength and put it into a straight left. It took the Ripton man in the throat, and drove him back a step. He came on again. Again Sheen stopped him.

It was his last effort. He could do no more. Everything seemed black to him. He leaned against the ropes and drank in the air in great gulps.

'Time!' said the referee.

The word was lost in the shouts that rose from the packed seats.

Sheen tottered to his corner and sat down.

'Keep it up, sir, keep it up,' said a voice. 'Bear't that the opposed may beware of thee. Don't forget the guard. And the straight left beats the world.'

It was Joe – at the eleventh hour.

With a delicious feeling of content Sheen leaned back in his chair. It would be all right now. He felt that the matter had been taken out of his hands. A more experienced brain than his would look after the generalship of the fight.

As the moments of the half-minute's rest slid away he discovered the truth of Joe's remarks on the value of a good second. In his other fights the flapping of the towel had hardly stirred the hair on his forehead. Joe's energetic arms set a perfect gale blowing. The cool air revived him. He opened his mouth and drank it in. A spongeful of cold water completed the cure. Long before the call of Time he was ready for the next round.

'Keep away from him, sir,' said Joe, 'and score with that left of yours. Don't try the right yet. Keep it for guarding. Box clever. Don't let him corner you. Slip him when he rushes. Cool and steady does it. Don't aim at his face too much. Go down below. That's the *de*-partment. And use your feet. Get about quick, and you'll find he don't like that. Hullo, says he, I can't touch him. Then, when he's tired, go in.'

The pupil nodded with closed eyes. [...]

Sheen came up for the second round fresh and confident. His head was clear, and his breath no longer came in gasps. There was to be no rallying this time. He had had the worst of the first round, and meant to make up his lost points.

Peteiro, losing no time, dashed in. Sheen met him with a left in the face, and gave way a foot. Again Peteiro rushed, and again he was stopped. As he bored in for the third time Sheen slipped him. The Ripton man paused, and dropped his guard for a moment.

Sheen's left shot out once more, and found its mark. Peteiro swung his right viciously but without effect. Another swift counter added one more point to Sheen's score.

Sheen nearly chuckled. It was all so beautifully simple. What a fool he had been to mix it up in the first round. If he only kept his head and stuck to out-fighting he could win with ease. The man couldn't box. He was nothing more than a slogger. Here he came, as usual, with the old familiar rush. Out went his left. But it missed its billet. Peteiro had checked his rush after the first movement, and now he came in with both hands. It was the first time during the round that he had got to close quarters, and he made the most of it. Sheen's blows were as frequent, but his were harder. He drove at the body, right and left; and once again the call of Time extricated Sheen from an awkward position. As far as points were concerned he had had the best of the round, but he was very sore and bruised. His left side was one dull ache.

'Keep away from him, sir,' said Joe Bevan. 'You were ahead on that round. Keep away all the time unless he gets tired. But if you see me signalling, then go in all you can and have a fight.'

There was a suspicion of weariness about the look of the Ripton champion as he shook hands for the last round. He had not had an expert in his corner, and he was beginning to feel the effects of his hurricane fighting in the opening rounds. He began quietly, sparring for an opening. Sheen led with his left. Peteiro was too late with his guard. Sheen tried again – a double lead. His opponent guarded the first blow, but the second went home heavily on the body, and he gave way a step.

Then from the corner of his eye Sheen saw Bevan gesticulating wildly, so, taking his life in his hands, he abandoned his waiting game, dropped his guard, and dashed in to fight. Peteiro met him doggedly. For a few moments the exchanges were even. Then suddenly the Riptonian's blows began to weaken. He got home his right on the head, and Sheen hardly felt it. And in a flash there came to him the glorious certainty that the game was his.

He was winning – winning – winning.

'That's enough,' said the referee.

The Ripton man was leaning against the ropes, utterly spent, at almost the same spot where Sheen had leaned at the end of the first round. The last attack had finished him. His seconds helped him to his corner.

The referee waved his hand.

'Sheen wins,' he said.

And that was the greatest moment of his life.

'THE ROUT AT RIPTON': RUGBY IN *THE WHITE FEATHER*

This chapter from The White Feather *digresses from the central drama of Sheen in order to depict a number of his Wrykyn classmates – Allardyce, Barry, Drummond, Atell – failing ignominiously yet entertainingly on the rugby field, during a grudge match with the now-familiar rivals of Ripton school.*

Here as previous, Wodehouse seems to focus on the gruelling aspects of a rugby match: a preference that would recur. As late as his 1930 story 'The Ordeal of Young Tuppy', he had Bertie Wooster opine perplexedly on the rules of the game like so:

'I know that the main scheme is to work the ball down the field somehow and deposit it over the line at the other end, and that, in order to squelch this programme, each side is allowed to put in a certain amount of assault and battery and do things to its fellow man which, if done elsewhere, would result in fourteen days without the option, coupled with some strong remarks from the Bench.'

Here, then, is the tale of how Wrykyn got squelched by Ripton.

Of the two Ripton matches, the one played at Wrykyn was always the big event of the football year; but the other came next in importance, and the telegram which was despatched to the school shop at the close of the game was always awaited with anxiety. This year Wrykyn looked forward to the return match with a certain amount of apathy, due partly to the fact that the school was in a slack, unpatriotic state, and partly to the hammering the team had received in the previous term, when the Ripton centre three-quarters had run through and scored with monotonous regularity. 'We're bound to get sat on,' was the general verdict of the school.

Allardyce, while thoroughly agreeing with this opinion, did his best to conceal the fact from the rest of the team. He had certainly done his duty by them. Every day for the past fortnight the forwards and outsides had turned out to run and pass, and on the Saturdays there had been matches with Corpus, Oxford, and the Cambridge Old Wrykynians. In both games the school had been beaten. In fact, it seemed as if they could only perform really well when they had no opponents. To see the three-quarters racing down the field (at practice) and scoring innumerable (imaginary) tries, one was apt to be misled into considering them a fine quartette. But when there was a match, all the beautiful dash and precision of the passing faded away, and the last thing they did was to run straight. Barry was the only one of the four who played the game properly.

But, as regarded condition, there was nothing wrong with the team. Even Trevor could not have made them train harder; and Allardyce in his more sanguine moments had a shadowy hope that the Ripton score might, with care, be kept in the teens.

Barry had bought a *Sportsman* at the station, and he unfolded it as the train began to move. Searching the left-hand column of the middle page, as we all do when we buy the *Sportsman* on Saturday – to see how our names look in print, and what sort of a team the enemy has got – he made a remarkable discovery. At the same moment Drummond, on the other side of the carriage, did the same.

'I say,' he said, 'they must have had a big clear-out at Ripton. Have you seen the team they've got out today?'

'I was just looking at it,' said Barry.

'What's up with it?' inquired Allardyce. 'Let's have a look.'

'They've only got about half their proper team. They've got a different back – Grey isn't playing.'

'Both their centres are, though,' said Drummond.

'More fun for us, Drum, old chap,' said Attell. 'I'm going home again. Stop the train.'

Drummond said nothing. He hated Attell most when he tried to be facetious.

'Dunn isn't playing, nor is Waite,' said Barry, 'so they haven't got either of their proper halves. I say, we might have a chance of doing something today.'

'Of course we shall,' said Allardyce. 'You've only got to buck up and we've got them on toast.'

The atmosphere in the carriage became charged with optimism. It seemed a simple thing to defeat a side which was practically a Ripton 'A' team. The centre three-quarters were there still, it was true, but Allardyce and Drummond ought to be able to prevent the halves ever getting the ball out to them. The team looked on those two unknown halves as timid novices, who would lose their heads at the kick-off. As a matter of fact, the system of football teaching at Ripton was so perfect, and the keenness so great, that the second fifteen was nearly as good as the first every year. But the Wrykyn team did not know this, with the exception of Allardyce, who kept his knowledge to himself; and they arrived at Ripton jaunty and confident.

Keith, the Ripton captain, who was one of the centre three-quarters who had made so many holes in the Wrykyn defence in the previous term, met the team at the station, and walked up to the school with them, carrying Allardyce's bag.

'You seem to have lost a good many men at Christmas,' said Allardyce. 'We were reading the *Sportsman* in the train. Apparently, you've only got ten of your last term's lot. Have they all left?'

The Ripton captain grinned ruefully.

'Not much,' he replied. 'They're all here. All except Dunn. You remember Dunn? Little thick-set chap who played half. He always had his hair quite tidy and parted exactly in the middle all through the game.'

'Oh, yes, I remember Dunn. What's he doing now?'

'Gone to Cooper's Hill. Rot, his not going to the 'Varsity. He'd have walked into his Blue.'

Allardyce agreed. He had marked Dunn in the match of the previous term, and that immaculate sportsman had made things not a little warm for him.

'Where are all the others, then?' he asked. 'Where's that other half of yours? And the rest of the forwards?'

'Mumps,' said Keith.

'What!'

'It's a fact. Rot, isn't it? We've had a regular bout of it. Twenty fellows got it altogether. Naturally, four of those were in the team. That's the way things happen. I only wonder the whole scrum didn't have it.'

'What beastly luck,' said Allardyce. 'We had measles like that a couple of years ago in the summer term, and had to play the Incogs and Zingari with a sort of second eleven. We got mopped.'

'That's what we shall get this afternoon, I'm afraid,' said Keith.

'Oh no,' said Allardyce. 'Of course you won't.'

And, as events turned out, that was one of the truest remarks he had ever made in his life.

One of the drawbacks to playing Ripton on its own ground was the crowd. Another was the fact that one generally got beaten. But your sportsman can put up with defeat. What he does not like is a crowd that regards him as a subtle blend of incompetent idiot and malicious scoundrel and says so very loud and clear. It was not, of course, the school that did this. They spent their time blushing for the shouters. It was the patriotic inhabitants of Ripton town who made the school wish that they could be saved from their friends. The football ground at Ripton was at the edge of the school fields, separated from the road by narrow iron railings; and along these railings the choicest spirits of the town would line up, and smoke and yell and spit and yell again. As Wordsworth wrote, 'There are two voices.' They were on something like the following lines.

Inside the railings: 'Sch-oo-oo-oo-oo-l! Buck up Sch-oo-oo-oo-oo-l!! Get it out, Schoo-oo-oo-oo-l!!!'

Outside the railings: 'Gow it, Ripton! That's the way, Ripton! Twist his good-old-English-adjectived neck, Ripton! Sit on his forcibly described head, Ripton! Gow it, Ripton! Haw, Haw, Haw! They ain't no use, Ripton! Kick 'im in the eye, Ripton! Haw, Haw, Haw!'

The bursts of merriment signalised the violent downfall of some dangerous opponent.

The school loathed these humble supporters, and occasionally fastidious juniors would go the length of throwing chunks of mud at them through the railings. But nothing discouraged them or abated their fervid desire to see the school win. Every year they seemed to increase in zeal, and they were always in great form at the Wrykyn match.

It would be charitable to ascribe to this reason the gruesome happenings of that afternoon. They needed some explaining away.

Allardyce won the toss, and chose to start downhill, with the wind in his favour. It is always best to get these advantages at the beginning of the game. If one starts against the wind, it usually changes ends at half-time. Amidst a roar from both touch-lines and a volley of howls from the road, a Ripton forward kicked off. The ball flew in the direction of Stanning, on the right wing. A storm of laughter arose from the road as he dropped it. The first scrum was formed on the Wrykyn twenty-five line.

The Ripton forwards got the ball, and heeled with their usual neatness. The Ripton half who was taking the scrum gathered it cleanly, and passed to his colleague. He was a sturdy youth with a dark, rather forbidding face, in which the acute observer might have read signs of the savage. He was of the breed which is vaguely described at public schools as 'nigger', a term covering every variety of shade from ebony to light lemon. As a matter of fact he was a half-caste, sent home to England to be educated. Drummond recognised him as he dived forward to tackle him. The last place where they had met had been the roped ring at Aldershot. It was his opponent in the final of the Feathers.

He reached him as he swerved, and they fell together. The ball bounded forward.

'Hullo, Peteiro,' he said. 'Thought you'd left.'

The other grinned recognition.

'Hullo, Drummond.'

'Going up to Aldershot this year?'

'Yes. Light-weight.'

'So am I.'

The scrum had formed by now, and further conversation was impossible. Drummond looked a little thoughtful as he put the ball in. He had been told that Peteiro was leaving Ripton at Christmas. It was a nuisance his being still at school. Drummond was not afraid of him – he would have fought a champion of the world if the school had expected him to – but he could not help remembering that it was only by the very narrowest margin, and after a terrific three rounds, that he had beaten him in the Feathers the year before. It would be too awful for words if the decision were to be reversed in the coming competition.

But he was not allowed much leisure for pondering on the future. The present was too full of incident and excitement. The withdrawal of the four invalids and the departure of Dunn had not reduced the Ripton team to that wreck of its former self which the Wrykyn fifteen had looked for. On the contrary, their play seemed, if anything, a shade better than it had been in the former match. There was all the old aggressiveness, and Peteiro and his partner, so far from being timid novices and losing their heads, eclipsed the exhibition given at Wrykyn by Waite and Dunn. Play had only been in progress six minutes when Keith, taking a pass on the twenty-five line, slipped past Attell, ran round the back, and scored between the posts. Three minutes later the other Ripton centre scored. At the end of twenty minutes the Wrykyn line had been crossed five times, and each of the tries had been converted.

'*Can't* you fellows get that ball in the scrum?' demanded Allardyce plaintively, as the team began for the fifth time the old familiar walk to the half-way line. 'Pack tight, and get the first shove.'

The result of this address was to increase the Ripton lead by four points. In his anxiety to get the ball, one of the Wrykyn forwards started heeling before it was in, and the referee promptly gave a free kick to Ripton for 'foot up'. As this event took place within easy reach of the Wrykyn goal, and immediately in front of the same, Keith had no difficulty in bringing off the penalty.

By half-time the crowd in the road, hoarse with laughter, had exhausted all their adjectives and were repeating themselves. The Ripton score was six goals, a penalty goal, and two tries to *nil*, and the Wrykyn team was a demoralised rabble.

The fact that the rate of scoring slackened somewhat after the interval may be attributed to the disinclination of the Riptonians to exert themselves unduly. They ceased playing in the stern and scientific spirit in which they had started; and, instead of adhering to an orthodox game, began to enjoy themselves. The forwards no longer heeled like a machine. They broke through ambitiously, and tried to score on their own account. When the outsides got as far as the back, they did not pass. They tried to drop goals. In this way only twenty-two points were scored after half-time. Allardyce and Drummond battled on nobly, but with their pack hopelessly out-classed it was impossible for them to do anything of material use. Barry, on the wing, tackled his man whenever the latter got the ball, but, as a rule, the centres did not pass, but attacked by them-selves. At last, by way of a fitting conclusion to the rout, the Ripton back, catching a high punt, ran instead of kicking, and, to the huge delight of the town contingent, scored. With this incident the visiting team drained the last dregs of the bitter cup. Humiliation could go no further. Almost immediately afterwards the referee blew his whistle for 'No side.'

'Three cheers for Wrykyn,' said Keith.

To the fifteen victims it sounded ironical.

The return journey of a school team after a crushing defeat in a foreign match is never a very exhilarating business. Those members of the side who have not yet received their colours are wondering which of them is to be sacrificed to popular indignation and 'chucked': the rest, who have managed to get their caps, are feeling that even now two-thirds of the school will be saying that they are not worth a place in the third fifteen; while the captain, brooding apart, is becoming soured at the thought that Posterity will forget what little good he may have done, and remember only that it was in his year that the school got so many points taken off them by So-and-So. Conversation does not ripple and sparkle during these home-comings. The Wrykyn team made the journey in almost unbroken silence. They were all stiff and sore, and their feelings were such as to unfit them for talking to people.

The school took the thing very philosophically – a bad sign. When a school is in a healthy, normal condition, it should be stirred up by a bad defeat by another school, like a disturbed wasps' nest. Wrykyn made one or two remarks about people who could not play footer for toffee, and then let the thing drop.

'A CRICKET GENIUS':
VARIOUS INNINGS BY
MIKE

The highest accomplishment of Wodehouse's cricket writing is surely in the sequence of fictions published between 1907 and 1910, aimed at a school-age readership and starring young Mike Jackson, who constitutes Wodehouse's major study in white flannels, and is, arguably, the most winning hero in his oeuvre until Bertie Wooster comes along.

Mike was introduced in 'Jackson Junior', a serial tale for the Captain *in 1907. Its sequel 'The Lost Lambs' followed in 1908, and these two pieces were published together as the novel* Mike *in 1909, and then separately in 1953 as* Mike at Wrykyn *and* Mike and Psmith.

Malcolm Muggeridge, in his autobiography The Infernal Grove, *recalls a meeting with Wodehouse and George Orwell in Paris in 1944, during which the latter pair 'just talked cricket' in clear and shared adoration of the game. Afterwards Muggeridge, bewildered, told Orwell that Wodehouse rated the 'surely immature schoolboy story'* Mike *to be his 'best ever book'; that in its author's estimation it fully captured the 'ring of a ball on a cricket bat, the green of the pitch, the white of the flannels, the cheers of the crowd'. Muggeridge was then knocked flat once more by Orwell's response: 'Wodehouse is perfectly right.* Mike *is undoubtedly his very best book.'*

This is how it begins. Young Master Mike is about to head off to Wkykyn school. He has four older brothers, Bob, Joe, Reggie and Frank, all of whom excel at cricket, and it is soon apparent to his sister Marjory that in Mike the apple hasn't fallen far from the tree. We meet the boy on his home turf but under the seasoned eye of a professional from Surrey CCC.

After breakfast, Mike and Marjory went off together to the meadow at the end of the garden. Saunders, the professional, assisted by the gardener's boy, was engaged in putting up the net. Mr Jackson believed in private coaching; and every spring since Joe, the eldest of the family, had been able to use a bat a man had come down from the Oval to teach him the best way to do so. Each of the boys in turn had passed from spectators to active participants in the net practice in the meadow. For several years now Saunders had been the chosen man, and his attitude towards the Jacksons was that of the Faithful Old Retainer in melodrama. Mike was his special favourite. He felt that in him he had material of the finest order to work upon. There was nothing the matter with Bob. In Bob he would turn out a good, sound article. Bob would be a Blue in his third or fourth year, and probably a creditable performer among the rank and file of a county team later on. But he was not a cricket genius, like Mike. Saunders would lie awake at night sometimes thinking of the possibilities that were in Mike. The strength could only come with years, but the style was there already. Joe's style, with improvements.

Mike put on his pads; and Marjory walked with the professional to the bowling crease.

'Mike's going to Wrykyn next term, Saunders,' she said. 'All the boys were there, you know. So was father, ages ago.'

'Is he, miss? I was thinking he would be soon.'

'Do you think he'll get into the school team?'

'School team, miss! Master Mike get into a school team! He'll be playing for England in another eight years. That's what he'll be playing for.'

'Yes, but I meant next term. It would be a record if he did. Even Joe only got in after he'd been at school two years. Don't you think he might, Saunders? He's awfully good, isn't he? He's better than Bob, isn't he? And Bob's almost certain to get in this term.'

Saunders looked a little doubtful.

'Next term!' he said. 'Well, you see, miss, it's this way. It's all there, in a manner of speaking, with Master Mike. He's got as much style as Mr Joe's got, every bit. The whole thing is, you see, miss, you get these young gentlemen of eighteen, and nineteen perhaps, and it stands to reason they're stronger. There's a young gentleman, perhaps, doesn't know as much about what I call real playing as Master Mike's forgotten; but then he can hit 'em harder when he does hit 'em, and that's where the runs come in. They aren't going to play Master Mike because he'll be in the England team when he leaves school. They'll give the cap to somebody that can make a few then and there.'

'But Mike's jolly strong.'

'Ah, I'm not saying it mightn't be, miss. I was only saying don't count on it, so you won't be disappointed if it doesn't happen. It's quite likely that it will, only all I say is don't count on it. I only hope that they won't knock all the style out of him before they're done with him. You know these school professionals, miss.'

'No, I don't, Saunders. What are they like?'

'Well, there's too much of the come-right-out-at-everything about 'em for my taste. Seem to think playing forward the alpha and omugger of batting. They'll make him pat balls back to the bowler which he'd cut for twos and threes if he was left to himself. Still, we'll hope for the best, miss. Ready, Master Mike? Play.'

As Saunders had said, it was all there. Of Mike's style there could be no doubt. Today, too, he was playing more strongly than usual. Marjory had to run to the end of the meadow to fetch one straight drive. 'He hit that hard enough, didn't he, Saunders?' she asked, as she returned the ball.

'If he could keep on doing ones like that, miss,' said the professional, 'they'd have him in the team before you could say knife.'

Marjory sat down again beside the net, and watched more hopefully.

*

At Wrykyn, Mike's elder brothers are already 'objects of veneration to most Wrykynians' and so upon his settling into the school Mike bears a certain burden of expectation, but also benefits by a helping hand from a kindly senior, and a sibling or two.

It was Wyatt who gave him his first chance at cricket. There were nets on the first afternoon of term for all old colours of the three teams and a dozen or so of those most likely to fill the vacant places. Wyatt was there, of course. He had got his first eleven cap in the previous season as a mighty hitter and a fair slow bowler. Mike met him crossing the field with his cricket bag.

'Hullo, where are you off to?' asked Wyatt. 'Coming to watch the nets?'

Mike had no particular programme for the afternoon. Junior cricket had not begun, and it was a little difficult to know how to fill in the time.

'I tell you what,' said Wyatt, 'nip into the house and shove on some things, and I'll try and get Burgess to let you have a knock later on.'

This suited Mike admirably. A quarter of an hour later he was sitting at the back of the first eleven net, watching the practice.

Burgess, the captain of the Wrykyn team, made no pretence of being a bat. He was the school fast bowler and concentrated his energies on that department of the game. He sometimes took ten minutes at the wicket after everybody else had had an innings, but it was to bowl that he came to the nets.

He was bowling now to one of the old colours whose name Mike did not know. Wyatt and one of the professionals were the other two bowlers.

Two nets away Firby-Smith, who had changed his pince-nez for a pair of huge spectacles, was performing rather ineffectively against some very bad bowling. Mike fixed his attention on the first eleven man. He was evidently a good bat. There was style and power in his batting. He had a way of gliding Burgess's fastest to leg which Mike admired greatly. He was succeeded at the end of a quarter of an hour by another eleven man, and then Bob appeared.

It was soon made evident that this was not Bob's day. Nobody is at his best on the first day of term; but Bob was worse than he had any right to be. He scratched forward at nearly everything, and when Burgess, who had been resting, took up the ball again, he had each stump uprooted in a regular series in seven balls. Once he skied one of Wyatt's slows over the net behind the wicket; and Mike, jumping up, caught him neatly.

'Thanks,' said Bob austerely, as Mike returned the ball to him. He seemed depressed.

Towards the end of the afternoon, Wyatt went up to Burgess.

'Burgess,' he said, 'see that kid sitting behind the net?'

'With the naked eye,' said Burgess. 'Why?'

'He's just come to Wain's. He's Bob Jackson's brother, and I've a sort of idea that he's a bit of a bat. I told him I'd ask you if he could have a knock. Why not send him in at the end net? There's nobody there now.'

Burgess's amiability off the field equalled his ruthlessness when bowling.

'All right,' he said. 'Only if you think that I'm going to sweat to bowl to him, you're making a fatal error.'

'You needn't do a thing. Just sit and watch. I rather fancy this kid's something special.'

Mike put on Wyatt's pads and gloves, borrowed his bat, and walked round into the net.

'Not in a funk, are you?' asked Wyatt, as he passed.

Mike grinned. The fact was that he had far too good an opinion of himself to be nervous. An entirely modest person seldom makes a good batsman. Batting is one of those things which demand first and foremost a thorough belief in oneself. It need not be aggressive, but it must be there.

Wyatt and the professional were the bowlers. Mike had seen enough of Wyatt's bowling to know that it was merely ordinary 'slow tosh,' and the professional did not look as difficult as Saunders. The first half-dozen balls he played carefully. He was on trial, and he meant to take no risks. Then the professional over-pitched one slightly on the off. Mike jumped out, and got the full face of the bat on to it. The ball hit one of the ropes of the net, and nearly broke it.

'How's that?' said Wyatt, with the smile of an impresario on the first night of a successful piece.

'Not bad,' admitted Burgess.

A few moments later he was still more complimentary. He got up and took a ball himself.

Mike braced himself up as Burgess began his run. This time he was more than a trifle nervous. The bowling he had had so far had been tame. This would be the real ordeal.

As the ball left Burgess's hand he began instinctively to shape for a forward stroke. Then suddenly he realised that the thing was going to be a yorker, and banged his bat down in the block just as the ball arrived. An unpleasant sensation as of having been struck by a thunderbolt was succeeded by a feeling of relief that he had kept the ball out of his wicket. There are easier things in the world than stopping a fast yorker.

'Well played,' said Burgess.

Mike felt like a successful general receiving the thanks of the nation.

The fact that Burgess's next ball knocked middle and off stumps out of the ground saddened him somewhat; but this was the last tragedy that occurred. He could not do much with the bowling beyond stopping it and feeling repetitions of the thunderbolt experience, but he kept up his end; and a short conversation which he had with Burgess at the end of his innings was full of encouragement to one skilled in reading between the lines.

'Thanks awfully,' said Mike, referring to the square manner in which the captain had behaved in letting him bat.

'What school were you at before you came here?' asked Burgess.

'A private school in Hampshire,' said Mike. 'King-Hall's. At a place called Emsworth.'

'Get much cricket there?'

'Yes, a good lot. One of the masters, a chap called Westbrook, was an awfully good slow bowler.'

Burgess nodded.

'You don't run away, which is something,' he said.

Mike turned purple with pleasure at this stately compliment. Then, having waited for further remarks, but gathering from the captain's silence that the audience was at an end, he proceeded to unbuckle his pads. Wyatt overtook him on his way to the house.

'Well played,' he said. 'I'd no idea you were such hot stuff. You're a regular pro.'

'I say,' said Mike gratefully, 'it was most awfully decent of you getting Burgess to let me go in. It was simply ripping of you.'

'Oh, that's all right. If you don't get pushed a bit here you stay for ages in the hundredth game with the cripples and the kids. Now you've shown them what you can do you ought to get into the Under Sixteen team straight away. Probably into the third, too.'

'By Jove, that would be all right.'

'I asked Burgess afterwards what he thought of your batting, and he said, "Not bad." But he says that about everything. It's his highest form of praise. He says it when he wants to let himself go and simply butter up a thing. If you took him to see N. A. Knox bowl, he'd say he wasn't bad. What he meant was that he was jolly struck with your batting, and is going to play you for the Under Sixteen.'

'I hope so,' said Mike.

The prophecy was fulfilled. On the following Wednesday there was a match between the Under Sixteen and a scratch side. Mike's name was among the Under Sixteen. And on the Saturday he was playing for the third eleven in a trial game.

'This place is ripping,' he said to himself, as he saw his name on the list. 'Thought I should like it.'

And that night he wrote a letter to his father, notifying him of the fact.

*

In due course Mike gets his chance at a First XI game: a prestigious contest against the MCC.

If the day happens to be fine, there is a curious, dream-like atmosphere about the opening stages of a first eleven match. Everything seems hushed and expectant. The rest of the school have gone in after the interval at eleven o'clock, and you are alone on the grounds with a cricket-bag. The only signs of life are a few pedestrians on the road beyond the railings and one or two blazer and flannel-clad forms in the pavilion. The sense of isolation is trying to the nerves, and a school team usually bats twenty-five per cent. Better after lunch, when the strangeness has worn off.

Mike walked across from Wain's, where he had changed, feeling quite hollow. He could almost have cried with pure fright. Bob had shouted after him from a window as he passed Donaldson's, to wait, so that they could walk over together; but conversation was the last thing Mike desired at that moment.

He had almost reached the pavilion when one of the M.C.C. team came down the steps, saw him, and stopped dead.

'By Jove, Saunders!' cried Mike.

'Why, Master Mike!'

The professional beamed, and quite suddenly, the lost, hopeless feeling left Mike. He felt as cheerful as if he and Saunders had met in the meadow at home, and were just going to begin a little quiet net-practice.

'Why, Master Mike, you don't mean to say you're playing for the school already?'

Mike nodded happily.

'Isn't it ripping,' he said.

Saunders slapped his leg in a sort of ecstasy.

'Didn't I always say it, sir,' he chuckled. 'Wasn't I right? I used to say to myself it 'ud be a pretty good school team that 'ud leave you out.'

'Of course, I'm only playing as a sub., you know. Three chaps are in extra, and I got one of the places.'

'Well, you'll make a hundred today, Master Mike, and then they'll have to put you in.'

'Wish I could!'

'Master Joe's come down with the Club,' said Saunders.

'Joe! Has he really? How ripping! Hullo, here he is. Hullo, Joe?'

The greatest of all the Jacksons was descending the pavilion steps with the gravity befitting an All England batsman. He stopped short, as Saunders had done.

'Mike! You aren't playing!'

'Yes.'

'Well, I'm hanged! Young marvel, isn't he, Saunders?'

'He is, sir,' said Saunders. 'Got all the strokes. I always said it, Master Joe. Only wants the strength.'

Joe took Mike by the shoulder, and walked him off in the direction of a man in a Zingari blazer who was bowling slows to another of the M.C.C. team. Mike recognised him with awe as one of the three best amateur wicket-keepers in the country.

'What do you think of this?' said Joe, exhibiting Mike, who grinned bashfully. 'Aged ten last birthday, and playing for the school. You are only ten, aren't you, Mike?'

'Brother of yours?' asked the wicket-keeper.

'Probably too proud to own the relationship, but he is.'

'Isn't there any end to you Jacksons?' demanded the wicket-keeper in an aggrieved tone. 'I never saw such a family.'

'This is our star. You wait till he gets at us today. Saunders is our only bowler, and Mike's been brought up on Saunders. You'd better win the toss if you want a chance of getting a knock and lifting your average out of the minuses.'

'I *have* won the toss,' said the other with dignity. 'Do you think I don't know the elementary duties of a captain?'

The school went out to field with mixed feelings. The wicket was hard and true, which would have made it pleasant to be going in first. On the other hand, they would feel decidedly better and fitter for centuries after the game had been in progress an hour or so. Burgess was glad as a private individual, sorry as a captain. For himself, the sooner he got hold of the ball and began to bowl the better he liked it. As a captain, he realised that a side with Joe Jackson on it, not to mention the other first-class men, was not a side to which he would have preferred to give away an advantage. Mike was feeling that by no possibility could he hold the simplest catch, and hoping that nothing would come his way. Bob, conscious of being an uncertain field, was feeling just the same.

The M.C.C. opened with Joe and a man in an Oxford Authentic cap. The beginning of the game was quiet. Burgess's yorker was nearly too much for the latter in the first over, but he contrived to chop it away, and the pair gradually settled down. At twenty, Joe began to open his shoulders. Twenty became forty with disturbing swiftness, and Burgess tried a change of bowling.

It seemed for one instant as if the move had been a success, for Joe, still taking risks, tried to late-cut a rising ball, and snicked it straight into Bob's hands at second slip. It was the easiest of slip-catches, but Bob fumbled it, dropped it, almost held it a second time, and finally let it fall miserably to the ground. It was a moment too painful for words. He rolled the ball back to the bowler in silence.

One of those weary periods followed when the batsman's defence seems to the fieldsmen absolutely impregnable. There was a sickening inevitableness in the way in which every ball was played with the very centre of the bat. And, as usual, just when things seemed most hopeless, relief came. The Authentic, getting in front of his wicket, to pull one of the simplest long-hops ever seen on a cricket field, missed it, and was l.b.w. And the next ball upset the newcomer's leg stump.

The school revived. Bowlers and field were infused with a new life. Another wicket – two stumps knocked out of the ground by Burgess – helped the thing on. When the bell rang for the end of morning school, five wickets were down for a hundred and thirteen.

But from the end of school till lunch things went very wrong indeed.

Joe was still in at one end, invincible; and at the other was the great wicket-keeper. And the pair of them suddenly began to force the pace till the bowling was in a tangled knot. Four after four, all round the wicket, with never a chance or a mishit to vary the monotony. Two hundred went up, and two hundred and fifty. Then Joe reached his century, and was stumped next ball. Then came lunch.

The rest of the innings was like the gentle rain after the thunderstorm. Runs came with fair regularity, but wickets fell at intervals, and when the wicket-keeper was run out at length for a lively sixty-three, the end was very near. Saunders, coming in last, hit two boundaries, and was then caught by Mike. His second hit had just lifted the M.C.C. total over the three hundred.

Three hundred is a score that takes some making on any ground, but on a fine day it was not an unusual total for the Wrykyn eleven. Some years before, against Ripton, they had run up four hundred and sixteen; and only last season had massacred a very weak team of Old Wrykynians with a score that only just missed the fourth hundred.

Unfortunately, on the present occasion, there was scarcely time, unless the bowling happened to get completely collared, to make the runs. It was a quarter to four when the innings began, and stumps were to be drawn at a quarter to seven. A hundred an hour is quick work.

Burgess, however, was optimistic, as usual. 'Better have a go for them,' he said to Berridge and Marsh, the school first pair.

Following out this courageous advice, Berridge, after hitting three boundaries in his first two overs, was stumped half-way through the third.

After this, things settled down. Morris, the first-wicket man, was a thoroughly sound bat, a little on the slow side, but exceedingly hard to shift. He and Marsh proceeded to play themselves in, until it looked as if they were likely to stay till the drawing of stumps.

A comfortable, rather somnolent feeling settled upon the school. A long stand at cricket is a soothing sight to watch. There was an absence of hurry about the batsmen which harmonised well with the drowsy summer afternoon. And yet runs were coming at a fair pace. The hundred went up at five o'clock, the hundred and fifty at half-past.

Both batsmen were completely at home, and the M.C.C. third-change bowlers had been put on.

Then the great wicket-keeper took off the pads and gloves, and the fieldsmen retired to posts at the extreme edge of the ground.

'Lobs,' said Burgess. 'By Jove, I wish I was in.'

It seemed to be the general opinion among the members of the Wrykyn eleven on the pavilion balcony that Morris and Marsh were in luck. The team did not grudge them their good fortune, because they had earned it; but they were distinctly envious.

Lobs are the most dangerous, insinuating things in the world. Everybody knows in theory the right way to treat them. Everybody knows that the man who is content not to try to score more than a single cannot get out to them. Yet nearly everybody does get out to them.

It was the same story today. The first over yielded six runs, all through gentle taps along the ground. In the second, Marsh hit an over-pitched one along the ground to the terrace bank. The next ball he swept round to the leg boundary. And that was the end of Marsh. He saw himself scoring at the rate of twenty-four an over. Off the last ball he was stumped by several feet, having done himself credit by scoring seventy.

The long stand was followed, as usual, by a series of disasters.

Marsh's wicket had fallen at a hundred and eighty. Ellerby left at a hundred and eighty-six. By the time the scoring-board registered two hundred, five wickets were down, three of them victims to the lobs.

Morris was still in at one end. He had refused to be tempted. He was jogging on steadily to his century.

Bob Jackson went in next, with instructions to keep his eye on the lob-man.

For a time things went well. Saunders, who had gone on to bowl again after a rest, seemed to give Morris no trouble, and Bob put him through the slips with apparent ease. Twenty runs were added, when the lob-bowler once more got in his deadly work. Bob, letting alone a ball wide of the off-stump under the impression that it was going to break away, was disagreeably surprised to find it break in instead, and hit the wicket. The bowler smiled sadly, as if he hated to have to do these things.

Mike's heart jumped as he saw the bails go. It was his turn next.

'Two hundred and twenty-nine,' said Burgess, 'and it's ten past six. No good trying for the runs now. Stick in,' he added to Mike. 'That's all you've got to do.'

All! … Mike felt as if he was being strangled. His heart was racing like the engines of a motor. He knew his teeth were chattering. He wished he could stop them. What a time Bob was taking to get back to the pavilion! He wanted to rush out, and get the thing over.

At last he arrived, and Mike, fumbling at a glove, tottered out into the sunshine. He heard miles and miles away a sound of clapping, and a thin, shrill noise as if somebody were screaming in the distance. As a matter of fact, several members of his form and of the junior day-room at Wain's nearly burst themselves at that moment.

At the wickets, he felt better. Bob had fallen to the last ball of the over, and Morris, standing ready for Saunders's delivery, looked so calm and certain of himself that it was impossible to feel entirely without hope and self-confidence. Mike knew that Morris had made ninety-eight, and he supposed that Morris knew that he was very near his century; yet he seemed to be absolutely undisturbed. Mike drew courage from his attitude.

Morris pushed the first ball away to leg. Mike would have liked to have run two, but short leg had retrieved the ball as he reached the crease.

The moment had come, the moment which he had experienced only in dreams. And in the dreams he was always full of confidence, and invariably hit a boundary. Sometimes a drive, sometimes a cut, but always a boundary.

'To leg, sir,' said the umpire.

'Don't be in a funk,' said a voice. 'Play straight, and you can't get out.'

It was Joe, who had taken the gloves when the wicket-keeper went on to bowl.

Mike grinned, wryly but gratefully.

Saunders was beginning his run. It was all so home-like that for a moment Mike felt himself again. How often he had seen those two little skips and the jump. It was like being in the paddock again, with Marjory and the dogs waiting by the railings to fetch the ball if he made a drive.

Saunders ran to the crease, and bowled.

Now, Saunders was a conscientious man, and, doubtless, bowled the very best ball that he possibly could. On the other hand, it was Mike's first appearance for the school, and Saunders, besides being conscientious, was undoubtedly kind-hearted. It is useless to specu-late as to whether he was trying to bowl his best that ball. If so, he failed signally. It was a half-volley, just the right distance away from the off-stump; the sort of ball Mike was wont to send nearly through the net at home ...

The next moment the dreams had come true. The umpire was signalling to the scoring-box, the school was shouting, extra-cover was trotting to the boundary to fetch the ball, and Mike was blush-ing and wondering whether it was bad form to grin.

From that ball onwards all was for the best in this best of all possible worlds. Saunders bowled no more half-volleys; but Mike played everything that he did bowl. He met the lobs with a bat like a barn-door. Even the departure of Morris, caught in the slips off Saunders's next over for a chanceless hundred and five, did not disturb him. All nervousness had left him. He felt equal to the situation.

Burgess came in, and began to hit out as if he meant to knock off the runs. The bowling became a shade loose. Twice he was given full tosses to leg, which he hit to the terrace bank. Half-past six chimed, and two hundred and fifty went up on the telegraph board. Burgess continued to hit. Mike's whole soul was concentrated on keeping up his wicket.

There was only Reeves to follow him, and Reeves was a victim to the first straight ball. Burgess had to hit because it was the only game he knew; but he himself must simply stay in.

The hands of the clock seemed to have stopped. Then suddenly he heard the umpire say 'Last over,' and he settled down to keep those six balls out of his wicket.

The lob-bowler had taken himself off, and the Oxford Authentic had gone on, fast left-hand.

The first ball was short and wide of the off-stump. Mike let it alone.

Number two: yorker. Got him! Three: straight half-volley. Mike played it back to the bowler. Four: beat him, and missed the wicket by an inch. Five: another yorker. Down on it again in the old familiar way.

All was well. The match was a draw now whatever happened to him. He hit out, almost at a venture, at the last ball, and mid-off, jumping, just failed to reach it. It hummed over his head, and ran like a streak along the turf and up the bank, and a great howl of delight went up from the school as the umpire took off the bails.

Mike walked away from the wickets with Joe and the wicket-keeper.

'I'm sorry about your nose, Joe,' said the wicket-keeper in tones of grave solicitude.

'What's wrong with it?'

'At present,' said the wicket-keeper, 'nothing. But in a few years I'm afraid it's going to be put badly out of joint.'

*

For all his aptitude, Mike's progress is not seamless. As he soon learns, 'One had to take the rungs of the ladder singly at Wrykyn.' But his next big chance and test of mettle is an inter-school match with Ripton, that nemesis in the Wodehouse sports canon.

The Ripton match was a special event, and the man who performed any outstanding feat against that school was treated as a sort of Horatius. Honours were heaped upon him. If he could only make a century! or even fifty. Even twenty, if it got the school out of a tight place. He was as nervous on the Saturday morning as he had been on the morning of the M.C.C. match. It was Victory or Westminster Abbey now. To do only averagely well, to be among the ruck, would be as useless as not playing at all, as far as his chance of his first was concerned.

It was evident to those who woke early on the Saturday morning that this Ripton match was not likely to end in a draw. During the Friday rain had fallen almost incessantly in a steady drizzle. It had stopped late at night; and at six in the morning there was every prospect of another hot day. There was that feeling in the air which shows that the sun is trying to get through the clouds. The sky was a dull grey at breakfast time, except where a flush of deeper colour gave a hint of the sun. It was a day on which to win the toss, and go in first. At eleven-thirty, when the match was timed to begin, the wicket would be too wet to be difficult. Runs would come easily till the sun came out and began to dry the ground. When that happened there would be trouble for the side that was batting.

Burgess, inspecting the wicket with Mr Spence during the quarter to eleven interval, was not slow to recognise this fact.

'I should win the toss today, if I were you, Burgess,' said Mr Spence.

'Just what I was thinking, sir.'

'That wicket's going to get nasty after lunch, if the sun comes out. A regular Rhodes wicket it's going to be.'

'I wish we *had* Rhodes,' said Burgess. 'Or even Wyatt. It would just suit him, this.'

Mr Spence, as a member of the staff, was not going to be drawn into discussing Wyatt and his premature departure, so he diverted the conversation on to the subject of the general aspect of the school's attack.

'Who will go on first with you, Burgess?'

'Who do you think, sir? Ellerby? It might be his wicket.'

Ellerby bowled medium inclining to slow. On a pitch that suited him he was apt to turn from leg and get people out caught at the wicket or short slip.

'Certainly, Ellerby. This end, I think. The other's yours, though I'm afraid you'll have a poor time bowling fast today. Even with plenty of sawdust I doubt if it will be possible to get a decent foothold till after lunch.'

'I must win the toss,' said Burgess. 'It's a nuisance too, about our batting. Marsh will probably be dead out of form after being in the Infirmary so long. If he'd had a chance of getting a bit of practice yesterday, it might have been all right.'

'That rain will have a lot to answer for if we lose. On a dry, hard wicket I'm certain we should beat them four times out of six. I was talking to a man who played against them for the Nomads. He said that on a true wicket there was not a great deal of sting in their bowling, but that they've got a slow leg-break man who might be dangerous on a day like this. A boy called de Freece. I don't know of him. He wasn't in the team last year.'

'I know the chap. He played wing three for them at footer against us this year on their ground. He was crocked when they came here.

He's a pretty useful chap all round, I believe. Plays racquets for them too.'

'Well, my friend said he had one very dangerous ball, of the Bosanquet type. Looks as if it were going away, and comes in instead.'

'I don't think a lot of that,' said Burgess ruefully. 'One consolation is, though, that that sort of ball is easier to watch on a slow wicket. I must tell the fellows to look out for it.'

'I should. And, above all, win the toss.'

Burgess and Maclaine, the Ripton captain, were old acquaintances. They had been at the same private school, and they had played against one another at football and cricket for two years now.

'We'll go in first, Mac,' said Burgess, as they met on the pavilion steps after they had changed.

'It's awfully good of you to suggest it,' said Maclaine. 'but I think we'll toss. It's a hobby of mine. You call.'

'Heads.'

'Tails it is. I ought to have warned you that you hadn't a chance. I've lost the toss five times running, so I was bound to win today.'

'You'll put us in, I suppose?'

'Yes – after us.'

'Oh, well, we sha'n't have long to wait for our knock, that's a comfort. Buck up and send someone in, and let's get at you.'

And Burgess went off to tell the ground-man to have plenty of sawdust ready, as he would want the field paved with it.

The policy of the Ripton team was obvious from the first over. They meant to force the game. Already the sun was beginning to peep through the haze. For about an hour run-getting ought to be a tolerably simple process; but after that hour singles would be as valuable as threes and boundaries an almost unheard-of luxury.

So Ripton went in to hit.

The policy proved successful for a time, as it generally does. Burgess, who relied on a run that was a series of tiger-like leaps culminating in a spring that suggested that he meant to lower the long jump record, found himself badly handicapped by the state of the ground. In spite of frequent libations of sawdust, he was compelled to tread cautiously, and this robbed his bowling of much of its pace. The score mounted rapidly. Twenty came in ten minutes. At thirty-five the first wicket fell, run out.

At sixty Ellerby, who had found the pitch too soft for him and had been expensive, gave place to Grant. Grant bowled what were supposed to be slow leg-breaks, but which did not always break. The change worked.

Maclaine, after hitting the first two balls to the boundary, skied the third to Bob Jackson in the deep, and Bob, for whom constant practice had robbed this sort of catch of its terrors, held it.

A yorker from Burgess disposed of the next man before he could settle down; but the score, seventy-four for three wickets, was large enough in view of the fact that the pitch was already becoming more difficult, and was certain to get worse, to make Ripton feel that the advantage was with them. Another hour of play remained before lunch. The deterioration of the wicket would be slow during that period. The sun, which was now shining brightly, would put in its deadliest work from two o'clock onwards. Maclaine's instructions to his men were to go on hitting.

A too liberal interpretation of the meaning of the verb 'to hit' led to the departure of two more Riptonians in the course of the next two overs. There is a certain type of school batsman who considers that to force the game means to swipe blindly at every ball on the chance of taking it half-volley. This policy sometimes leads to a boundary or two, as it did on this occasion, but it means that wickets will fall, as also happened now. Seventy-four for three became eighty-six for five. Burgess began to look happier.

His contentment increased when he got the next man leg-before-wicket with the total unaltered. At this rate Ripton would be out before lunch for under a hundred.

But the rot stopped with the fall of that wicket. Dashing tactics were laid aside. The pitch had begun to play tricks, and the pair now in settled down to watch the ball. They plodded on, scoring slowly and jerkily till the hands of the clock stood at half-past one. Then Ellerby, who had gone on again instead of Grant, beat the less steady of the pair with a ball that pitched on the middle stump and shot into the base of the off. A hundred and twenty had gone up on the board at the beginning of the over.

That period which is always so dangerous, when the wicket is bad, the ten minutes before lunch, proved fatal to two more of the enemy. The last man had just gone to the wickets, with the score at a hundred and thirty-one, when a quarter to two arrived, and with it the luncheon interval.

So far it was anybody's game.

The Ripton last-wicket man was de Freece, the slow bowler. He was apparently a young gentleman wholly free from the curse of nervousness. He wore a cheerful smile as he took guard before receiving the first ball after lunch, and Wrykyn had plenty of opportunity of seeing that that was his normal expression when at the wickets. There is often a certain looseness about the attack after lunch, and the bowler of googlies took advantage of it now. He seemed to be a batsman with only one hit; but he had also a very accurate eye, and his one hit, a semicircular stroke, which suggested the golf links rather than the cricket field, came off with distressing frequency. He mowed Burgess's first ball to the square-leg boundary, missed his second, and snicked the third for three over long-slip's head. The other batsman played out the over, and de Freece proceeded to treat Ellerby's bowling with equal familiarity. The scoring-board showed an increase of twenty as the result of three overs. Every run was invaluable now, and the Ripton contingent made the pavilion re-echo as a fluky shot over mid-on's head sent up the hundred and fifty.

There are few things more exasperating to the fielding side than a last-wicket stand. It resembles in its effect the dragging-out of a book or play after the *denouement* has been reached. At the fall of the ninth wicket the fieldsmen nearly always look on their outing as finished. Just a ball or two to the last man, and it will be their turn to bat. If the last man insists on keeping them out in the field, they resent it.

What made it especially irritating now was the knowledge that a straight yorker would solve the whole thing. But when Burgess bowled a yorker, it was not straight. And when he bowled a straight ball, it was not a yorker. A four and a three to de Freece, and a four bye sent up a hundred and sixty.

It was beginning to look as if this might go on for ever, when Ellerby, who had been missing the stumps by fractions of an inch, for the last ten minutes, did what Burgess had failed to do. He bowled a straight, medium-paced yorker, and de Freece, swiping at it with a bright smile, found his leg-stump knocked back. He had made twenty-eight. His record score, he explained to Mike, as they walked to the pavilion, for this or any ground.

The Ripton total was a hundred and sixty-six.

With the ground in its usual true, hard condition, Wrykyn would have gone in against a score of a hundred and sixty-six with the cheery intention of knocking off the runs for the loss of two or three wickets. It would have been a gentle canter for them.

But ordinary standards would not apply here. On a good wicket Wrykyn that season were a two hundred and fifty to three hundred side. On a bad wicket – well, they had met the Incogniti on a bad wicket, and their total – with Wyatt playing and making top score – had worked out at a hundred and seven.

A grim determination to do their best, rather than confidence that their best, when done, would be anything record-breaking, was the spirit which animated the team when they opened their innings.

And in five minutes this had changed to a dull gloom.

The tragedy started with the very first ball. It hardly seemed that the innings had begun, when Morris was seen to leave the crease, and make for the pavilion.

'It's that googly man,' said Burgess blankly.

'What's happened?' shouted a voice from the interior of the first eleven room.

'Morris is out.'

'Good gracious! How?' asked Ellerby, emerging from the room with one pad on his leg and the other in his hand.

'L.b.w. First ball.'

'My aunt! Who's in next? Not me?'

'No. Berridge. For goodness sake, Berry, stick a bat in the way, and not your legs. Watch that de Freece man like a hawk. He breaks like sin all over the shop. Hullo, Morris! Bad luck! Were you out, do you think?' A batsman who has been given l.b.w. is always asked this question on his return to the pavilion, and he answers it in nine cases out of ten in the negative. Morris was the tenth case. He thought it was all right, he said.

'Thought the thing was going to break, but it didn't.'

'Hear that, Berry? He doesn't always break. You must look out for that,' said Burgess helpfully. Morris sat down and began to take off his pads.

'That chap'll have Berry, if he doesn't look out,' he said.

But Berridge survived the ordeal. He turned his first ball to leg for a single.

This brought Marsh to the batting end; and the second tragedy occurred.

It was evident from the way he shaped that Marsh was short of practice. His visit to the Infirmary had taken the edge off his batting. He scratched awkwardly at three balls without hitting them.

The last of the over had him in two minds. He started to play forward, changed his stroke suddenly and tried to step back, and the next moment the bails had shot up like the *debris* of a small explosion, and the wicket-keeper was clapping his gloved hands gently and slowly in the introspective, dreamy way wicket-keepers have on these occasions.

A silence that could be felt brooded over the pavilion.

The voice of the scorer, addressing from his little wooden hut the melancholy youth who was working the telegraph-board, broke it.

'One for two. Last man duck.'

Ellerby echoed the remark. He got up, and took off his blazer.

'This is all right,' he said, 'isn't it! I wonder if the man at the other end is a sort of young Rhodes too!'

Fortunately he was not. The star of the Ripton attack was evidently de Freece. The bowler at the other end looked fairly plain. He sent them down medium-pace, and on a good wicket would probably have been simple. But today there was danger in the most guileless-looking deliveries.

Berridge relieved the tension a little by playing safely through the over, and scoring a couple of twos off it. And when Ellerby not only survived the destructive de Freece's second over, but actually lifted a loose ball on to the roof of the scoring-hut, the cloud began perceptibly to lift. A no-ball in the same over sent up the first ten. Ten for two was not good; but it was considerably better than one for two.

With the score at thirty, Ellerby was missed in the slips off de Freece. He had been playing with slowly increasing confidence till then, but this seemed to throw him out of his stride. He played inside the next ball, and was all but bowled: and then, jumping out to drive, he was smartly stumped. The cloud began to settle again.

Bob was the next man in.

Ellerby took off his pads, and dropped into the chair next to Mike's.

Mike was silent and thoughtful. He was in after Bob, and to be on the eve of batting does not make one conversational.

'You in next?' asked Ellerby.

Mike nodded.

'It's getting trickier every minute,' said Ellerby. 'The only thing is, if we can only stay in, we might have a chance. The wicket'll get better, and I don't believe they've any bowling at all bar de Freece. By George, Bob's out! ... No, he isn't.'

Bob had jumped out at one of de Freece's slows, as Ellerby had done, and had nearly met the same fate. The wicket-keeper, however, had fumbled the ball.

'That's the way I was had,' said Ellerby. 'That man's keeping such a jolly good length that you don't know whether to stay in your ground or go out at them. If only somebody would knock him off his length, I believe we might win yet.'

The same idea apparently occurred to Burgess. He came to where Mike was sitting.

'I'm going to shove you down one, Jackson,' he said. 'I shall go in next myself and swipe, and try and knock that man de Freece off.'

'All right,' said Mike. He was not quite sure whether he was glad or sorry at the respite.

'It's a pity old Wyatt isn't here,' said Ellerby. 'This is just the sort of time when he might have come off.'

'Bob's broken his egg,' said Mike.

'Good man. Every little helps ... Oh, you silly ass, get *back*!'

Berridge had called Bob for a short run that was obviously no run.

Third man was returning the ball as the batsmen crossed. The next moment the wicket-keeper had the bails off. Berridge was out by a yard.

'Forty-one for four,' said Ellerby. 'Help!'

Burgess began his campaign against de Freece by skying his first ball over cover's head to the boundary. A howl of delight went up from the school, which was repeated, *fortissimo*, when, more by accident than by accurate timing, the captain put on two more fours past extra-cover. The bowler's cheerful smile never varied.

Whether Burgess would have knocked de Freece off his length or not was a question that was destined to remain unsolved, for in the middle of the other bowler's over Bob hit a single; the batsmen crossed; and Burgess had his leg-stump uprooted while trying a gigantic pull-stroke.

The melancholy youth put up the figures, 54, 5, 12, on the board.

Mike, as he walked out of the pavilion to join Bob, was not conscious of any particular nervousness. It had been an ordeal having to wait and look on while wickets fell, but now that the time of inaction was at an end he felt curiously composed. When he had gone out to bat against the M.C.C. on the occasion of his first appearance for the school, he experienced a quaint sensation of unreality. He seemed to be watching his body walking to the wickets, as if it were someone else's. There was no sense of individuality.

But now his feelings were different. He was cool. He noticed small things – mid-off chewing bits of grass, the bowler re-tying the scarf round his waist, little patches of brown where the turf had been worn away. He took guard with a clear picture of the positions of the fieldsmen photographed on his brain.

Fitness, which in a batsman exhibits itself mainly in an increased power of seeing the ball, is one of the most inexplicable things connected with cricket. It has nothing, or very little, to do with actual health. A man may come out of a sick-room with just that extra quickness in sighting the ball that makes all the difference; or he may be in perfect training and play inside straight half-volleys. Mike would not have said that he felt more than ordinarily well that day.

Indeed, he was rather painfully conscious of having bolted his food at lunch. But something seemed to whisper to him, as he settled himself to face the bowler, that he was at the top of his batting form. A difficult wicket always brought out his latent powers as a bat. It was a standing mystery with the sporting Press how Joe Jackson managed to collect fifties and sixties on wickets that completely upset men who were, apparently, finer players. On days when the Olympians of the cricket world were bringing their averages down with ducks and singles, Joe would be in his element, watching the ball and pushing it through the slips as if there were no such thing as a tricky wicket.

And Mike took after Joe.

A single off the fifth ball of the over opened his score and brought him to the opposite end. Bob played ball number six back to the bowler, and Mike took guard preparatory to facing de Freece.

The Ripton slow bowler took a long run, considering his pace. In the early part of an innings he often trapped the batsmen in this way, by leading them to expect a faster ball than he actually sent down. A queer little jump in the middle of the run increased the difficulty of watching him.

The smiting he had received from Burgess in the previous over had not had the effect of knocking de Freece off his length. The ball was too short to reach with comfort, and not short enough to take liberties with. It pitched slightly to leg, and whipped in quickly. Mike had faced half-left, and stepped back. The increased speed of the ball after it had touched the ground beat him. The ball hit his right pad.

"'S that?' shouted mid-on. Mid-on has a habit of appealing for l.b.w. in school matches.

De Freece said nothing. The Ripton bowler was as conscientious in the matter of appeals as a good bowler should be. He had seen that the ball had pitched off the leg-stump.

The umpire shook his head. Mid-on tried to look as if he had not spoken.

Mike prepared himself for the next ball with a glow of confidence. He felt that he knew where he was now. Till then he had not thought the wicket was so fast. The two balls he had played at the other end had told him nothing. They had been well pitched up, and he had smothered them. He knew what to do now. He had played on wickets of this pace at home against Saunders's bowling, and Saunders had shown him the right way to cope with them.

The next ball was of the same length, but this time off the off-stump. Mike jumped out, and hit it before it had time to break. It flew along the ground through the gap between cover and extra-cover, a comfortable three.

Bob played out the over with elaborate care.

Off the second ball of the other man's over Mike scored his first boundary. It was a long-hop on the off. He banged it behind point to the terrace-bank. The last ball of the over, a half-volley to leg, he lifted over the other boundary.

'Sixty up,' said Ellerby, in the pavilion, as the umpire signalled another no-ball. 'By George! I believe these chaps are going to knock off the runs. Young Jackson looks as if he was in for a century.'

'You ass,' said Berridge. 'Don't say that, or he's certain to get out.'

Berridge was one of those who are skilled in cricket superstitions.

But Mike did not get out. He took seven off de Freece's next over by means of two cuts and a drive. And, with Bob still exhibiting a stolid and rock-like defence, the score mounted to eighty, thence to ninety, and so, mainly by singles, to a hundred.

At a hundred and four, when the wicket had put on exactly fifty, Bob fell to a combination of de Freece and extra-cover. He had stuck like a limpet for an hour and a quarter, and made twenty-one.

Mike watched him go with much the same feelings as those of a man who turns away from the platform after seeing a friend off on a long railway journey. His departure upset the scheme of things. For himself he had no fear now. He might possibly get out off his next ball, but he felt set enough to stay at the wickets till nightfall. He had had narrow escapes from de Freece, but he was full of that conviction, which comes to all batsmen on occasion, that this was his day. He had made twenty-six, and the wicket was getting easier. He could feel the sting going out of the bowling every over.

Henfrey, the next man in, was a promising rather than an effective bat. He had an excellent style, but he was uncertain. (Two years later, when he captained the Wrykyn teams, he made a lot of runs.) But this season his batting had been spasmodic.

Today he never looked like settling down. He survived an over from de Freece, and hit a fast change bowler who had been put on at the other end for a couple of fluky fours. Then Mike got the bowling for three consecutive overs, and raised the score to a hundred and twenty-six. A bye brought Henfrey to the batting end again, and de Freece's pet googly, which had not been much in evidence hitherto, led to his snicking an easy catch into short-slip's hands.

A hundred and twenty-seven for seven against a total of a hundred and sixty-six gives the impression that the batting side has the advantage. In the present case, however, it was Ripton who were really in the better position. Apparently, Wrykyn had three more wickets to fall. Practically they had only one, for neither Ashe, nor Grant, nor Devenish had any pretensions to be considered batsmen. Ashe was the school wicket-keeper. Grant and Devenish were bowlers. Between them the three could not be relied on for a dozen in a decent match.

Mike watched Ashe shape with a sinking heart. The wicket-keeper looked like a man who feels that his hour has come. Mike could see him licking his lips. There was nervousness written all over him.

He was not kept long in suspense. De Freece's first ball made a hideous wreck of his wicket.

'Over,' said the umpire.

Mike felt that the school's one chance now lay in his keeping the bowling. But how was he to do this? It suddenly occurred to him that it was a delicate position that he was in. It was not often that he was troubled by an inconvenient modesty, but this happened now. Grant was a fellow he hardly knew, and a school prefect to boot. Could he go up to him and explain that he, Jackson, did not consider him competent to bat in this crisis? Would not this get about and be accounted to him for side? He had made forty, but even so ...

Fortunately Grant solved the problem on his own account. He came up to Mike and spoke with an earnestness born of nerves. 'For goodness sake,' he whispered, 'collar the bowling all you know, or we're done. I shall get outed first ball.'

'All right,' said Mike, and set his teeth. Forty to win! A large order. But it was going to be done. His whole existence seemed to concentrate itself on those forty runs.

The fast bowler, who was the last of several changes that had been tried at the other end, was well-meaning but erratic. The wicket was almost true again now, and it was possible to take liberties.

Mike took them.

A distant clapping from the pavilion, taken up a moment later all round the ground, and echoed by the Ripton fieldsmen, announced that he had reached his fifty.

The last ball of the over he mishit. It rolled in the direction of third man.

'Come on,' shouted Grant.

Mike and the ball arrived at the opposite wicket almost simultaneously. Another fraction of a second, and he would have been run out.

The last balls of the next two overs provided repetitions of this performance. But each time luck was with him, and his bat was across the crease before the bails were off. The telegraph-board showed a hundred and fifty.

The next over was doubly sensational. The original medium-paced bowler had gone on again in place of the fast man, and for the first five balls he could not find his length. During those five balls Mike raised the score to a hundred and sixty.

But the sixth was of a different kind. Faster than the rest and of a perfect length, it all but got through Mike's defence. As it was, he stopped it. But he did not score. The umpire called 'Over!' and there was Grant at the batting end, with de Freece smiling pleasantly as he walked back to begin his run with the comfortable reflection that at last he had got somebody except Mike to bowl at.

That over was an experience Mike never forgot.

Grant pursued the Fabian policy of keeping his bat almost immovable and trusting to luck. Point and the slips crowded round. Mid-off and mid-on moved half-way down the pitch. Grant looked embarrassed, but determined. For four balls he baffled the attack, though once nearly caught by point a yard from the wicket. The fifth curled round his bat, and touched the off-stump. A bail fell silently to the ground.

Devenish came in to take the last ball of the over.

It was an awe-inspiring moment. A great stillness was over all the ground. Mike's knees trembled. Devenish's face was a delicate grey.

The only person unmoved seemed to be de Freece. His smile was even more amiable than usual as he began his run.

The next moment the crisis was past. The ball hit the very centre of Devenish's bat, and rolled back down the pitch.

The school broke into one great howl of joy. There were still seven runs between them and victory, but nobody appeared to recognise this fact as important. Mike had got the bowling, and the bowling was not de Freece's.

It seemed almost an anti-climax when a four to leg and two two's through the slips settled the thing.

Devenish was caught and bowled in de Freece's next over; but the Wrykyn total was one hundred and seventy-two.

'Good game,' said Maclaine, meeting Burgess in the pavilion. 'Who was the man who made all the runs? How many, by the way?'

'Eighty-three. It was young Jackson. Brother of the other one.'

'That family! How many more of them are you going to have here?'

'He's the last. I say, rough luck on de Freece. He bowled rippingly.'

Politeness to a beaten foe caused Burgess to change his usual 'not bad.'

'The funny part of it is,' continued he, 'that young Jackson was only playing as a sub.'

'You've got a rum idea of what's funny,' said Maclaine.

MIKE AND PSMITH

Wodehouse limns Mike's progress at Wrykyn to the point where, a couple of years on from arrival, he is on the verge of captaining the first XI – when his father sees a school report that laments Mike's level of academic attainment, and so decides to uproot him to Sedleigh school instead.

There Mike makes a friend in another new boy, the monocle-wearing ex-Etonian dandy Rupert Psmith (of which the P is affected and silent, 'as in pshrimp'.) Evelyn Waugh was famously of the view that Psmith's entry to proceedings marks a decisive turn in Wodehouse's work – a moment when 'the light is kindled', the Wodehousian wit distilled, and the great later work augured. The 'languid grace' of Psmith certainly makes an impression; and he and an unhappy Mike initially eschew cricket at Sedleigh in favour of the archaeological society. Thus no one at Sedleigh is aware of the cricketing genius that walks among them. But inevitably Mike feels an itch of regret, and the call to strap on his pads duly arrives when he is asked to play for his 'Outwood' house in a match against the rival side captained by Adair but headed by housemaster Mr Downing, an authority figure who is felt to deserve a comeuppance on account of showing excessive favouritism to his own charges.

*

When you have been impressing upon a non-cricketing boy for nearly a month that (a) the school is above all a keen school, (b) that all members of it should play cricket, and (c) that by not playing cricket he is ruining his chances in this world and imperilling them in the next; and when, quite unexpectedly, you come upon this boy dressed in cricket flannels, wearing cricket boots and carrying a cricket bag, it seems only natural to assume that you have converted him, that the seeds of your eloquence have fallen on fruitful soil and sprouted.

Mr Downing assumed it.

He was walking to the field with Adair and another member of his team when he came upon Mike.

'What!' he cried. 'Our Jackson clad in suit of mail and armed for the fray!'

This was Mr Downing's No. 2 manner – the playful.

'This is indeed Saul among the prophets. Why this sudden enthusiasm for a game which I understood that you despised? Are our opponents so reduced?'

Psmith, who was with Mike, took charge of the affair with a languid grace which had maddened hundreds in its time, and which never failed to ruffle Mr Downing.

'We are, above all, sir,' he said, 'a keen house. Drones are not welcomed by us. We are essentially versatile. Jackson, the archaeologist of yesterday, becomes the cricketer of today. It is the right spirit, sir,' said Psmith earnestly. 'I like to see it.'

'Indeed, Smith? You are not playing yourself, I notice. Your enthusiasm has bounds.'

'In our house, sir, competition is fierce, and the Selection Committee unfortunately passed me over.'

There were a number of pitches dotted about over the field, for there was always a touch of the London Park about it on Mid-term

Service day. Adair, as captain of cricket, had naturally selected the best for his own match. It was a good wicket, Mike saw. As a matter of fact the wickets at Sedleigh were nearly always good. Adair had infected the ground-man with some of his own keenness, with the result that that once-leisurely official now found himself sometimes, with a kind of mild surprise, working really hard. At the beginning of the previous season Sedleigh had played a scratch team from a neighbouring town on a wicket which, except for the creases, was absolutely undistinguishable from the surrounding turf, and behind the pavilion after the match Adair had spoken certain home truths to the ground-man. The latter's reformation had dated from that moment.

Barnes, timidly jubilant, came up to Mike with the news that he had won the toss, and the request that Mike would go in first with him.

In stories of the 'Not Really a Duffer' type, where the nervous new boy, who has been found crying in the boot-room over the photograph of his sister, contrives to get an innings in a game, nobody suspects that he is really a prodigy till he hits the Bully's first ball out of the ground for six.

With Mike it was different. There was no pitying smile on Adair's face as he started his run preparatory to sending down the first ball. Mike, on the cricket field, could not have looked anything but a cricketer if he had turned out in a tweed suit and hobnail boots. Cricketer was written all over him – in his walk, in the way he took guard, in his stand at the wickets. Adair started to bowl with the feeling that this was somebody who had more than a little knowledge of how to deal with good bowling and punish bad.

Mike started cautiously. He was more than usually anxious to make runs today, and he meant to take no risks till he could afford to do so. He had seen Adair bowl at the nets, and he knew that he was good.

The first over was a maiden, six dangerous balls beautifully played. The fieldsmen changed over.

The general interest had now settled on the match between Outwood's and Downing's. The fact in Mike's case had gone round the field, and, as several of the other games had not yet begun, quite a large crowd had collected near the pavilion to watch. Mike's masterly treatment of the opening over had impressed the spectators, and there was a popular desire to see how he would deal with Mr Downing's slows. It was generally anticipated that he would do something special with them.

Off the first ball of the master's over a leg-bye was run.

Mike took guard.

Mr Downing was a bowler with a style of his own. He took two short steps, two long steps, gave a jump, took three more short steps, and ended with a combination of step and jump, during which the ball emerged from behind his back and started on its slow career to the wicket. The whole business had some of the dignity of the old-fashioned minuet, subtly blended with the careless vigour of a cake-walk. The ball, when delivered, was billed to break from leg, but the programme was subject to alterations.

If the spectators had expected Mike to begin any firework effects with the first ball, they were disappointed. He played the over through with a grace worthy of his brother Joe. The last ball he turned to leg for a single.

His treatment of Adair's next over was freer. He had got a sight of the ball now. Half-way through the over a beautiful square cut forced a passage through the crowd by the pavilion, and dashed up against the rails. He drove the sixth ball past cover for three.

The crowd was now reluctantly dispersing to its own games, but it stopped as Mr Downing started his minuet-cake-walk, in the hope that it might see something more sensational.

This time the hope was fulfilled.

The ball was well up, slow, and off the wicket on the on-side. Perhaps if it had been allowed to pitch, it might have broken in and become quite dangerous. Mike went out at it, and hit it a couple of feet from the ground. The ball dropped with a thud and a spurting of dust in the road that ran along one side of the cricket field.

It was returned on the instalment system by helpers from other games, and the bowler began his manoeuvres again. A half-volley this time.

Mike slammed it back, and mid-on, whose heart was obviously not in the thing, failed to stop it.

'Get to them, Jenkins,' said Mr Downing irritably, as the ball came back from the boundary. 'Get to them.'

'Sir, please, sir—'

'Don't talk in the field, Jenkins.'

Having had a full-pitch hit for six and a half-volley for four, there was a strong probability that Mr Downing would pitch his next ball short.

The expected happened. The third ball was a slow long-hop, and hit the road at about the same spot where the first had landed. A howl of untuneful applause rose from the watchers in the pavilion, and Mike, with the feeling that this sort of bowling was too good to be true, waited in position for number four.

There are moments when a sort of panic seizes a bowler. This happened now with Mr Downing. He suddenly abandoned science and ran amok. His run lost its stateliness and increased its vigour. He charged up to the wicket as a wounded buffalo sometimes charges a gun. His whole idea now was to bowl fast.

When a slow bowler starts to bowl fast, it is usually as well to be batting, if you can manage it.

By the time the over was finished, Mike's score had been increased by sixteen, and the total of his side, in addition, by three wides.

And a shrill small voice, from the neighbourhood of the pavilion, uttered with painful distinctness the words, 'Take him off!'

That was how the most sensational day's cricket began that Sedleigh had known.

A description of the details of the morning's play would be monotonous. It is enough to say that they ran on much the same lines as the third and fourth overs of the match. Mr Downing bowled one more over, off which Mike helped himself to sixteen runs, and then retired moodily to cover-point, where, in Adair's fifth over, he missed Barnes – the first occasion since the game began on which that mild batsman had attempted to score more than a single. Scared by this escape, Outwood's captain shrank back into his shell, sat on the splice like a limpet, and, offering no more chances, was not out at lunch time with a score of eleven.

Mike had then made a hundred and three.

As Mike was taking off his pads in the pavilion, Adair came up.

'Why did you say you didn't play cricket?' he asked abruptly.

When one has been bowling the whole morning, and bowling well, without the slightest success, one is inclined to be abrupt.

Mike finished unfastening an obstinate strap. Then he looked up.

'I didn't say anything of the kind. I said I wasn't going to play here. There's a difference. As a matter of fact, I was in the Wrykyn team before I came here. Three years.'

Adair was silent for a moment.

'Will you play for us against the Old Sedleighans tomorrow?' he said at length.

Mike tossed his pads into his bag and got up.

'No, thanks.'

There was a silence.

'Above it, I suppose?'

'Not a bit. Not up to it. I shall want a lot of coaching at that end net of yours before I'm fit to play for Sedleigh.'

There was another pause.

'Then you won't play?' asked Adair.

'I'm not keeping you, am I?' said Mike, politely.

It was remarkable what a number of members of Outwood's house appeared to cherish a personal grudge against Mr Downing. It had been that master's somewhat injudicious practice for many years to treat his own house as a sort of Chosen People. Of all masters, the most unpopular is he who by the silent tribunal of a school is convicted of favouritism. And the dislike deepens if it is a house which he favours and not merely individuals. On occasions when boys in his own house and boys from other houses were accomplices and partners in wrong-doing, Mr Downing distributed his thunderbolts unequally, and the school noticed it. The result was that not only he himself, but also – which was rather unfair – his house, too, had acquired a good deal of unpopularity.

The general consensus of opinion in Outwood's during the luncheon interval was that, having got Downing's up a tree, they would be fools not to make the most of the situation.

Barnes's remark that he supposed, unless anything happened and wickets began to fall a bit faster, they had better think of declaring somewhere about half-past three or four, was met with a storm of opposition.

'Declare!' said Robinson. 'Great Scott, what on earth are you talking about?'

'Declare!' Stone's voice was almost a wail of indignation. 'I never saw such a chump.'

'They'll be rather sick if we don't, won't they?' suggested Barnes.

'Sick! I should think they would,' said Stone. 'That's just the gay idea. Can't you see that by a miracle we've got a chance of getting a jolly good bit of our own back against those Downing's ticks? What we've got to do is to jolly well keep them in the field all day if we can, and be jolly glad it's so beastly hot. If they lose about a dozen pounds each through sweating about in the sun after Jackson's drives, perhaps they'll stick on less side about things in general in future. Besides, I want an innings against that bilge of old Downing's, if I can get it.'

'So do I,' said Robinson.

'If you declare, I swear I won't field. Nor will Robinson.'

'Rather not.'

'Well, I won't then,' said Barnes unhappily. 'Only you know they're rather sick already.'

'Don't you worry about that,' said Stone with a wide grin. 'They'll be a lot sicker before we've finished.'

And so it came about that that particular Mid-term Service-day match made history. Big scores had often been put up on Mid-term Service day. Games had frequently been one-sided. But it had never happened before in the annals of the school that one side, going in first early in the morning, had neither completed its innings nor declared it closed when stumps were drawn at six-thirty. In no previous Sedleigh match, after a full day's play, had the pathetic words 'Did not bat' been written against the whole of one of the contending teams.

These are the things which mark epochs.

Play was resumed at two-fifteen. For a quarter of an hour Mike was comparatively quiet. Adair, fortified by food and rest, was bowling really well, and his first half-dozen overs had to be watched carefully. But the wicket was too good to give him a chance, and Mike, playing himself in again, proceeded to get to business once more.

Bowlers came and went. Adair pounded away at one end with brief intervals between the attacks. Mr Downing took a couple more overs, in one of which a horse, passing in the road, nearly had its useful life cut suddenly short. Change-bowlers of various actions and paces, each weirder and more futile than the last, tried their luck. But still the first-wicket stand continued.

The bowling of a house team is all head and no body. The first pair probably have some idea of length and break. The first-change pair are poor. And the rest, the small change, are simply the sort of things one sees in dreams after a heavy supper, or when one is out without one's gun.

Time, mercifully, generally breaks up a big stand at cricket before the field has suffered too much, and that is what happened now.

At four o'clock, when the score stood at two hundred and twenty for no wicket, Barnes, greatly daring, smote lustily at a rather wide half-volley and was caught at short-slip for thirty-three. He retired blushfully to the pavilion, amidst applause, and Stone came out.

As Mike had then made a hundred and eighty-seven, it was assumed by the field, that directly he had topped his second century, the closure would be applied and their ordeal finished. There was almost a sigh of relief when frantic cheering from the crowd told that the feat had been accomplished. The fieldsmen clapped in quite an indulgent sort of way, as who should say, 'Capital, capital. And now let's start *our* innings.' Some even began to edge towards the pavilion.

But the next ball was bowled, and the next over, and the next after that, and still Barnes made no sign. (The conscience-stricken captain of Outwood's was, as a matter of fact, being practically held down by Robinson and other ruffians by force.)

A grey dismay settled on the field.

The bowling had now become almost unbelievably bad. Lobs were being tried, and Stone, nearly weeping with pure joy, was playing an innings of the How-to-brighten-cricket type. He had an unorthodox style, but an excellent eye, and the road at this period of the game became absolutely unsafe for pedestrians and traffic.

Mike's pace had become slower, as was only natural, but his score, too, was mounting steadily.

'This is foolery,' snapped Mr Downing, as the three hundred and fifty went up on the board. 'Barnes!' he called.

There was no reply. A committee of three was at that moment engaged in sitting on Barnes's head in the first eleven changing-room, in order to correct a more than usually feverish attack of conscience.

'Barnes!'

'Please, sir,' said Stone, some species of telepathy telling him what was detaining his captain. 'I think Barnes must have left the field. He has probably gone over to the house to fetch something.'

'This is absurd. You must declare your innings closed. The game has become a farce.'

'Declare! Sir, we can't unless Barnes does. He might be awfully annoyed if we did anything like that without consulting him.'

'Absurd.'

'He's very touchy, sir.'

'It is perfect foolery.'

'I think Jenkins is just going to bowl, sir.'

Mr Downing walked moodily to his place.

*

In a neat wooden frame in the senior day-room at Outwood's, just above the mantelpiece, there was on view, a week later, a slip of paper. The writing on it was as follows:

OUTWOOD'S _v_. DOWNING'S
Outwood's. First innings._

J. P. Barnes, _c._ Hammond, _b._ Hassall 33
M. Jackson, not out 277
W. J. Stone, not out................................. 124
Extras.. 37
—
Total (for one wicket)................................ 471
Downing's did not bat.

*

The frosty relations between Mike and Adair, Sedleigh's captain of cricket, have thawed by the end of the tale. A further turnaround is that Psmith has revealed himself to be a skilful bowler, and so both Mike and Psmith take the field for a climactic contest between Sedleigh and Mike's former school, Wrykyn.

The Wrykyn match was three-parts over, and things were going badly for Sedleigh. In a way one might have said that the game was over, and that Sedleigh had lost; for it was a one day match, and Wrykyn, who had led on the first innings, had only to play out time to make the game theirs.

Sedleigh were paying the penalty for allowing themselves to be influenced by nerves in the early part of the day. Nerves lose more school matches than good play ever won. There is a certain type of school batsman who is a gift to any bowler when he once lets his imagination run away with him. Sedleigh, with the exception of Adair, Psmith, and Mike, had entered upon this match in a state of the most azure funk. Ever since Mike had received Strachan's answer and Adair had announced on the notice-board that on Saturday, July the twentieth, Sedleigh would play Wrykyn, the team had been all on the jump. It was useless for Adair to tell them, as he did repeatedly, on Mike's authority, that Wrykyn were weak this season, and that on their present form Sedleigh ought to win easily. The team listened, but were not comforted. Wrykyn might be below their usual strength, but then Wrykyn cricket, as a rule, reached such a high standard that this probably meant little. However weak Wrykyn might be – for them – there was a very firm impression among the members of the Sedleigh first eleven that the other school was quite strong enough to knock the cover off *them*. Experience counts enormously in school matches.

Sedleigh had never been proved. The teams they played were the sort of sides which the Wrykyn second eleven would play. Whereas Wrykyn, from time immemorial, had been beating Ripton teams and Free Foresters teams and M.C.C. teams packed with county men and sending men to Oxford and Cambridge who got their Blues as freshmen.

Sedleigh had gone on to the field that morning a depressed side.

It was unfortunate that Adair had won the toss. He had had no choice but to take first innings. The weather had been bad for the last week, and the wicket was slow and treacherous. It was likely to get worse during the day, so Adair had chosen to bat first.

Taking into consideration the state of nerves the team was in, this in itself was a calamity. A school eleven are always at their worst and nerviest before lunch. Even on their own ground they find the surroundings lonely and unfamiliar. The subtlety of the bowlers becomes magnified. Unless the first pair make a really good start, a collapse almost invariably ensues.

Today the start had been gruesome beyond words. Mike, the bulwark of the side, the man who had been brought up on Wrykyn bowling, and from whom, whatever might happen to the others, at least a fifty was expected – Mike, going in first with Barnes and taking first over, had played inside one from Bruce, the Wrykyn slow bowler, and had been caught at short slip off his second ball.

That put the finishing-touch on the panic. Stone, Robinson, and the others, all quite decent punishing batsmen when their nerves allowed them to play their own game, crawled to the wickets, declined to hit out at anything, and were clean bowled, several of them, playing back to half-volleys. Adair did not suffer from panic, but his batting was not equal to his bowling, and he had fallen after hitting one four.

Seven wickets were down for thirty when Psmith went in.

Psmith had always disclaimed any pretensions to batting skill, but he was undoubtedly the right man for a crisis like this. He had an enormous reach, and he used it. Three consecutive balls from Bruce he turned into full-tosses and swept to the leg-boundary, and, assisted by Barnes, who had been sitting on the splice in his usual manner, he raised the total to seventy-one before being yorked, with his score at thirty-five. Ten minutes later the innings was over, with Barnes not out sixteen, for seventy-nine.

Wrykyn had then gone in, lost Strachan for twenty before lunch, and finally completed their innings at a quarter to four for a hundred and thirty-one.

This was better than Sedleigh had expected. At least eight of the team had looked forward dismally to an afternoon's leather-hunting. But Adair and Psmith, helped by the wicket, had never been easy, especially Psmith, who had taken six wickets, his slows playing havoc with the tail.

It would be too much to say that Sedleigh had any hope of pulling the game out of the fire; but it was a comfort, they felt, at any rate, having another knock. As is usual at this stage of a match, their nervousness had vanished, and they felt capable of better things than in the first innings.

It was on Mike's suggestion that Psmith and himself went in first. Mike knew the limitations of the Wrykyn bowling, and he was convinced that, if they could knock Bruce off, it might be possible to rattle up a score sufficient to give them the game, always provided that Wrykyn collapsed in the second innings. And it seemed to Mike that the wicket would be so bad then that they easily might.

So he and Psmith had gone in at four o'clock to hit. And they had hit. The deficit had been wiped off, all but a dozen runs, when Psmith was bowled, and by that time Mike was set and in his best vein. He treated all the bowlers alike. And when Stone came in, restored to his proper frame of mind, and lashed out stoutly, and after him Robinson and the rest, it looked as if Sedleigh had a chance again. The score was a hundred and twenty when Mike, who had just reached his fifty, skied one to Strachan at cover. The time was twenty-five past five.

As Mike reached the pavilion, Adair declared the innings closed.

Wrykyn started batting at twenty-five minutes to six, with sixty-nine to make if they wished to make them, and an hour and ten minutes during which to keep up their wickets if they preferred to take things easy and go for a win on the first innings.

At first it looked as if they meant to knock off the runs, for Strachan forced the game from the first ball, which was Psmith's, and which he hit into the pavilion. But, at fifteen, Adair bowled him. And when, two runs later, Psmith got the next man stumped, and finished up his over with a c.-and-b., Wrykyn decided that it was not good enough.

Seventeen for three, with an hour all but five minutes to go, was getting too dangerous. So Drummond and Rigby, the next pair, proceeded to play with caution, and the collapse ceased.

This was the state of the game at the point at which this chapter opened. Seventeen for three had become twenty-four for three, and the hands of the clock stood at ten minutes past six. Changes of bowling had been tried, but there seemed no chance of getting past the batsmen's defence. They were playing all the good balls, and refused to hit at the bad.

A quarter past six struck, and then Psmith made a suggestion which altered the game completely.

'Why don't you have a shot this end?' he said to Adair, as they were crossing over. 'There's a spot on the off which might help you a lot. You can break like blazes if only you land on it. It doesn't help my leg-breaks a bit, because they won't hit at them.'

Barnes was on the point of beginning to bowl, when Adair took the ball from him. The captain of Outwood's retired to short leg with an air that suggested that he was glad to be relieved of his prominent post.

The next moment Drummond's off-stump was lying at an angle of forty-five. Adair was absolutely accurate as a bowler, and he had dropped his first ball right on the worn patch.

Two minutes later Drummond's successor was retiring to the pavilion, while the wicket-keeper straightened the stumps again.

There is nothing like a couple of unexpected wickets for altering the atmosphere of a game. Five minutes before, Sedleigh had been lethargic and without hope. Now there was a stir and buzz all round the ground.

There were twenty-five minutes to go, and five wickets were down.

Sedleigh was on top again.

The next man seemed to take an age coming out. As a matter of fact, he walked more rapidly than a batsman usually walks to the crease.

Adair's third ball dropped just short of the spot. The batsman, hitting out, was a shade too soon. The ball hummed through the air a couple of feet from the ground in the direction of mid-off, and Mike, diving to the right, got to it as he was falling, and chucked it up.

After that the thing was a walk-over. Psmith clean bowled a man in his next over; and the tail, demoralised by the sudden change in the game, collapsed uncompromisingly. Sedleigh won by thirty-five runs with eight minutes in hand.

Psmith and Mike sat in their study after lock-up, discussing things in general and the game in particular.

'I feel like a beastly renegade, playing against Wrykyn,' said Mike. 'Still, I'm glad we won. Adair's a jolly good sort, and it'll make him happy for weeks.'

'When I last saw Comrade Adair,' said Psmith, 'he was going about in a sort of trance, beaming vaguely and wanting to stand people things at the shop.'

'He bowled awfully well.'

'Yes,' said Psmith. 'I say, I don't wish to cast a gloom over this joyful occasion in any way, but you say Wrykyn are going to give Sedleigh a fixture again next year?'

'Well?'

'Well, have you thought of the massacre which will ensue? You will have left, Adair will have left. Incidentally, I shall have left. Wrykyn will swamp them.'

'I suppose they will. Still, the great thing, you see, is to get the thing started. That's what Adair was so keen on. Now Sedleigh has beaten Wrykyn, he's satisfied. They can get on fixtures with decent clubs, and work up to playing the big schools. You've got to start somehow. So it's all right, you see.'

'And, besides,' said Psmith, reflectively, 'in an emergency they can always get Comrade Downing to bowl for them, what? Let us now sally out and see if we can't promote a rag of some sort in this abode of wrath. Comrade Outwood has gone over to dinner at the School House, and it would be a pity to waste a somewhat golden opportunity. Shall we stagger?'

They staggered.

FROM
PSMITH IN THE CITY

In the later chronicles of Mike and Psmith, the latter was to move increasingly to the fore, and the work published as Psmith in the City *really focuses on Psmith's post-Sedleigh exploits as a banker and bright young thing about London. Mike, too, is forced by circumstance to go into banking, a turn of events markedly similar to Wodehouse's own biography. The disagreeable feel of that endeavour is foreshadowed early as we find Mike playing a country-house match for Ilsworth, a team run by Psmith's father, 'a man of vast but volatile brain'. Mike is in customary form, until an unwelcome off-pitch intervention from 'a blighter of the name of Bickersdyke'.*

On this Saturday, as Mike buckled on his pads, Mr Smith bounded up, full of advice and encouragement.

'My boy,' he said, 'we rely on you. These others' – he indicated with a disparaging wave of the hand the rest of the team, who were visible through the window of the changing-room – 'are all very well. Decent club bats. Good for a few on a billiard-table. But you're our hope on a wicket like this. I have studied cricket all my life' – till that summer it is improbable that Mr Smith had ever handled a bat – 'and I know a first-class batsman when I see one. I've seen your brothers play. Pooh, you're better than any of them. That century of yours against the Green Jackets was a wonderful innings, wonderful. Now look here, my boy. I want you to be careful. We've a lot of runs to make, so we mustn't take any risks. Hit plenty of boundaries, of course, but be careful. Careful. Dash it, there's a youngster trying to climb up the elm. He'll break his neck. It's young Giles, my keeper's boy. Hi! Hi, there!'

He scudded out to avert the tragedy, leaving Mike to digest his expert advice on the art of batting on bad wickets.

Possibly it was the excellence of this advice which induced Mike to play what was, to date, the best innings of his life. There are moments when the batsman feels an almost super-human fitness. This came to Mike now. The sun had begun to shine strongly. It made the wicket more difficult, but it added a cheerful touch to the scene. Mike felt calm and masterful. The bowling had no terrors for him. He scored nine off his first over and seven off his second, half-way through which he lost his partner. He was to undergo a similar bereavement several times that afternoon, and at frequent intervals. However simple the bowling might seem to him, it had enough sting in it to worry the rest of the team considerably. Batsmen came and went at the other end with such rapidity that it seemed hardly worth while their troubling to come in at all.

Every now and then one would give promise of better things by lifting the slow bowler into the pavilion or over the boundary, but it always happened that a similar stroke, a few balls later, ended in an easy catch. At five o'clock the Ilsworth score was eighty-one for seven wickets, last man nought, Mike not out fifty-nine. As most of the house team, including Mike, were dispersing to their homes or were due for visits at other houses that night, stumps were to be drawn at six. It was obvious that they could not hope to win. Number nine on the list, who was Bagley, the ground-man, went in with instructions to play for a draw, and minute advice from Mr Smith as to how he was to do it. Mike had now begun to score rapidly, and it was not to be expected that he could change his game; but Bagley, a dried-up little man of the type which bowls for five hours on a hot August day without exhibiting any symptoms of fatigue, put a much-bound bat stolidly in front of every ball he received; and the Hall's prospects of saving the game grew brighter.

At a quarter to six the professional left, caught at very silly point for eight. The score was a hundred and fifteen, of which Mike had made eighty-five.

A lengthy young man with yellow hair, who had done some good fast bowling for the Hall during the week, was the next man in. In previous matches he had hit furiously at everything, and against the Green Jackets had knocked up forty in twenty minutes while Mike was putting the finishing touches to his century. Now, however, with his host's warning ringing in his ears, he adopted the unspectacular, or Bagley, style of play. His manner of dealing with the ball was that of one playing croquet. He patted it gingerly back to the bowler when it was straight, and left it icily alone when it was off the wicket. Mike, still in the brilliant vein, clumped a half-volley past point to the boundary, and with highly scientific late cuts and glides brought his score to ninety-eight. With Mike's score at this, the total at a hundred and thirty, and the hands of the clock at five minutes to six, the yellow-haired croquet exponent fell, as Bagley had fallen, a victim to silly point, the ball being the last of the over.

Mr Smith, who always went in last for his side, and who so far had not received a single ball during the week, was down the pavilion steps and half-way to the wicket before the retiring batsman had taken half a dozen steps.

'Last over,' said the wicket-keeper to Mike. 'Any idea how many you've got? You must be near your century, I should think.'

'Ninety-eight,' said Mike. He always counted his runs.

'By Jove, as near as that? This is something like a finish.'

Mike left the first ball alone, and the second. They were too wide of the off-stump to be hit at safely. Then he felt a thrill as the third ball left the bowler's hand. It was a long-hop. He faced square to pull it.

And at that moment Mr John Bickersdyke walked into his life across the bowling-screen.

He crossed the bowler's arm just before the ball pitched. Mike lost sight of it for a fraction of a second, and hit wildly. The next moment his leg stump was askew; and the Hall had lost the match.

'I'm sorry,' he said to Mr Smith. 'Some silly idiot walked across the screen just as the ball was bowled.'

'What!' shouted Mr Smith. 'Who was the fool who walked behind the bowler's arm?' he yelled appealingly to Space.

'Here he comes, whoever he is,' said Mike.

A short, stout man in a straw hat and a flannel suit was walking towards them. As he came nearer Mike saw that he had a hard, thin-lipped mouth, half-hidden by a rather ragged moustache, and that behind a pair of gold spectacles were two pale and slightly protruding eyes, which, like his mouth, looked hard.

'How are you, Smith?' he said.

'Hullo, Bickersdyke.' There was a slight internal struggle, and then Mr Smith ceased to be the cricketer and became the host. He chatted amiably to the new-comer.

'You lost the game, I suppose,' said Mr Bickersdyke.

The cricketer in Mr Smith came to the top again, blended now, however, with the host. He was annoyed, but restrained in his annoyance.

'I say, Bickersdyke, you know, my dear fellow,' he said complainingly, 'you shouldn't have walked across the screen. You put Jackson off, and made him get bowled.'

'The screen?'

'That curious white object,' said Mike. 'It is not put up merely as an ornament. There's a sort of rough idea of giving the batsman a chance of seeing the ball, as well. It's a great help to him when people come charging across it just as the bowler bowls.'

Mr Bickersdyke turned a slightly deeper shade of purple, and was about to reply, when what sporting reporters call 'the veritable ovation' began.

Quite a large crowd had been watching the game, and they expressed their approval of Mike's performance.

There is only one thing for a batsman to do on these occasions. Mike ran into the pavilion, leaving Mr Bickersdyke standing.

*

It's not long after this regrettable incident that Mike and Psmith must both go to business in the City; and Bickersdyke, inevitably, is their boss at the New Asiatic Bank. Mike likes the banking life about as much as Wodehouse did, and when the weather turns seasonable he hankers after cricket. One day his brother Joe offers him a place in a county game at Lord's. Mike accepts, and bunks off work for the day, only for his enemy Bickersdyke to get wind.

Mike got to Lord's just as the umpires moved out into the field. He raced round to the pavilion. Joe met him on the stairs.

'It's all right,' he said. 'No hurry. We've won the toss. I've put you in fourth wicket.'

'Right ho,' said Mike. 'Glad we haven't to field just yet.'

'We oughtn't to have to field today if we don't chuck our wickets away.'

'Good wicket?'

'Like a billiard-table. I'm glad you were able to come. Have any difficulty in getting away?'

Joe Jackson's knowledge of the workings of a bank was of the slightest. He himself had never, since he left Oxford, been in a position where there were obstacles to getting off to play in first-class cricket. By profession he was agent to a sporting baronet whose hobby was the cricket of the county, and so, far from finding any difficulty in playing for the county, he was given to understand by his employer that that was his chief duty. It never occurred to him that Mike might find his bank less amenable in the matter of giving leave. His only fear, when he rang Mike up that morning, had been that this might be a particularly busy day at the New Asiatic Bank. If there was no special rush of work, he took it for granted that Mike would simply go to the manager, ask for leave to play in the match, and be given it with a beaming smile.

Mike did not answer the question, but asked one on his own account.

'How did you happen to be short?' he said.

'It was rotten luck. It was like this. We were altering our team after the Sussex match, to bring in Ballard, Keene, and Willis. They couldn't get down to Brighton, as the 'Varsity had a match, but there was nothing on for them in the last half of the week, so they'd promised to roll up.'

Ballard, Keene, and Willis were members of the Cambridge team, all very capable performers and much in demand by the county, when they could get away to play for it.

'Well?' said Mike.

'Well, we all came up by train from Brighton last night. But these three asses had arranged to motor down from Cambridge early today, and get here in time for the start. What happens? Why, Willis, who fancies himself as a chauffeur, undertakes to do the driving; and naturally, being an absolute rotter, goes and smashes up the whole concern just outside St Albans. The first thing I knew of it was when I got to Lord's at half-past ten, and found a wire waiting for me to say that they were all three of them crocked, and couldn't possibly play. I tell you, it was a bit of a jar to get half an hour before the match started. Willis has sprained his ankle, apparently; Keene's damaged his wrist; and Ballard has smashed his collar-bone. I don't suppose they'll be able to play in the 'Varsity match. Rotten luck for Cambridge. Well, fortunately we'd had two reserve pros, with us at Brighton, who had come up to London with the team in case they might be wanted, so, with them, we were only one short. Then I thought of you. That's how it was.'

'I see,' said Mike. 'Who are the pros?'

'Davis and Brockley. Both bowlers. It weakens our batting a lot. Ballard or Willis might have got a stack of runs on this wicket. Still, we've got a certain amount of batting as it is. We oughtn't to do badly, if we're careful. You've been getting some practice, I suppose, this season?'

'In a sort of a way. Nets and so on. No matches of any importance.'

'Dash it, I wish you'd had a game or two in decent-class cricket. Still, nets are better than nothing, I hope you'll be in form. We may want a pretty long knock from you, if things go wrong. These men seem to be settling down all right, thank goodness,' he added, looking out of the window at the county's first pair, Warrington and Mills, two professionals, who, as the result of ten minutes' play, had put up twenty.

'I'd better go and change,' said Mike, picking up his bag. 'You're in first wicket, I suppose?'

'Yes. And Reggie, second wicket.'

Reggie was another of Mike's brothers, not nearly so fine a player as Joe, but a sound bat, who generally made runs if allowed to stay in.

Mike changed, and went out into the little balcony at the top of the pavilion. He had it to himself. There were not many spectators in the pavilion at this early stage of the game.

There are few more restful places, if one wishes to think, than the upper balconies of Lord's pavilion. Mike, watching the game making its leisurely progress on the turf below, set himself seriously to review the situation in all its aspects. The exhilaration of bursting the bonds had begun to fade, and he found himself able to look into the matter of his desertion and weigh up the consequences. There was no doubt that he had cut the painter once and for all. Even a friendly-disposed management could hardly overlook what he had done.

And the management of the New Asiatic Bank was the very reverse of friendly. Mr Bickersdyke, he knew, would jump at this chance of getting rid of him. He realised that he must look on his career in the bank as a closed book. It was definitely over, and he must now think about the future.

It was not a time for half-measures. He could not go home. He must carry the thing through, now that he had begun, and find something definite to do, to support himself.

There seemed only one opening for him. What could he do, he asked himself. Just one thing. He could play cricket. It was by his cricket that he must live. He would have to become a professional. Could he get taken on? That was the question. It was impossible that he should play for his own county on his residential qualification. He could not appear as a professional in the same team in which his brothers were playing as amateurs. He must stake all on his birth qualification for Surrey.

On the other hand, had he the credentials which Surrey would want? He had a school reputation. But was that enough? He could not help feeling that it might not be.

Thinking it over more tensely than he had ever thought over anything in his whole life, he saw clearly that everything depended on what sort of show he made in this match which was now in progress. It was his big chance. If he succeeded, all would be well. He did not care to think what his position would be if he did not succeed.

A distant appeal and a sound of clapping from the crowd broke in on his thoughts. Mills was out, caught at the wicket. The telegraph-board gave the total as forty-eight. Not sensational. The success of the team depended largely on what sort of a start the two professionals made.

The clapping broke out again as Joe made his way down the steps. Joe, as an All England player, was a favourite with the crowd.

Mike watched him play an over in his strong, graceful style: then it suddenly occurred to him that he would like to know how matters had gone at the bank in his absence.

He went down to the telephone, rang up the bank, and asked for Psmith.

Presently the familiar voice made itself heard.

'Hullo, Smith.'

'Hullo. Is that Comrade Jackson? How are things progressing?'

'Fairly well. We're in first. We've lost one wicket, and the fifty's just up. I say, what's happened at the bank?'

'I broke the news to Comrade Gregory. A charming personality. I feel that we shall be friends.'

'Was he sick?'

'In a measure, yes. Indeed, I may say he practically foamed at the mouth. I explained the situation, but he was not to be appeased. He jerked me into the presence of Comrade Bickersdyke, with whom I had a brief but entertaining chat. He had not a great deal to say, but he listened attentively to my narrative, and eventually told me off to take your place in the Fixed Deposits. That melancholy task I am now performing to the best of my ability. I find the work a little trying. There is too much ledger-lugging to be done for my simple tastes. I have been hauling ledgers from the safe all the morning. The cry is beginning to go round, 'Psmith is willing, but can his physique stand the strain?' In the excitement of the moment just now I dropped a somewhat massive tome on to Comrade Gregory's foot, unfortunately, I understand, the foot in which he has of late been suffering twinges of gout. I passed the thing off with ready tact, but I cannot deny that there was a certain temporary coolness, which, indeed, is not yet past. These things, Comrade Jackson, are the whirlpools in the quiet stream of commercial life.'

'Have I got the sack?'

'No official pronouncement has been made to me as yet on the subject, but I think I should advise you, if you are offered another job in the course of the day, to accept it. I cannot say that you are precisely the pet of the management just at present. However, I have ideas for your future, which I will divulge when we meet. I propose to slide coyly from the office at about four o'clock. I am meeting my father at that hour. We shall come straight on to Lord's.'

'Right ho,' said Mike. 'I'll be looking out for you.'

'Is there any little message I can give Comrade Gregory from you?'

'You can give him my love, if you like.'

'It shall be done. Good-bye.'

'Good-bye.'

Mike replaced the receiver, and went up to his balcony again.

As soon as his eye fell on the telegraph-board he saw with a start that things had been moving rapidly in his brief absence. The numbers of the batsmen on the board were three and five.

'Great Scott!' he cried. 'Why, I'm in next. What on earth's been happening?'

He put on his pads hurriedly, expecting every moment that a wicket would fall and find him unprepared. But the batsmen were still together when he rose, ready for the fray, and went downstairs to get news.

He found his brother Reggie in the dressing-room,

'What's happened?' he said. 'How were you out?'

'L.b.w.,' said Reggie. 'Goodness knows how it happened. My eyesight must be going. I mistimed the thing altogether.'

'How was Warrington out?'

'Caught in the slips.'

'By Jove!' said Mike. 'This is pretty rocky. Three for sixty-one. We shall get mopped.'

'Unless you and Joe do something. There's no earthly need to get out. The wicket's as good as you want, and the bowling's nothing special. Well played, Joe!'

A beautiful glide to leg by the greatest of the Jacksons had rolled up against the pavilion rails. The fieldsmen changed across for the next over.

'If only Peters stops a bit—' began Mike, and broke off. Peters' off stump was lying at an angle of forty-five degrees.

'Well, he hasn't,' said Reggie grimly. 'Silly ass, why did he hit at that one? All he'd got to do was to stay in with Joe. Now it's up to you. Do try and do something, or we'll be out under the hundred.'

Mike waited till the outcoming batsman had turned in at the professionals' gate. Then he walked down the steps and out into the open, feeling more nervous than he had felt since that far-off day when he had first gone in to bat for Wrykyn against the M.C.C. He found his thoughts flying back to that occasion. Today, as then, everything seemed very distant and unreal. The spectators were miles away. He had often been to Lord's as a spectator, but the place seemed entirely unfamiliar now. He felt as if he were in a strange land.

He was conscious of Joe leaving the crease to meet him on his way. He smiled feebly. 'Buck up,' said Joe in that robust way of his which was so heartening. 'Nothing in the bowling, and the wicket like a shirt-front. Play just as if you were at the nets. And for goodness' sake don't try to score all your runs in the first over. Stick in, and we've got them.'

Mike smiled again more feebly than before, and made a weird gurgling noise in his throat.

It had been the Middlesex fast bowler who had destroyed Peters. Mike was not sorry. He did not object to fast bowling. He took guard, and looked round him, taking careful note of the positions of the slips.

As usual, once he was at the wicket the paralysed feeling left him. He became conscious again of his power. Dash it all, what was there to be afraid of? He was a jolly good bat, and he would jolly well show them that he was, too.

The fast bowler, with a preliminary bound, began his run. Mike settled himself into position, his whole soul concentrated on the ball. Everything else was wiped from his mind. [...]

For nearly two hours Mike had been experiencing the keenest pleasure that it had ever fallen to his lot to feel. From the moment he took his first ball till the luncheon interval he had suffered the acutest discomfort. His nervousness had left him to a great extent, but he had never really settled down. Sometimes by luck, and sometimes by skill, he had kept the ball out of his wicket; but he was scratching, and he knew it. Not for a single over had he been comfortable. On several occasions he had edged balls to leg and through the slips in quite an inferior manner, and it was seldom that he managed to hit with the centre of the bat.

Nobody is more alive to the fact that he is not playing up to his true form than the batsman. Even though his score mounted little by little into the twenties, Mike was miserable. If this was the best he could do on a perfect wicket, he felt there was not much hope for him as a professional.

The poorness of his play was accentuated by the brilliance of Joe's. Joe combined science and vigour to a remarkable degree. He laid on the wood with a graceful robustness which drew much cheering from the crowd. Beside him Mike was oppressed by that leaden sense of moral inferiority which weighs on a man who has turned up to dinner in ordinary clothes when everybody else has dressed. He felt awkward and conspicuously out of place.

Then came lunch – and after lunch a glorious change.

Volumes might be written on the cricket lunch and the influence it has on the run of the game; how it undoes one man, and sends another back to the fray like a giant refreshed; how it turns the brilliant fast bowler into the sluggish medium, and the nervous bat into the masterful smiter.

On Mike its effect was magical. He lunched wisely and well, chewing his food with the concentration of a thirty-three-bites a mouthful crank, and drinking dry ginger-ale. As he walked out with Joe after the interval he knew that a change had taken place in him. His nerve had come back, and with it his form.

It sometimes happens at cricket that when one feels particularly fit one gets snapped in the slips in the first over, or clean bowled by a full toss; but neither of these things happened to Mike. He stayed in, and began to score. Now there were no edgings through the slips and snicks to leg. He was meeting the ball in the centre of the bat, and meeting it vigorously. Two boundaries in successive balls off the fast bowler, hard, clean drives past extra-cover, put him at peace with all the world. He was on top. He had found himself.

Joe, at the other end, resumed his brilliant career. His century and Mike's fifty arrived in the same over. The bowling began to grow loose.

Joe, having reached his century, slowed down somewhat, and Mike took up the running. The score rose rapidly.

A leg-theory bowler kept down the pace of the run-getting for a time, but the bowlers at the other end continued to give away runs. Mike's score passed from sixty to seventy, from seventy to eighty, from eighty to ninety. When the Smiths, father and son, came on to the ground the total was ninety-eight. Joe had made a hundred and thirty-three.

Mike reached his century just as Psmith and his father took their seats. A square cut off the slow bowler was just too wide for point to get to. By the time third man had sprinted across and returned the ball the batsmen had run two.

Mr Smith was enthusiastic.

'I tell you,' he said to Psmith, who was clapping in a gently encouraging manner, 'the boy's a wonderful bat. I said so when he was down with us. I remember telling him so myself. "I've seen your brothers play," I said, "and you're better than any of them." I remember it distinctly. He'll be playing for England in another year or two. Fancy putting a cricketer like that into the City! It's a crime.'

'I gather,' said Psmith, 'that the family coffers had got a bit low. It was necessary for Comrade Jackson to do something by way of saving the Old Home.'

'He ought to be at the University. Look, he's got that man away to the boundary again. They'll never get him out.'

At six o'clock the partnership was broken, Joe running himself out in trying to snatch a single where no single was. He had made a hundred and eighty-nine.

Mike flung himself down on the turf with mixed feelings. He was sorry Joe was out, but he was very glad indeed of the chance of a rest. He was utterly fagged. A half-day match once a week is no training for first-class cricket. Joe, who had been playing all the season, was as tough as india-rubber, and trotted into the pavilion as fresh as if he had been having a brief spell at the nets. Mike, on the other hand, felt that he simply wanted to be dropped into a cold bath and left there indefinitely. There was only another half-hour's play, but he doubted if he could get through it.

He dragged himself up wearily as Joe's successor arrived at the wickets. He had crossed Joe before the latter's downfall, and it was his turn to take the bowling.

Something seemed to have gone out of him. He could not time the ball properly. The last ball of the over looked like a half-volley, and he hit out at it. But it was just short of a half-volley, and his stroke arrived too soon. The bowler, running in the direction of mid-on, brought off an easy c.-and-b.

Mike turned away towards the pavilion. He heard the gradually swelling applause in a sort of dream. It seemed to him hours before he reached the dressing-room.

He was sitting on a chair, wishing that somebody would come along and take off his pads, when Psmith's card was brought to him. A few moments later the old Etonian appeared in person.

'Hullo, Smith,' said Mike, 'By Jove! I'm done.'

'"How Little Willie Saved the Match",' said Psmith. 'What you want is one of those gin and ginger-beers we hear so much about. Remove those pads, and let us flit downstairs in search of a couple. Well, Comrade Jackson, you have fought the good fight this day. My father sends his compliments. He is dining out, or he would have come up. He is going to look in at the flat latish.'

'How many did I get?' asked Mike. 'I was so jolly done I didn't think of looking.'

'A hundred and forty-eight of the best,' said Psmith. 'What will they say at the old homestead about this? Are you ready? Then let us test this fruity old ginger-beer of theirs.'

Postscript:

Psmith went merrily onward as a titular returning character in Wodehouse; Mike retired to the supporting cast. But what became of him? Well, Wodehouse had Mike attend Cambridge, funded by Mr Smith, where, as one would expect, he starred for the Varsity XI and for the MCC. But, as things fell, Mike would end up making his living as a Lincolnshire farmer rather than an England batsman – consoled, no doubt, by memories of the glory days of his youth.

'REGINALD'S RECORD KNOCK'

This cricket story, first published in Pearson's *magazine, signals for us a shift in Wodehouse from the boyish world of the school stories to the sighting of 'love interest', and a certain kind of romantic embarrassment that would come to be another speciality of the author. When females appear in Wodehouse's sporting stories, this is quite often so as to make possible a particular narrative in which the hero's fortunes on the field are paralleled with his (awkward) romantic relations; and different problems in both departments might be solved by a single sporting stroke.*

The reader might wonder what was Wodehouse's own record knock? Asked by an interviewer in 1955 if he had ever played a really big and notable innings, he responded: 'Never! I was a fast bowler and almost a total loss as a bat. I once made a century for the Globe *printers against the* Evening News *printers and once ninety-seven for the bank against another bank, but the bowling was not so hot ... '*

Reginald Humby was one of those men who go in just above the byes, and are to tired bowlers what the dew is to parched earth at the close of an August afternoon. When a boy at school he once made nine not out in a house match, but after that he went all to pieces. His adult cricket career was on the one-match one-ball principle. Whether it was that Reginald hit too soon at them or did not hit soon enough, whether it was that his bat deviated from the dotted line which joined the two points A and B in the illustrated plate of the man making the forward stroke in the 'Hints on Cricket' book, or whether it was that each ball swerved both ways at once and broke a yard and a quarter, I do not know. Reginald rather favoured the last theory.

The important point is that Reginald, after an almost unbroken series of eggs in the first two months of the season, turned out for Chigley Heath versus The Hearty Lunchers in the early part of July, went in first, and knocked up a hundred and thirteen.

Reginald, mark you, whose normal batting style was a sort of cross between hop-scotch, diabolo, and a man with gout in one leg trying to dance the Salome Dance.

When great events happen the public generally shows an anxiety to discover their cause. In the case of Reginald's century, on the face of it the most remarkable event since the Flood, the miracle may be attributed directly to his personal popularity.

Carpers may cavil at this statement. It is possible, too, that cavillers may carp. I seem to see them at it. All around me, I repeat, I seem to hear the angry murmur of carpers cavilling and cavillers carping. I seem to hear them asking how it is possible for a man to make a century by being popular.

'Can a batsman,' they ask, 'by sheer amiability stop a yorker on the leg stump?'

Nevertheless it is true. The facts are these:

Everybody who plays club cricket knows the Hearty Lunchers. Inveterate free-drinkers to a man, they wander about the country playing-villages. They belong to the school of thought which holds that the beauty of cricket is that, above all other games, it offers such magnificent opportunities for a long drink and a smoke in the shade. The Hearty Lunchers do not take their cricket in that spirit of deadly and business-like earnest which so many people consider is spoiling the game. A Hearty Luncher who has been given out caught at the wicket does not explain on arriving at the pavilion that he was nowhere near the ball, and that the umpire has had a personal grudge against him since boyhood. No, he sinks into a deck chair, removes his pads, and remarks that if anyone was thinking of buying him a stone ginger with the merest dash of gin in it, now is his time.

It will therefore readily be understood that Reginald's inability to lift his average out of the minuses did not handicap him with the Hearty Lunchers, as it might have handicapped him with some clubs. The genial sportsmen took him to their bosoms to a man and looked on him as a brother. Reginald's was one of those noble natures which are always good for five shillings at any hour of the day, and the Hearty Lunchers were not slow to appreciate it. They all loved Reginald.

Reginald was seated in his room one lovely evening at the beginning of July oiling a bat – he was a confirmed bat-oiler – when the telephone bell rang. He went to the instrument and was hailed by the comfortable voice of Westaway, the Hearty Lunchers' secretary.

'Is that Humby?' asked Westaway. 'I say, Reggie, I'm booking you for the Chigley Heath match next Saturday. Train, Waterloo, ten-fifteen.'

'Oh, I say,' replied Reginald, a note of penitence in his voice, 'I'm afraid I can't – fact is, I'm playing for Chigley.'

'You're what?'

'They asked me last week – they seemed very keen that I should play.'

'Why, haven't they seen you play?'

'I'm awfully sorry.'

'Oh, all right. How do you come to be mixed up with Chigley Heath?'

'My *fiancée* lives down there.'

'I see. Well, so long.'

'So long.'

'You're all right for the Saturday after against Porkley-in-the-Wold, I suppose?'

'Yes, rather!'

'Good! So long.'

'So long.'

And Reginald, replacing the instrument, resumed the oiling of the bat.

Now Westaway happened to be of a romantic and sentimental nature. He was inclined to be stout, and all rather stout men are sentimental. Westaway was the sort of man who keeps old ball-programmes and bundles of letters tied round with lilac ribbon. At country houses, when they lingered on the terrace after dinner to watch the moonlight flooding the quiet garden, it was Westaway and his colleagues who lingered longest. Westaway knew Tennyson's 'Maud' by heart, and could take Browning without gas.

It is not to be wondered at, therefore, that Reginald's remark about his *fiancée* living at Chigley Heath should give him food for thought. It appealed to him.

He reflected on it a good deal during the evening, and running across Blagdon, the Hearty Lunchers' captain, after dinner that night at the Club, he spoke of the matter to him. It so happened that both had dined excellently and were looking on the world with a sort of cosy benevolence. They were in the mood when men give small boys sixpences.

'I rang up Reggie Humby today,' said Westaway.

'One of the best, Reggie,' said Blagdon. 'Waiter, coffee and – what's yours? Coffee for two, a Maraschino, a liqueur brandy, and two of those old-shape Larranagas. Yes, dear old chap, Reggie.'

'Did you know he was engaged?'

'I did hear something about it – girl of the name of Belleville or something like that – Melville, that's it! Charming girl. Fond of poetry and all that, I believe.'

'She lives at Chigley Heath.'

'Then Reggie'll get a chance of seeing her next Saturday.'

'He tells me he's promised to play for Chigley Heath against us.'

'Confound him, the renegade! Still, we needn't scratch because of that, need we?'

Westaway sucked at his cigar in silence for a while, watching with dreamy eyes the blue smoke as it curled ceilingwards. When he spoke his voice was singularly soft.

'Do you know, Blagdon,' he said, sipping his Maraschino with a sort of gentle melancholy, 'do you know, there is something wonderfully pathetic to me in this business. I see the whole thing so clearly. There was a kind of quiver in poor Reggie's voice when he said: "I am playing for Chigley Heath, my *fiancée* lives down there," which told me more than any words could have done. It is a tragedy in its way, Blagdon. We may smile at it, think it trivial; but it is none the less a tragedy. That warm-hearted, enthusiastic girl, all eagerness to see the man she loves do well. Reggie, poor old Reggie, all on fire to prove to her that her trust in him is not misplaced, and the end – Disillusionment – Disappointment – Unhappiness.'

'He might be duck not out,' said the more practical Blagdon.

'He won't go in last for Chigley Heath; probably they think a lot of him. He may be their hope. Quite possibly he may go in first.'

'If Reggie's mug enough to let himself be shoved in first,' said Blagdon decidedly, 'he deserves all he gets. Waiter, two whiskeys and soda, large.'

Westaway was in no mood to subscribe to this stony-hearted view.

'I tell you,' he said, 'I'm sorry for Reggie! I'm sorry for the poor old chap, and I'm more than sorry for the girl.'

'Well, I don't see what we can do,' said Blagdon. 'Not all the soda, thanks. We can hardly be expected to bowl badly just to let Reggie show off before his girl.'

Westaway paused in the act of lighting his cigar, as one smitten with a great thought.

'Why not?' he said. 'Why not, Blagdon? Blagdon, you've hit it!'

'My dear chap!'

'You have! I tell you, Blagdon, you've solved the whole thing. Reggie's a dashed good sort, one of the very absolute! Why not give him a benefit? Why not let him knock up a few for a change? It'll be the only chance he'll ever get of making a decent score. You aren't going to tell me at your time of life that you care whether we beat Chigley Heath or not!'

'I was thinking more of the dashing about in a hot sun while Reggie made his runs – I'm all against too much exercise.'

Blagdon was one of the non-stooping brigade. He liked best to field point with a good cover behind him.

'Oh, nonsense!' said Westaway. 'There won't be too much of that, we can be getting the rest of them out all the while; and, besides, fifty will satisfy poor old Reggie. We needn't let him make a hundred.'

Blagdon's benevolence was expanding under the influence of the whiskey and soda (large) and the old-shape Larranaga. Little acts of kindness on Reggie's part, here a cigar, there a lunch, at another time a box at a theatre, began to rise to the surface of his memory like rainbow-coloured bubbles. Having grown accustomed to the basic bizarreness of the hon. secretary's idea, he began now, as it were, to out-Westaway Westaway.

'No!' he said, 'let us do the thing in style. Reggie shall have his knock and he shall make a century, unless, of course, they put him in last. If they do that he will have to be satisfied with twenty or so.'

'As to squaring the bowlers,' said Westaway, 'can that be managed?'

'You and I will go on first, with Blake and Harris as first change. After Blake and Harris, Grigson can have an over, too. We will broach the matter to them at a dinner at which we will be joint hosts. They are all stout fellows who will be charmed to do a little thing like this for a sportsman like Reggie.'

'Yours is a noble nature, Blagdon,' said Westaway, reaching out for his glass.

'Oh, no,' said the paragon modestly. 'Have another cigar?'

In order that the reader may get that mental strangle-hold on the plot of this narrative which is so essential if a short story is to charm, elevate, and instruct, it is necessary now for the nonce (but only for the nonce) to inspect Reginald's past life.

Reginald, as stated by Blagdon, was engaged to a Miss Melville – Miss Margaret Melville. How few men, dear reader, are engaged to girls with svelte figures, brown hair, and large blue eyes, now sparkling and vivacious, now dreamy and soulful, but always large and blue! How few, I say. You are, dear reader, and so am I, but who else? Reginald, however, happened to be, and he considered himself uncommonly fortunate.

He was happy. It is true that Margaret's mother was not, as it were, wrapped up in him. She exhibited none of that effervescent joy at his appearance which we like to see in our mothers-in-law elect. On the contrary, she generally cried bitterly whenever she saw him, and at the end of ten minutes was apt to retire sobbing to her room, where she remained in a state of semi-coma till an advanced hour. She was by way of being a confirmed invalid, and something about Reginald seemed to get right in amongst her nerve centres, reducing them for the time being to a complicated hash. She did not like Reginald; she said she liked big, manly men. Behind his back she not infrequently referred to him as a 'poop'; sometimes even as 'that guffin'.

She did not do this to Margaret, for Margaret, besides being blue-eyed, was also a shade quick-tempered. Whenever she discussed Reginald, it was with her son Brewster – Brewster Melville, who thought Reginald a bit of an ass, was always ready to sit and listen to his mother on the subject, it being, however, an understood thing that at the conclusion of the séance she yielded one or two minted sovereigns towards his racing debts. For Brewster, having developed a habit of backing horses which either did not start at all or sat down and thought in the middle of a race, could always do with a pound or two. His prices for these interviews worked out, as a rule, at about two and a half guineas a thousand words.

In these circumstances it is not to be wondered at that Reginald and Margaret should prefer to meet, when they did meet, at some other spot than the latter's ancestral home. It suited both of them better that they should arrange a secret tryst each week. Reginald preferred it because being in the same room as Mrs Melville always made him feel like a murderer with particularly large feet; and Margaret preferred it because, as she told Reginald, these secret meetings lent a touch of poetry, a sort of atmosphere of Marcus Stone's pictures, to what might otherwise have been a commonplace engagement.

Reginald thought this charming; but at the same time he could not conceal from himself the fact that Margaret's passion for the poetic cut, as it were, both ways. He admired and loved the loftiness of her soul, but, on the other hand, it was the deuce of a business having to live up to it. For Reginald was a very ordinary young man. They had tried to inoculate him with a love of Poetry at school, but it had never 'taken'. Until he was twenty-six he had been satisfied to class all poetry (except that of Mr Doss Chiderdoss) under the heading of Rot. Then he met Margaret, and the trouble began. On the day he first met her, at a picnic, she had looked so soulful, so aloof from this world, that he had felt instinctively that here was a girl who expected more from a man than a mere statement that the weather was rippin'. It so chanced that he knew just one quotation from the Classics, to wit, Tennyson's critique of the Island Valley of Avilion. He knew this because he had had the passage to write out one hundred and fifty times at school, on the occasion of his being caught smoking by a master who happened to be a passionate admirer of 'The Idylls of the King'.

A remark of Margaret's that it was a splendid day for a picnic and that the country looked nice gave him his opportunity.

'It reminds me,' he said, 'of the Island Valley of Avilion, where falls not hail or rain or any snow, nor ever wind blows loudly; but it lies Deep-meadow'd, happy, fair, with orchard lawns ...'

He broke off here to squash a wasp; but Margaret had heard enough.

'Are you fond of poetry, Mr Humby?' she said, with a sort of far-off look.

'Er – oh, rather! I should think so!' said Reginald.

And that was how all the trouble had started. It had meant unremitting toil for Reginald. He felt that he had set himself a standard from which he must not fall. He bought every new volume of poetry which was praised in the Press, and learned the reviews of it by heart. Every evening he read painfully a portion of the Classics. He plodded through the poetry sections of Bartlett's 'Book of Quotations'. Margaret's devotion to the various bards was so enthusiastic, and her reading so wide, that there were times when

Reginald wondered if he could stand the strain. But he pegged away manfully.

He was helped by the fact that he actually saw Margaret but rarely. Being in a Government office he found it impossible to get away during the week, Chigley Heath being a matter of thirty miles or so from London. Sunday was, as a rule, the only day on which they met; and studious application to the poets during the week always enabled him to acquit himself with credit.

But the strain was fearful.

It occurred to Reginald on this particular Saturday that he was in a position to bring off a double event. The Hearty Lunchers' match was to begin at eleven-thirty. Consequently, if he arranged to meet Margaret at their usual Sunday meeting-place – Brown's boathouse, which was about a mile from the cricket-field – at four-thirty, he could have his game and still have plenty of time to pull her up the river to their favourite honeysuckled cottage for tea. If his side happened to be fielding at four o'clock he could get a substitute to act for him; and if Chigley Heath batted last he would get his captain to put him in early, so that he could get his innings over in good time.

Having laid these plans he caught his train on the Saturday morning with a light heart.

All went well from the start. The day was fine, the sun warm but tempered with a light breeze. The Hearty Lunchers batted first and lost six wickets before the interval for a hundred and twenty. The Chigley Heath crowd, mainly composed of small boys and octogenarians, who looked on the Hearty Lunchers as a first-class team because they wore bright blazers, were loud in their approval of their bowlers' performance in dismissing more than half the side for so few runs.

Reginald, who quite inadvertently had caught a hot catch at mid-on, went into the pavilion thoroughly pleased with himself. It was a red-letter day for him when he caught a catch, and this had been a particularly smart one. Indeed, he had not realised that the ball was coming in his direction at all till it hit him in the stomach.

At the festive board the Hearty Lunchers, as usual, justified their name, and it was not until a quarter to three that the match was resumed. The Hearty Lunchers believed in scientific stoking preparatory to the strenuous toil of the afternoon. The bill of fare was good and varied, and the only bitter drop in Reginald's cup was that he could not find his tobacco pouch. He had had it with him in the train, but now it had vanished. This rather saddened Reginald, for the pouch had been given to him by Margaret, and he had always thought it one more proof of the way her nature towered over the natures of other girls, that she had not woven a monogram on it in forget-me-nots. This record pouch, I say, was missing, and Reginald mourned for the loss.

He was still moody when the team went out to the field.

The remaining Hearty Lunchers did not offer very much resistance to the Chigley Heath fast bowler, and the whole side was out with the addition of forty runs.

It was now half-past three, and Reginald saw that if he was to do himself justice with the bat he must be put in early. Buttonholing the Chigley Heath captain he explained this to him, and the captain, a sympathetic soul, requested Reginald to get his pads on and come in first with him.

Having received one favour Reginald did not like to ask another, so greatly against his will he prepared himself to take first ball. He did this with grave care. Everyone who has seen Reginald Humby bat knows that his taking of guard is one of the most impressive sights ever witnessed on the cricket field. He tilted his cap over his eyes, waggled his bat about till the umpire was satisfied that he had got two-leg, scratched the crease with a bail, looked round at the field, walked out of his ground to pat down a blade of grass, picked.

up a fragment of mud, waved imperatively to two small boys who looked as if they might get behind the bowler's arm, and finally settled himself, left toe well in the air, to receive the first ball.

It was then that he noted for the first time that the bowler was Blagdon.

The sight sent a thrill through Reginald. He had seen Blagdon bowl at the nets, but he had never dared to hope that he might bat against him in a match. Exigencies of space forbid a detailed description of Blagdon's bowling. Suffice it to say that it was a shade inferior as bowling to Reginald's batting as batting.

It was Reginald's invariable custom to play forward, on principle, to each ball of his first over wherever it pitched. He called this playing himself in. In accordance with this rule he lunged grandly for six balls (three of which were long-hops to leg), and Blagdon registered a maiden. Four small boys near the pavilion clapped tentatively, but an octogenarian scowled, and, having said that cricket was a brighter game in his young days, went on to compare Reginald unfavourably with Alfred Mynn.

Scarcely had Reginald recovered from the pleasurable shock of finding Blagdon bowling at one end when he was amazed to find that Westaway was bowling at the other. Critics had often wrangled warmly as to the comparative merits of Blagdon and Westaway as bowlers; some thought that Blagdon had it, others that Westaway was the more putrid of the two; a third party called it a dead heat.

The Chigley Heath captain hit Westaway's first ball for three, and Reginald, coming to the batting end, suddenly resolved that this was an occasion on which conventional rules might be flung to the winds; instead, therefore, of playing forward at a full-pitch to leg, he waited for it, and lashing out sent it flying over short slip's head for a single.

That stroke marked an epoch. Reginald was now set.

The ordinary batsman, whose average always pans out at the end of the season between the twenties and the thirties, does not understand the whirl of mixed sensations which the really incompetent cricketer experiences on the rare occasions when he does notch a few. As ball follows ball, and he does not get out, a wild exhilaration surges through him, followed by a sort of awe as if he were doing something wrong, even irreligious. Then all these yeasty emotions subside, and are blended into one glorious sensation of grandeur and majesty, as of a giant among pygmies. This last state of mind does not come till the batsman's score has passed thirty.

By the time that Reginald, ballooning one of Blagdon's half-volleys over cover-point's head, had made his score thirty-two, he was in the full grip of this feeling. As he stood parting the pitch and waiting for the ball to be returned from the boundary, he felt that this was Life, that till now he had been a mere mollusc. His eye rolled proudly round the field.

As it did so it was caught by the clock of the adjacent church, and the sight of that clock was like a douche of cold water. The hands stood at a quarter past four.

Let us pause and ponder on this point for a while. Do not let us dismiss it as if it were some mere trivial everyday difficulty, because it is not. It is about the heftiest soul problem ever handed out to suffering man. You, dear reader, play a long and stylish innings every time you go to the wickets, and so do I; but Reginald was not like us. This was the first occasion on which the ball had seemed larger to him than a rather undersized marble. It was the first occasion on which he had ever hit at a ball with the chances in his favour of getting it anywhere near the centre of the bat.

On the other hand, he was passionately devoted to Margaret Melville, whom he was due to meet at Brown's boathouse at four-thirty sharp. It was now four-fifteen, and Brown's boathouse was still a mile away.

Reginald Humby was at the cross-roads.

The mental struggle was brief but keen. A sharp pang, and his mind was made up. Cost what it might he must stay at the wickets. Not even for Margaret could he wilfully put an end to an innings like this. If she broke off the engagement – well, it might be that Time would heal the wound, and that after many years he would find some other girl for whom he might come to care in a wrecked, broken sort of way. But a chance like this, a chance of batting thoroughly set, against the bowling of Blagdon, Westaway, Blake, and Harris, could never come again. Such things did not happen twice in a lifetime. Only to the very favoured did they happen once. What is Love compared to a chance of knocking up a really big score? ... Reginald prepared to face the bowling again.

Soon a burst of applause from the pavilion signalled the fact that Reginald had made the first fifty of his life.

The time was now twenty-five to five, and Brown's boathouse was exactly where it had been at a quarter past four, a mile away.

But there was no room now in Reginald's mind for even a passing thought about Brown's boathouse, for his gleaming eyes had seen that Grigson was being put on to bowl. Antony would have forgotten Cleopatra if he had had the chance of batting against Grigson.

If Grigson, as a bowler, had one fault more than another (which his friends denied), it was that he was too tantalising. In pace his deliveries were – from a batsman's point of view – ideal. It was in direction that they erred. His first ball soared languidly into the hands of second slip, without touching terra firma. His second was fielded and returned by point. Reginald watched these truants with growing impatience.

At the third ball he could restrain himself no longer. The sight of the square-leg umpire shaping for a catch maddened him. He bounded from his crease, pushed the official to one side, and was just in time at the end of this manoeuvre to smite the ball as it bounced and send it hurtling to the pavilion. There were cheers; the octogenarian who had compared him to his disadvantage with Alfred Mynn handsomely retracted his words; and two small boys in their enthusiasm fell out of a tree.

Of the remaining hour and ten minutes of his innings Reginald's recollections are like some blurred but beautiful dream. He remembers occasional outstanding hits – as when he scored a boundary off a ball of Grigson's which stopped dead two-thirds of the way down the pitch, and when he beat short-slip in a race for a delivery of Harris'. But the greater part of the innings has fled from him.

One moment, however, still stands out sharp and clear in his memory – the moment when a second burst of cheering, beside which the first was as nothing, informed him that his score had reached three figures. After that one or two more lofty hits, and finally the crash of the stumps and the triumphant return to the pavilion on the shoulders of a mixed bevy of Chigley Heathens and Hearty Lunchers.

For some fifteen minutes he sat on a bench in a moist, happy trance.

And then, suddenly, like a cold douche, came the thought of Margaret.

Reginald sprang for the dressing-room and changed his clothes, his brain working feverishly.

And as he laced his boots there came, like some knell, the sound of the clock outside striking six.

Margaret and her mother were seated in the drawing-room when Reginald arrived. Mrs Melville, who had elicited the information that Reginald had not kept his appointment, had been saying 'I told you so' for some time, and this had not improved Margaret's temper. When, therefore, Reginald, damp and dishevelled, was shown in, he felt like a man who has suddenly discovered the North Pole. Mrs Melville did her celebrated imitation of the Gorgon, while Margaret, lightly humming an air, picked up a weekly paper and became absorbed in it.

'Margaret, let me explain,' panted Reginald.

Mrs Melville was understood to remark that she dared say.

Margaret's attention was riveted by a fashion plate.

'Driving in a taximeter to Charing Cross this afternoon,' resumed Reginald, 'I had an accident.'

(Which was the net result of his feverish brain-work in the pavilion dressing-room.)

The weekly periodical flapped to the floor.

'Oh, Reggie, are you hurt?'

'A few scratches, nothing more; but it made me miss my train.'

'Oh, Reggie! But why didn't you wire? I have been worrying so.'

'I was too agitated, dearest.'

'What train did you catch?'

'The five-one.'

'Why, Brewster was coming home by the five-one. Did you see him?'

Reginald's jaw dropped slightly.

'Er – no,' he said.

'How curious,' said Margaret.

'Very curious,' said Reginald.

'Most curious,' said Mrs Melville.

They were still reflecting on the singularity of this fact when the door opened again, and the son of the house entered in person.

'Thought I should find you here, Humby,' he said. 'They gave me this at the station to give to you; you dropped it this morning when you got out of the train.'

He handed Reginald the missing pouch.

'Thanks,' said the latter, huskily. 'When you say this morning, of course you mean this evening but thanks, all the same – thanks – thanks.'

'No, Reginald Humby, he does not mean this evening,' said Mrs Melville. 'Brewster, speak! From what train did that guf – did Mr Humby alight when he dropped the tobacco pouch?'

'The ten-fifteen, the porter chap told me – said he would have given it back to him then only he nipped off in the deuce of a hurry in a cab.'

Six eyes focused themselves upon Reginald.

'Margaret,' he said, 'I will not try to deceive you—'

'You may try,' observed Mrs Melville, 'but you will not succeed.'

'Well, Reginald?'

Reginald fingered his collar.

'There was no taximeter accident.'

'Ah!' said Mrs Melville.

'The fact is, I've been playing cricket for Chigley Heath against the Hearty Lunchers.'

Margaret uttered an exclamation of surprise.

'Playing cricket!'

Reginald bowed his head with manly resignation.

'Why didn't you tell me? Why didn't you arrange for us to meet on the ground? I wanted to watch the match, only I couldn't get there in the morning, and it didn't seem worth it for such a little while in the afternoon.'

Reginald was amazed.

'You take an interest in cricket, Margaret? You! I thought you scorned it, considered it an unintellectual game.'

'Why, I play regularly in the ladies' match.'

'Margaret! Why didn't you tell me?'

'I thought you might not like it. You were so spiritual, so poetic. I feared you would despise me.'

Reginald took a step forward. His voice was tense and trembling.

'Margaret,' he said, and his accents thrilled with a dawning hope, 'this is no time for misunderstandings. We must be open with one another. Our happiness is at stake. Tell me honestly, do you like poetry really?'

Margaret hesitated, then answered bravely:

'No, Reginald,' she said. 'It is as you suspect. I am not worthy of you. I do not like poetry. Ah, you shudder! You turn away!'

'I don't,' yelled Reginald. 'I don't. You've made me another man. Margaret!'

She stared, wild-eyed, astonished.

'What! Do you mean that you, too—'

'I should jolly well think I do. I tell you I hate the beastly stuff. I only pretended to like it because I thought you did. The hours I've spent mugging it up! I wonder I've not got brain fever.'

'Reggie! Used you to read it up too? Oh, if I'd only known!'

'And you forgive me – this afternoon, I mean?'

'Of course. You couldn't leave a cricket match. By the way, did you make any runs?'

Reginald coughed.

'A few,' he said, modestly. 'One or two. In fact, rather a lot. As a matter of fact, I made a hundred and thirteen.'

'A hundred and thirteen!' whispered Margaret. 'My hero!'

'You won't be wanting me for a bit, will you?' asked Brewster, nonchalantly. 'Think I'll smoke a cigarette in the garden.'

And sobs from the staircase told that Mrs Melville was already on her way to her room.

CRICKET, BASEBALL, AND 'ROUNDERS': FROM *PICCADILLY JIM*

Amid the supporting cast of Wodehouse's 1917 novel is one 'Bingley Crocker, late of New York', a formerly on-his-uppers actor who lands in clover by marrying the wealthy Eugenia Pett and so finds himself exiled in London — to be precise, the fashionable address of Drexdale House on Grosvenor Square, where he is attended by a butler named Bayliss. But Bingley misses New York, and above all one special aspect of his homeland, as revealed in this celebrated sequence which begins at the Crocker breakfast table.

'Bingley! You aren't listening. What is that you are reading?'

Mr Crocker tore himself from the paper.

'This? Oh, I was looking at a report of that cricket game you made me go and see yesterday.'

'Oh? I am glad you have begun to take an interest in cricket. It is simply a social necessity in England. Why you ever made such a fuss about taking it up, I can't think. You used to be so fond of watching baseball and cricket is just the same thing.'

A close observer would have marked a deepening of the look of pain on Mr Crocker's face. Women say this sort of thing carelessly, with no wish to wound: but that makes it none the less hard to bear.

From the hall outside came faintly the sound of the telephone, then the measured tones of Bayliss answering it. Mr Crocker returned to his paper.

Bayliss entered.

'Lady Corstorphine desires to speak to you on the telephone, madam.'

Half-way to the door Mrs Crocker paused, as if recalling something that had slipped her memory.

'Is Mr James getting up, Bayliss?'

'I believe not, madam. I am informed by one of the house-maids who passed his door a short time back that there were no sounds.'

Mrs Crocker left the room. Bayliss, preparing to follow her example, was arrested by an exclamation from the table.

'Say!'

His master's voice.

'Say, Bayliss, come here a minute. Want to ask you something.'

The butler approached the table. It seemed to him that his employer was not looking quite himself this morning. There was something a trifle wild, a little haggard, about his expression. He had remarked on it earlier in the morning in the Servants' Hall.

As a matter of fact, Mr Crocker's ailment was a perfectly simple one. He was suffering from one of those acute spasms of home-sickness, which invariably racked him in the earlier summer months. Ever since his marriage five years previously and his simultaneous removal from his native land he had been a chronic victim to the complaint. The symptoms grew less acute in winter and spring, but from May onward he suffered severely.

Poets have dealt feelingly with the emotions of practically every variety except one. They have sung of Ruth, of Israel in bondage, of slaves pining for their native Africa, and of the miner's dream of home. But the sorrows of the baseball bug, compelled by fate to live three thousand miles away from the Polo Grounds, have been neglected in song. Bingley Crocker was such a one, and in summer his agonies were awful. He pined away in a country where they said 'Well played, sir!' when they meant "at-a-boy!'

'Bayliss, do you play cricket?'

'I am a little past the age, sir. In my younger days ...'

'Do you understand it?'

'Yes, sir. I frequently spend an afternoon at Lord's or the Oval when there is a good match.'

Many who enjoyed a merely casual acquaintance with the butler would have looked on this as an astonishingly unexpected revelation of humanity in Bayliss, but Mr Crocker was not surprised. To him, from the very beginning, Bayliss had been a man and a brother who was always willing to suspend his duties in order to answer questions dealing with the thousand and one problems which the social life of England presented. Mr Crocker's mind had adjusted itself with difficulty to the niceties of class distinction: and, while he had cured himself of his early tendency to address the butler as 'Bill', he never failed to consult him as man to man in his moments of perplexity.

Bayliss was always eager to be of assistance. He liked Mr Crocker. True, his manner might have struck a more sensitive man than his employer as a shade too closely resembling that of an indulgent father towards a son who was not quite right in the head: but it had genuine affection in it.

Mr Crocker picked up his paper and folded it back at the sporting page, pointing with a stubby forefinger.

'Well, what does all this mean? I've kept out of watching cricket since I landed in England, but yesterday they got the poison needle to work and took me off to see Surrey play Kent at that place Lord's where you say you go sometimes.'

'I was there yesterday, sir. A very exciting game.'

'Exciting? How do you make that out? I sat in the bleachers all afternoon, waiting for something to break loose. Doesn't anything ever happen at cricket?'

The butler winced a little, but managed to smile a tolerant smile. This man, he reflected, was but an American and as such more to be pitied than censured. He endeavoured to explain.

'It was a sticky wicket yesterday, sir, owing to the rain.'

'Eh?'

'The wicket was sticky, sir.'

'Come again.'

'I mean that the reason why the game yesterday struck you as slow was that the wicket – I should say the turf – was sticky – that is to say wet. Sticky is the technical term, sir. When the wicket is sticky, the batsmen are obliged to exercise a great deal of caution, as the stickiness of the wicket enables the bowlers to make the ball turn more sharply in either direction as it strikes the turf than when the wicket is not sticky.'

'That's it, is it?'

'Yes, sir.'

'Thanks for telling me.'

'Not at all, sir.'

Mr Crocker pointed to the paper.

'Well, now, this seems to be the box-score of the game we saw yesterday. If you can make sense out of that, go to it.'

The passage on which his finger rested was headed 'Final Score', and ran as follows:

SURREY
First Innings
Hayward, c Wooley, b Carr 67
Hobbs, run out 0
Hayes, st Huish, b Fielder 12

Ducat, b Fielder 33
Harrison, not out 11
Sandham, not out 6
Extras 10

Total (for four wickets) 139

Bayliss inspected the cipher gravely.

'What is it you wish me to explain, sir?'

'Why, the whole thing. What's it all about?'

'It's perfectly simple, sir. Surrey won the toss, and took first knock. Hayward and Hobbs were the opening pair. Hayward called Hobbs for a short run, but the latter was unable to get across and was thrown out by mid-on. Hayes was the next man in. He went out of his ground and was stumped. Ducat and Hayward made a capital stand considering the stickiness of the wicket, until Ducat was bowled by a good length off break and Hayward caught at second slip off a googly. Then Harrison and Sandham played out time.'

Mr Crocker breathed heavily through his nose.

'Yes!' he said. 'Yes! I had an idea that was it. But I think I'd like to have it once again, slowly. Start with these figures. What does that sixty-seven mean, opposite Hayward's name?'

'He made sixty-seven runs, sir.'

'Sixty-seven! In one game?'

'Yes, sir.'

'Why, Home-Run Baker couldn't do it!'

'I am not familiar with Mr Baker, sir.'

'I suppose you've never seen a ball-game?'

'Ball-game, sir?'

'A baseball game?'

'Never, sir.'

'Then, Bill,' said Mr Crocker, reverting in his emotion to the bad habit of his early London days, 'you haven't lived. See here!'

Whatever vestige of respect for class distinctions Mr Crocker had managed to preserve during the opening stages of the interview now definitely disappeared. His eyes shone wildly and he snorted like a war-horse. He clutched the butler by the sleeve and drew him closer to the table, then began to move forks, spoons, cups, and even the contents of his plate about the cloth with an energy little short of feverish.

'Bayliss!'

'Sir?'

'Watch!' said Mr Crocker, with the air of an excitable high priest about to initiate a novice into the Mysteries.

He removed a roll from the basket.

'You see this roll? That's the home plate. This spoon is first base. Where I'm putting this cup is second. This piece of bacon is third. There's your diamond for you. Very well, then. These lumps of sugar are the infielders and the outfielders. Now we're ready. Batter up? He stands here. Catcher behind him. Umps behind catcher.'

'Umps, I take it, sir, is what we would call the umpire?'

'Call him anything you like. It's part of the game. Now here's the box, where I've put this dab of marmalade, and here's the pitcher, winding up.'

'The pitcher would be equivalent to our bowler?'

'I guess so, though why you should call him a bowler gets past me.'

'The box, then, is the bowler's wicket?'

'Have it your own way. Now pay attention. Play ball! Pitcher's winding up. Put it over, Mike, put it over! Some speed, kid! Here it comes, right in the groove. Bing! Batter slams it and streaks for first. Outfielder – this lump of sugar – boots it. Bonehead! Batter touches second. Third? No! Get back! Can't be done. Play it safe.

Stick around the sack, old pal. Second batter up. Pitcher getting something on the ball now besides the cover. Whiffs him. Back to the bench, Cyril! Third batter up. See him rub his hands in the dirt. Watch this kid. He's good! He lets two alone, then slams the next right on the nose. Whizzes around to second. First guy, the one we left on second, comes home for one run. That's a game! Take it from me, Bill, that's a *game!*'

Somewhat overcome with the energy with which he had flung himself into his lecture, Mr Crocker sat down and refreshed himself with cold coffee.

'Quite an interesting game,' said Bayliss. 'But I find, now that you have explained it, sir, that it is familiar to me, though I have always known it under another name. It is played a great deal in this country.'

Mr Crocker started to his feet.

'It is? And I've been five years here without finding it out! When's the next game scheduled?'

'It is known in England as 'rounders', sir. Children play it with a soft ball and a racquet, and derive considerable enjoyment from it. I had never heard of it before as a pastime for adults.'

Two shocked eyes stared into the butler's face.

'Children?' The word came in a whisper. 'A racquet?'

'Yes, sir.'

'You – you didn't say a soft ball?'

'Yes, sir.'

A sort of spasm seemed to convulse Mr Crocker. He had lived five years in England, but not till this moment had he realised to the full how utterly alone he was in an alien land. Fate had placed him, bound and helpless, in a country where they called baseball 'rounders' and played it with a soft ball.

He sank back into his chair, staring before him. And as he sat the wall seemed to melt and he was gazing upon a green field, in the centre of which a man in a grey uniform was beginning a Salome dance. Watching this person with a cold and suspicious eye, stood another uniformed man, holding poised above his shoulder a sturdy club. Two Masked Marvels crouched behind him in attitudes of watchful waiting. On wooden seats all around sat a vast multitude of shirt-sleeved spectators, and the air was full of voices. One voice detached itself from the din.

'Pea-nuts! Get y'r pea-nuts!'

Something that was almost a sob shook Bingley Crocker's ample frame. Bayliss the butler gazed down upon him with concern. He was sure the master was unwell.

'A PLEA
FOR INDOOR GOLF'

By the autumn of 1914 Wodehouse had met and married Ethel Newton in New York, then set up home in Long Island. Another luminous date in his biography around this time is the debut appearance, in a short story of September 1915 entitled 'Extricating Young Gussie', of the manservant Jeeves, his name loaned from the great Warwickshire bowler Percy Jeeves. But in America cricket began to recede from Wodehouse's fiction, its place steadily assumed by golf – a game in which he made his early, tentative assays at the Sound View Golf Club in Great Neck, before embarking on the run of stories you are about to consume.

Now, this bit is very important. In Wodehouse's day, 'bogey' and 'par' were synonymous terms for the score on a hole that a player off scratch handicap was expected to make. Contemporary readers, moreover, might well find themselves in want of a key or glossary to the names given to golf clubs a century ago, and so appearing routinely in Wodehouse. While these clubs performed much the same functions as those you'd find in the modern bag, they went by different monikers.

So, starting from the tee, a driver then was a play club, the next wood up was a brassey, and the more lofted driving wood was a spoon. A

fairway wood was a baffing spoon or baffey. Moving to the irons, the
1 iron was a driving iron; the 2 iron a cleek, the 3 a mid-mashie, the 4
a mashie-iron, the 5 a mashie proper, and the 6 a spade mashie. Regard-
ing the lofted irons: the 7 iron was a mashie niblick, the 8 a pitching
niblick, the 9 just a niblick. A wedging or chipping club was a jigger.
And a putter was, reassuringly, just a putter.

But then for a good many people their first meeting with the tools of
the golf game comes via a spot of indoor putting, prior to any attempt
to drive the ball hundreds of yards from a tee-box. This carpet-based
practice gave Wodehouse the notion for the following piece, which was
subtitled 'a Plaintive Dirge – By a Golfing Neophyte – for the Passing
of Winter' and appeared in Vanity Fair *in May 1919.*

It might be supposed, by the vapid and unreflective, that in winter,
when the first snows have begun to fall and the last pros have
started flying South, the enthusiastic golfer would be to some extent
up against it. The fact is, however, that of the four seasons of the
golfing year – spring, when you lose your ball in the un-mown hay;
summer, when you lose it in the glare of the sun; autumn, when
you lose it under dead leaves; and winter, when you have a sporting
chance of not losing it at all – the last-named is, to the thoughtful
golfer, quite the pleasantest.

It is glorious, no doubt, on a lovely afternoon in summer, with
the sun shining down and a gentle breeze tempering the heat, to
slice your ball into the adjacent jungle and to feel that you are
thereby doing a bit of good to a small boy who needs the money
which he will get when – directly your back is turned – he finds
and sells the missing globule.

It is thrilling, on one of those still, crisp days in the fall, to drive
off the tee at eleven-fifteen and potter about the course till twelve-
forty-five, turning over leaves with a niblick in the hope that each
leaf be the one under which your ball has elected to nestle. But

both these pleasures are eclipsed by the delight of playing on a frosty morning in the winter.

In Winter You Get Good Visibility

There you stand – before you a prairie denuded of all vegetation. The trees, into which you used to send your second shot, have now no leaves, and it is quite possible to penetrate them with a well-judged stroke of the light iron. Your caddie broods dejectedly beside you. He knows that, even if you slice into the wood at the elbow-hole, you can find the ball for yourself.

And then you drive off.

It is one of your medium drives. You have violated, possibly, only eleven out of the twenty-three rules for correct driving. The ball soars in a lofty arc, edging off to the right. Sixty yards from the tee it touches earth, and bounds another fifty, when it hits the frozen surface of a puddle and skids against a tree-trunk, a further ninety yards ahead. The angle at which it hits the tree just corrects your slice to perfection, and there you are, in a dead straight line with the pin, with a two hundred and thirty yard drive to your credit.

This is Golf, in the true sense of the word.

Even now, however, your happiness is not complete. You have omitted to take into consideration the fact that you are playing what are called Winter Rules, which entitle you to tee your ball up in the fairway. So you remove the pill from the cuppy lie into which it has settled and look round you for a convenient hillock. You can usually find a worm-cast or a mole-hill of a convenient height, and from this you propel the ball onto the green.

The green is a trifle rough, perhaps, but, after all, what does that matter? Experts will try to tell you otherwise, but every beginner knows that putting is a pure game of chance, and that you are just as likely to hole out over rough ground as over smooth. I, personally, prefer a worm-cast or two on the green. They seem to lend zip to my putting.

Of course, there are weeks in the winter when golf on the links is impossible, unless you happen to be in such an advanced stage of mental decay that you can contemplate with equanimity a round in the snow with a red ball. The ordinary golfer, unequal to such excesses, will take, during these weeks, to indoor golf. There are two varieties of the indoor game, both almost equally enjoyable.

The Glories of Indoor Golf

The first, and more customary, kind of indoor golf is that played in department stores, where professionals live in little dens on the Toys and Sporting Goods floor and give instruction, at a dollar the half hour. You stand on a rubber mat: the ball is placed on an ordinary door-mat: and you swat it against a target painted on a mattress.

The merits of this plan are obvious.

It is almost impossible not to hit the mattress *somewhere*, and it makes just as satisfactory a thud whether you hit it in the middle or in one of the outlying suburbs. And in indoor golf, as played in department stores, the thud is everything. This indoor instruction is invaluable. I may say that I, myself, am what I am as a golfer almost entirely through indoor instruction.

In the fall of 1917 I was a steady hundred-and-twenty man. Sometimes I would get into difficulties at one or other of the holes, as the best players will do, and then my score would be a hundred and thirty. Sometimes, again, I would find my form early in the round and shoot a hundred and eighteen. But, take me for all in all, I averaged a hundred and twenty. After a steady winter of indoor instruction, I was going round, this spring, in a hundred and twelve.

These figures speak for themselves.

Of course, the drawback to department-store golf is that it is so difficult to reproduce the same conditions when you get out on the links. I have been in a variety of lies, good and bad, in my time, but never yet have I had the luck to drop my ball on a doormat. Why this should be so, it is hard to say. I suppose the fact is that, unless you actually pull the ball, off the first tee, at right angles between your legs, it is not easy to land on a door-mat. And, even then, it would probably be a rubber doormat, which is not at all the same thing.

Indoor Sport for the Housewreckers' Union

The other form of indoor golf is that which is played in the home. Whether you live in a palace or a hovel, an indoor golf-course, be it only of nine holes, is well within your reach. A house offers greater facilities than an apartment, and I have found my game greatly improved since I went to live in the country. I can, perhaps, scarcely do better than give a brief description of the sporting nine-hole course which I have recently laid out in my present residence.

All authorities agree that the first hole on every links should be moderately easy, in order to give the nervous player a temporary and fictitious confidence.

At Wodehouse Manor, therefore, we drive off from the front door – in order to get the benefit of the door-mat – down an entry fairway, carpeted with rugs, and without traps. The hole – a loving-cup from the Inebriates' Daughters of Communipaw for my services in combating the drink evil – is just under the stairs; and a good player ought to have no difficulty in doing it in two.

The second hole, a short one, takes you into the telephone booth. This also is simple. Trouble begins with the third, a long dog-leg hole through the kitchen into the dining-room. This hole is well trapped with table-legs, kitchen utensils, and a moving hazard in the person of Clarence the cat, who is generally wandering about the fairway. The hole is under the glass-and-china cupboard, where you are liable to be bunkered if you loft your approach-shot excessively. It is better to take your light iron and try a running-up approach, instead of becoming ambitious with the mashie-niblick.

The fourth and fifth holes call for no comment. They are straight-forward holes without traps, the only danger being that you may lose a stroke through hitting the maid if she happens to be coming down the back stairs while you are taking a mashie-shot. This is a penalty under the local rule.

A Word as to the Water Hazard

The sixth is the indispensable water-hole. It is short, but tricky. Teeing off from just outside the bathroom door, you have to loft the ball over the side of the bath, holing out in the little vent pipe, at the end where the water runs out. It is apparently a simple shot, but I have known many fine players, notably Ouimet, and Chick Evans, who have taken threes and fours over it. It is a niblick shot, and to use a full swing with the brassey is courting disaster. (In the Open Championship of 1914 Ouimet broke all precedents by taking a shovel for his tee-shot, and the subsequent controversy and the final ruling of the Golf Association will be fresh in the memory of all.)

The seventh is the longest hole on the course. Starting at the entrance of the best bedroom, a full drive takes you to the head of the stairs, whence you will need at least two more strokes to put you dead on the pin in the drawing-room. In the drawing-room the fairway is trapped with photograph frames – with glass, complete – these serving as casual water; and anyone who can hole out on the piano in five or under is a player of class. Bogey is six, and I have known even such a capable exponent of the game as my Uncle Reginald, who is plus two on his home links on Park Avenue, to take twenty-seven at the hole. But on that occasion he had the misfortune to be bunkered in a photograph of my Aunt Clara and took no fewer than eleven strokes with his niblick to extricate himself from it.

The eighth and ninth holes are straightforward, and can be done in two and three respectively, provided you swing easily and avoid the canary's cage. Once trapped there, it is better to give up the hole without further effort. It is almost impossible to get out in less than fifty-six, and after you have taken about thirty the bird gets visibly annoyed.

'A WOMAN IS ONLY A WOMAN'

In his 1986 essay 'Golf in Writing', John Updike pays generous tribute to Wodehouse's contributions to the genre, though he does not stint from identifying certain narrative plot formulae on which the great man depended for his effects: to wit, 'mock-epic Wodehousian matches, often played for the hand of a comely girl'. This is perhaps the first and finest of such – also a suitable introduction to the returning figure of the Oldest Member, the retired sage who sees all from the clubhouse terrace.

On a fine day in the spring, summer, or early autumn, there are few spots more delightful than the terrace in front of our Golf Club. It is a vantage-point peculiarly fitted to the man of philo-sophic mind: for from it may be seen that varied, never-ending pageant, which men call Golf, in a number of its aspects. To your right, on the first tee, stand the cheery optimists who are about to make their opening drive, happily conscious that even a topped shot will trickle a measurable distance down the steep hill. Away in the valley, directly in front of you, is the lake-hole, where these same optimists will be converted to pessimism by the wet splash of a new ball. At your side is the ninth green, with its sinuous undulations which have so often wrecked the returning traveller in sight of home. And at various points within your line of vision are the third tee, the sixth tee, and the sinister bunkers about the eighth green – none of them lacking in food for the reflective mind.

It is on this terrace that the Oldest Member sits, watching the younger generation knocking at the divot. His gaze wanders from Jimmy Fothergill's two-hundred-and-twenty-yard drive down the hill to the silver drops that flash up in the sun, as young Freddie Woosley's mashie-shot drops weakly into the waters of the lake. Returning, it rests upon Peter Willard, large and tall, and James Todd, small and slender, as they struggle up the fairway of the ninth.

*

Love (says the Oldest Member) is an emotion which your true golfer should always treat with suspicion. Do not misunderstand me. I am not saying that love is a bad thing, only that it is an unknown quantity. I have known cases where marriage improved a man's game, and other cases where it seemed to put him right off his stroke. There seems to be no fixed rule. But what I do say is that a golfer should be cautious. He should not be led away by the first pretty face. I will tell you a story that illustrates the point. It is the story of those two men who have just got on to the ninth green – Peter Willard and James Todd.

There is about great friendships between man and man (said the Oldest Member) a certain inevitability that can only be compared with the age-old association of ham and eggs. No one can say when it was that these two wholesome and palatable food-stuffs first came together, nor what was the mutual magnetism that brought their deathless partnership about. One simply feels that it is one of the things that must be so.

Similarly with men. Who can trace to its first beginnings the love of Damon for Pythias, of David for Jonathan, of Swan for Edgar? Who can explain what it was about Crosse that first attracted Blackwell? We simply say, 'These men are friends,' and leave it at that.

In the case of Peter Willard and James Todd, one may hazard the guess that the first link in the chain that bound them together was the fact that they took up golf within a few days of each other, and contrived, as time went on, to develop such equal form at the game that the most expert critics are still baffled in their efforts to decide which is the worse player. I have heard the point argued a hundred times without any conclusion being reached. Supporters of Peter claim that his driving off the tee entitles him to an unchallenged pre-eminence among the world's most hopeless foozlers – only to be discomfited later when the advocates of James show, by means of diagrams, that no one has ever surpassed their man in absolute incompetence with the spoon. It is one of those problems where debate is futile.

Few things draw two men together more surely than a mutual inability to master golf, coupled with an intense and ever-increasing love for the game. At the end of the first few months, when a series of costly experiments had convinced both Peter and James that there was not a tottering grey-beard nor a toddling infant in the neighbourhood whose downfall they could encompass, the two became inseparable. It was pleasanter, they found, to play together, and go neck and neck round the eighteen holes, than to take on some lissome youngster who could spatter them all over the course with one old ball and a cut-down cleek stolen from his father; or some spavined elder who not only rubbed it into them, but was apt, between strokes, to bore them with personal reminiscences of the Crimean War. So they began to play together early and late. In the small hours before breakfast, long ere the first faint piping of the waking caddie made itself heard from the caddie-shed, they were half-way through their opening round. And at close of day, when bats wheeled against the steely sky and the 'pros' had stolen home to rest, you might see them in the deepening dusk, going through the concluding exercises of their final spasm. After dark, they visited each other's houses and read golf books.

If you have gathered from what I have said that Peter Willard and James Todd were fond of golf, I am satisfied. That is the impression I intended to convey. They were real golfers, for real golf is a thing of the spirit, not of mere mechanical excellence of stroke.

It must not be thought, however, that they devoted too much of their time and their thoughts to golf – assuming, indeed, that such a thing is possible. Each was connected with a business in the metropolis; and often, before he left for the links, Peter would go to the trouble and expense of ringing up the office to say he would not be coming in that day; while I myself have heard James – and this not once, but frequently – say, while lunching in the club-house, that he had half a mind to get Gracechurch Street on the 'phone and ask how things were going. They were, in fact, the type of men of whom England is proudest – the back-bone of a great country, toilers in the mart, untired businessmen, keen red-blooded men of affairs. If they played a little golf besides, who shall blame them?

So they went on, day by day, happy and contented. And then the Woman came into their lives, like the Serpent in the Links of Eden, and perhaps for the first time they realised that they were not one entity – not one single, indivisible Something that made for topped drives and short putts – but two individuals, in whose breasts Nature had implanted other desires than the simple ambition some day to do the dog-leg hole on the second nine in under double figures. My friends tell me that, when I am relating a story, my language is inclined at times a little to obscure my meaning;

but, if you understand from what I have been saying that James Todd and Peter Willard both fell in love with the same woman – all right, let us carry on. That is precisely what I was driving at.

I have not the pleasure of an intimate acquaintance with Grace Forrester. I have seen her in the distance, watering the flowers in her garden, and on these occasions her stance struck me as graceful. And once, at a picnic, I observed her killing wasps with a teaspoon, and was impressed by the freedom of the wrist-action of her back-swing.

Beyond this, I can say little. But she must have been attractive, for there can be no doubt of the earnestness with which both Peter and James fell in love with her. I doubt if either slept a wink the night of the dance at which it was their privilege first to meet her.

The next afternoon, happening to encounter Peter in the bunker near the eleventh green, James said:

'That was a nice girl, that Miss What's-her-name.'

And Peter, pausing for a moment from his trench-digging, replied:

'Yes.'

And then James, with a pang, knew that he had a rival, for he had not mentioned Miss Forrester's name, and yet Peter had divined that it was to her that he had referred.

Love is a fever which, so to speak, drives off without wasting time on the address. On the very next morning after the conversation which I have related, James Todd rang Peter Willard up on the 'phone and cancelled their golf engagements for the day, on the plea of a sprained wrist. Peter, acknowledging the cancellation, stated that he himself had been on the point of ringing James up to say that he would be unable to play owing to a slight headache. They met at tea-time at Miss Forrester's house. James asked how Peter's headache was, and Peter said it was a little better. Peter inquired after James's sprained wrist, and was told it seemed on the mend. Miss Forrester dispensed tea and conversation to both impartially.

They walked home together. After an awkward silence of twenty minutes, James said:

'There is something about the atmosphere – the aura, shall I say? – that emanates from a good woman that makes a man feel that life has a new, a different meaning.'

Peter replied:

'Yes.'

When they reached James's door, James said:

'I won't ask you in tonight, old man. You want to go home and rest and cure that headache.'

'Yes,' said Peter.

There was another silence. Peter was thinking that, only a couple of days before, James had told him that he had a copy of Sandy MacBean's 'How to Become a Scratch Man Your First Season by Studying Photographs' coming by parcel-post from town, and they had arranged to read it aloud together. By now, thought Peter, it must be lying on his friend's table. The thought saddened him. And James, guessing what was in Peter's mind, was saddened too. But he did not waver. He was in no mood to read MacBean's masterpiece that night. In the twenty minutes of silence after leaving Miss Forrester he had realised that 'Grace' rhymes with 'face', and he wanted to sit alone in his study and write poetry. The two men parted with a distant nod. I beg your pardon? Yes, you are right. Two distant nods. It was always a failing of mine to count the score erroneously.

It is not my purpose to weary you by a minute recital of the happenings of each day that went by. On the surface, the lives of these two men seemed unchanged. They still played golf together, and during the round achieved towards each other a manner that, superficially, retained all its ancient cheeriness and affection. If – I should say – when, James topped his drive, Peter never failed to say 'Hard luck!' And when – or, rather, if Peter managed not to top his, James invariably said 'Great!' But things were not the same, and they knew it.

It so happened, as it sometimes will on these occasions, for Fate is a dramatist who gets his best effects with a small cast, that Peter Willard and James Todd were the only visible aspirants for the hand of Miss Forrester. Right at the beginning young Freddie Woosley had seemed attracted by the girl, and had called once or twice with flowers and chocolates, but Freddie's affections never centred themselves on one object for more than a few days, and he had dropped out after the first week. From that time on it became clear to all of us that, if Grace Forrester intended to marry anyone in the place, it would be either James or Peter; and a good deal of interest was taken in the matter by the local sportsmen. So little was known of the form of the two men, neither having figured as principal in a love-affair before, that even money was the best you could get, and the market was sluggish. I think my own flutter of twelve golf-balls, taken up by Percival Brown, was the most substantial of any of the wagers. I selected James as the winner. Why, I can hardly say, unless that he had an aunt who contributed occasional stories to the 'Woman's Sphere'. These things sometimes weigh with a girl. On the other hand, George Lucas, who had half-a-dozen of ginger-ale on Peter, based his calculations on the fact that James wore knickerbockers on the links, and that no girl could possibly love a man with calves like that. In short, you see, we really had nothing to go on.

Nor had James and Peter. The girl seemed to like them both equally. They never saw her except in each other's company. And it was not until one day when Grace Forrester was knitting a sweater that there seemed a chance of getting a clue to her hidden feelings.

When the news began to spread through the place that Grace was knitting this sweater there was a big sensation. The thing seemed to us practically to amount to a declaration.

That was the view that James Todd and Peter Willard took of it, and they used to call on Grace, watch her knitting, and come away with their heads full of complicated calculations. The whole thing hung on one point – to wit, what size the sweater was going to be. If it was large, then it must be for Peter; if small, then James was the lucky man. Neither dared to make open inquiries, but it began to seem almost impossible to find out the truth without them. No masculine eye can reckon up purls and plains and estimate the size of chest which the garment is destined to cover. Moreover, with amateur knitters there must always be allowed a margin for involuntary error. There were many cases during the war where our girls sent sweaters to their sweethearts which would have induced strangulation in their young brothers. The amateur sweater of those days was, in fact, practically tantamount to German propaganda.

Peter and James were accordingly baffled. One evening the sweater would look small, and James would come away jubilant; the next it would have swollen over a vast area, and Peter would walk home singing. The suspense of the two men can readily be imagined. On the one hand, they wanted to know their fate; on the other, they fully realised that whoever the sweater was for would have to wear it. And, as it was a vivid pink and would probably not fit by a mile, their hearts quailed at the prospect.

In all affairs of human tension there must come a breaking point. It came one night as the two men were walking home.

'Peter,' said James, stopping in mid-stride. He mopped his forehead. His manner had been feverish all the evening.

'Yes?' said Peter.

'I can't stand this any longer. I haven't had a good night's rest for weeks. We must find out definitely which of us is to have that sweater.'

'Let's go back and ask her,' said Peter.

So they turned back and rang the bell and went into the house and presented themselves before Miss Forrester.

'Lovely evening,' said James, to break the ice.

'Superb,' said Peter.

'Delightful,' said Miss Forrester, looking a little surprised at finding the troupe playing a return date without having booked it in advance.

'To settle a bet,' said James, 'will you please tell us who – I should say, whom – you are knitting that sweater for?'

'It is not a sweater,' replied Miss Forrester, with a womanly candour that well became her. 'It is a sock. And it is for my cousin Juliet's youngest son, Willie.'

'Good-night,' said James.

'Good-night,' said Peter.

'Good-night,' said Grace Forrester.

It was during the long hours of the night, when ideas so often come to wakeful men, that James was struck by an admirable solution of his and Peter's difficulty. It seemed to him that, were one or the other to leave Woodhaven, the survivor would find himself in a position to conduct his wooing as wooing should be conducted. Hitherto, as I have indicated, neither had allowed the other to be more than a few minutes alone with the girl. They watched each other like hawks. When James called, Peter called. When Peter dropped in, James invariably popped round. The thing had resolved itself into a stalemate.

The idea which now came to James was that he and Peter should settle their rivalry by an eighteen-hole match on the links. He thought very highly of the idea before he finally went to sleep, and in the morning the scheme looked just as good to him as it had done overnight.

James was breakfasting next morning, preparatory to going round to disclose his plan to Peter, when Peter walked in, looking happier than he had done for days.

"Morning,' said James.

"Morning,' said Peter.

Peter sat down and toyed absently with a slice of bacon.

'I've got an idea,' he said.

'One isn't many,' said James, bringing his knife down with a jerk-shot on a fried egg. 'What is your idea?'

'Got it last night as I was lying awake. It struck me that, if either of us was to clear out of this place, the other would have a fair chance. You know what I mean – with Her. At present we've got each other stymied. Now, how would it be,' said Peter, abstractedly spreading marmalade on his bacon, 'if we were to play an eighteen-hole match, the loser to leg out of the neighbourhood and stay away long enough to give the winner the chance to find out exactly how things stood?'

James started so violently that he struck himself in the left eye with his fork.

'That's exactly the idea I got last night, too.'

'Then it's a go?'

'It's the only thing to do.'

There was silence for a moment. Both men were thinking. Remember, they were friends. For years they had shared each other's sorrows, joys, and golf-balls, and sliced into the same bunkers.

Presently Peter said:

'I shall miss you.'

'What do you mean, miss me?'

'When you're gone. Woodhaven won't seem the same place. But of course you'll soon be able to come back. I sha'n't waste any time proposing.'

'Leave me your address,' said James, 'and I'll send you a wire when you can return. You won't be offended if I don't ask you to be best man at the wedding? In the circumstances it might be painful to you.'

Peter sighed dreamily.

'We'll have the sitting-room done in blue. Her eyes are blue.'

'Remember,' said James, 'there will always be a knife and fork for you at our little nest. Grace is not the woman to want me to drop my bachelor friends.'

'Touching this match,' said Peter. 'Strict Royal and Ancient rules, of course?'

'Certainly.'

'I mean to say – no offence, old man – but no grounding niblicks in bunkers.'

'Precisely. And, without hinting at anything personal, the ball shall be considered holed-out only when it is in the hole, not when it stops on the edge.'

'Undoubtedly. And – you know I don't want to hurt your feelings – missing the ball counts as a stroke, not as a practice-swing.'

'Exactly. And – you'll forgive me if I mention it – a player whose ball has fallen in the rough, may not pull up all the bushes within a radius of three feet.'

'In fact, strict rules.'

'Strict rules.'

They shook hands without more words. And presently Peter walked out, and James, with a guilty look over his shoulder, took down Sandy MacBean's great work from the bookshelf and began to study the photograph of the short approach-shot showing Mr MacBean swinging from Point A, through dotted line B-C, to Point D, his head the while remaining rigid at the spot marked with a cross. He felt a little guiltily that he had stolen a march on his friend, and that the contest was as good as over.

*

I cannot recall a lovelier summer day than that on which the great Todd-Willard eighteen-hole match took place. It had rained during the night, and now the sun shone down from a clear blue sky on to turf that glistened more greenly than the young grass of early spring.

Butterflies flitted to and fro; birds sang merrily. In short, all Nature smiled. And it is to be doubted if Nature ever had a better excuse for smiling – or even laughing outright; for matches like that between James Todd and Peter Willard do not occur every day.

Whether it was that love had keyed them up, or whether hours of study of Braid's 'Advanced Golf' and the Badminton Book had produced a belated effect, I cannot say; but both started off quite reasonably well. Our first hole, as you can see, is a bogey four, and James was dead on the pin in seven, leaving Peter, who had twice hit the United Kingdom with his mashie in mistake for the ball, a difficult putt for the half. Only one thing could happen when you left Peter a difficult putt; and James advanced to the lake-hole one up, Peter, as he followed, trying to console himself with the thought that many of the best golfers prefer to lose the first hole and save themselves for a strong finish.

Peter and James had played over the lake-hole so often that they had become accustomed to it, and had grown into the habit of sinking a ball or two as a preliminary formality with much the same stoicism displayed by those kings in ancient and superstitious times who used to fling jewellery into the sea to propitiate it before they took a voyage. But today, by one of those miracles without which golf would not be golf, each of them got over with his first shot – and not only over, but dead on the pin. Our 'pro' himself could not have done better.

I think it was at this point that the two men began to go to pieces. They were in an excited frame of mind, and this thing unmanned them. You will no doubt recall Keats's poem about stout Cortez staring with eagle eyes at the Pacific while all his men gazed at each other with a wild surmise, silent upon a peak in Darien. Precisely so did Peter Willard and James Todd stare with eagle eyes at the second lake-hole, and gaze at each other with a wild surmise, silent upon a tee in Woodhaven. They had dreamed of such a happening so often and woke to find the vision false, that at first they could not believe that the thing had actually occurred.

'I got over!' whispered James, in an awed voice.

'So did I!' muttered Peter.

'In one!'

'With my very first!'

They walked in silence round the edge of the lake, and holed out. One putt was enough for each, and they halved the hole with a two. Peter's previous record was eight, and James had once done a seven. There are times when strong men lose their self-control, and this was one of them. They reached the third tee in a daze, and it was here that mortification began to set in.

The third hole is another bogey four, up the hill and past the tree that serves as a direction-post, the hole itself being out of sight. On his day, James had often done it in ten and Peter in nine; but now they were unnerved. James, who had the honour, shook visibly as he addressed his ball. Three times he swung and only connected with the ozone; the fourth time he topped badly. The discs had been set back a little way, and James had the mournful distinction of breaking a record for the course by playing his fifth shot from the tee. It was a low, raking brassey-shot, which carried a heap of stones twenty feet to the right and finished in a furrow. Peter, meanwhile, had popped up a lofty ball which came to rest behind a stone.

It was now that the rigid rules governing this contest began to take their toll. Had they been playing an ordinary friendly round, each would have teed up on some convenient hillock and probably been past the tree with their second, for James would, in ordinary circumstances, have taken his drive back and regarded the strokes he had made as a little preliminary practice to get him into mid-season form. But today it was war to the niblick, and neither man asked nor expected quarter.

Peter's seventh shot dislodged the stone, leaving him a clear field, and James, with his eleventh, extricated himself from the furrow. Fifty feet from the tree James was eighteen, Peter twelve; but then the latter, as every golfer does at times, suddenly went right off his game. He hit the tree four times, then hooked into the sand-bunkers to the left of the hole. James, who had been playing a game that was steady without being brilliant, was on the green in twenty-six, Peter taking twenty-seven. Poor putting lost James the hole. Peter was down in thirty-three, but the pace was too hot for James. He missed a two-foot putt for the half, and they went to the fourth tee all square.

The fourth hole follows the curve of the road, on the other side of which are picturesque woods. It presents no difficulties to the expert, but it has pitfalls for the novice. The dashing player stands for a slice, while the more cautious are satisfied if they can clear the bunker that spans the fairway and lay their ball well out to the left, whence an iron shot will take them to the green. Peter and James combined the two policies. Peter aimed to the left and got a slice, and James, also aiming to the left, topped into the bunker. Peter, realising from experience the futility of searching for his ball in the woods, drove a second, which also disappeared into the jungle, as did his third. By the time he had joined James in the bunker he had played his sixth.

It is the glorious uncertainty of golf that makes it the game it is. The fact that James and Peter, lying side by side in the same bunker, had played respectively one and six shots, might have induced an unthinking observer to fancy the chances of the former. And no doubt, had he not taken seven strokes to extricate himself from the pit, while his opponent, by some act of God, contrived to get out in two, James's chances might have been extremely rosy. As it was, the two men staggered out on to the fairway again with a score of eight apiece.

Once past the bunker and round the bend of the road, the hole becomes simple. A judicious use of the cleek put Peter on the green in fourteen, while James, with a Braid iron, reached it in twelve. Peter was down in seventeen, and James contrived to halve. It was only as he was leaving the hole that the latter discovered that he had been putting with his niblick, which cannot have failed to exercise a prejudicial effect on his game. These little incidents are bound to happen when one is in a nervous and highly strung condition.

The fifth and sixth holes produced no unusual features. Peter won the fifth in eleven, and James the sixth in ten. The short seventh they halved in nine. The eighth, always a tricky hole, they took no liberties with, James, sinking a long putt with his twenty-third, just managing to halve. A ding-dong race up the hill for the ninth found James first at the pin, and they finished the first nine with James one up.

As they left the green James looked a little furtively at his companion.

'You might be strolling on to the tenth,' he said. 'I want to get a few balls at the shop. And my mashie wants fixing up. I sha'n't be long.'

'I'll come with you,' said Peter.

'Don't bother,' said James. 'You go on and hold our place at the tee.'

I regret to say that James was lying. His mashie was in excellent repair, and he still had a dozen balls in his bag, it being his prudent practice always to start out with eighteen. No! What he had said was mere subterfuge. He wanted to go to his locker and snatch a few minutes with Sandy MacBean's 'How to Become a Scratch Man'. He felt sure that one more glance at the photograph of Mr MacBean driving would give him the mastery of the stroke and so enable him to win the match. In this I think he was a little sanguine. The difficulty about Sandy MacBean's method of tuition was that he laid great stress on the fact that the ball should be directly in a line with a point exactly in the centre of the back of the player's neck; and so far James's efforts to keep his eye on the ball and on the back of his neck simultaneously had produced no satisfactory results.

*

It seemed to James, when he joined Peter on the tenth tee, that the latter's manner was strange. He was pale. There was a curious look in his eye.

'James, old man,' he said.

'Yes?' said James.

'While you were away I have been thinking. James, old man, do you really love this girl?'

James stared. A spasm of pain twisted Peter's face.

'Suppose,' he said in a low voice, 'she were not all you – we – think she is!'

'What do you mean?'

'Nothing, nothing.'

'Miss Forrester is an angel.'

'Yes, yes. Quite so.'

'I know what it is,' said James, passionately. 'You're trying to put me off my stroke. You know that the least thing makes me lose my form.'

'No, no!'

'You hope that you can take my mind off the game and make me go to pieces, and then you'll win the match.'

'On the contrary,' said Peter. 'I intend to forfeit the match.'

James reeled.

'What!'

'I give up.'

'But – but—' James shook with emotion. His voice quavered. 'Ah!' he cried. 'I see now: I understand! You are doing this for me because I am your pal. Peter, this is noble! This is the sort of thing you read about in books. I've seen it in the movies. But I can't accept the sacrifice.'

'You must!'

'No, no!'

'I insist!'

'Do you mean this?'

'I give her up, James, old man. I – I hope you will be happy.'

'But I don't know what to say. How can I thank you?'

'Don't thank me.'

'But, Peter, do you fully realise what you are doing? True, I am one up, but there are nine holes to go, and I am not right on my game today. You might easily beat me. Have you forgotten that I once took forty-seven at the dog-leg hole? This may be one of my bad days. Do you understand that if you insist on giving up I shall go to Miss Forrester tonight and propose to her?'

'I understand.'

'And yet you stick to it that you are through?'

'I do. And, by the way, there's no need for you to wait till tonight. I saw Miss Forrester just now outside the tennis-court. She's alone.'

James turned crimson.

'Then I think perhaps—'

'You'd better go to her at once.'

'I will.' James extended his hand. 'Peter, old man, I shall never forget this.'

'That's all right.'

'What are you going to do?'

'Now, do you mean? Oh, I shall potter round the second nine. If you want me, you'll find me somewhere about.'

'You'll come to the wedding, Peter?' said James, wistfully.

'Of course,' said Peter. 'Good luck.'

He spoke cheerily, but, when the other had turned to go, he stood looking after him thoughtfully. Then he sighed a heavy sigh.

*

James approached Miss Forrester with a beating heart. She made a charming picture as she stood there in the sunlight, one hand on her hip, the other swaying a tennis racket.

'How do you do?' said James.

'How are you, Mr Todd? Have you been playing golf?'

'Yes.'

'With Mr Willard?'

'Yes. We were having a match.'

'Golf,' said Grace Forrester, 'seems to make men very rude. Mr Willard left me without a word in the middle of our conversation.'

James was astonished.

'Were you talking to Peter?'

'Yes. Just now. I can't understand what was the matter with him. He just turned on his heel and swung off.'

'You oughtn't to turn on your heel when you swing,' said James; 'only on the ball of the foot.'

'I beg your pardon?'

'Nothing, nothing. I wasn't thinking. The fact is, I've something on my mind. So has Peter. You mustn't think too hardly of him.

We have been playing an important match, and it must have got on his nerves. You didn't happen by any chance to be watching us?'

'No.'

'Ah! I wish you had seen me at the lake-hole. I did it one under par.'

'Was your father playing?'

'You don't understand. I mean I did it in one better than even the finest player is supposed to do it. It's a mashie-shot, you know. You mustn't play too light, or you fall in the lake; and you mustn't play it too hard, or you go past the hole into the woods. It requires the nicest delicacy and judgment, such as I gave it. You might have to wait a year before seeing anyone do it in two again. I doubt if the 'pro' often does it in two. Now, directly we came to this hole today, I made up my mind that there was going to be no mistake. The great secret of any shot at golf is ease, elegance, and the ability to relax. The majority of men, you will find, think it important that their address should be good.'

'How snobbish! What does it matter where a man lives?'

'You don't absolutely follow me. I refer to the waggle and the stance before you make the stroke. Most players seem to fix in their minds the appearance of the angles which are presented by the position of the arms, legs, and club shaft, and it is largely the desire to retain these angles which results in their moving their heads and stiffening their muscles so that there is no freedom in the swing. There is only one point which vitally affects the stroke, and the only reason why that should be kept constant is that you are enabled to see your ball clearly. That is the pivotal point marked at the base of the neck, and a line drawn from this point to the ball should be at right angles to the line of flight.'

James paused for a moment for air, and as he paused Miss Forrester spoke.

'This is all gibberish to me,' she said.

'Gibberish!' gasped James. 'I am quoting verbatim from one of the best authorities on golf.'

Miss Forrester swung her tennis racket irritably.

'Golf,' she said, 'bores me pallid. I think it is the silliest game ever invented!'

The trouble about telling a story is that words are so feeble a means of depicting the supreme moments of life. That is where the artist has the advantage over the historian. Were I an artist, I should show James at this point falling backwards with his feet together and his eyes shut, with a semi-circular dotted line marking the progress of his flight and a few stars above his head to indicate moral collapse. There are no words that can adequately describe the sheer, black horror that froze the blood in his veins as this frightful speech smote his ears. He had never inquired into Miss Forrester's religious views before, but he had always assumed that they were sound. And now here she was polluting the golden summer air with the most hideous blasphemy. It would be incorrect to say that James's love was turned to hate. He did not hate Grace. The repulsion he felt was deeper than mere hate. What he felt was not altogether loathing and not wholly pity. It was a blend of the two.

There was a tense silence. The listening world stood still. Then, without a word, James Todd turned and tottered away.

*

Peter was working moodily in the twelfth bunker when his friend arrived. He looked up with a start. Then, seeing that the other was alone, he came forward hesitatingly.

'Am I to congratulate you?'

James breathed a deep breath.

'You are!' he said. 'On an escape!'

'She refused you?'

'She didn't get the chance. Old man, have you ever sent one right up the edge of that bunker in front of the seventh and just not gone in?'

'Very rarely.'

'I did once. It was my second shot, from a good lie, with the light iron, and I followed well through and thought I had gone just too far, and, when I walked up, there was my ball on the edge of the bunker, nicely teed up on a chunk of grass, so that I was able to lay it dead with my mashie-niblick, holing out in six. Well, what I mean to say is, I feel now as I felt then – as if some unseen power had withheld me in time from some frightful disaster.'

'I know just how you feel,' said Peter, gravely.

'Peter, old man, that girl said golf bored her pallid. She said she thought it was the silliest game ever invented.' He paused to mark the effect of his words. Peter merely smiled a faint, wan smile. 'You don't seem revolted,' said James.

'I am revolted, but not surprised. You see, she said the same thing to me only a few minutes before.'

'She did!'

'It amounted to the same thing. I had just been telling her how I did the lake-hole today in two, and she said that in her opinion golf was a game for children with water on the brain who weren't athletic enough to play Animal Grab.'

The two men shivered in sympathy.

'There must be insanity in the family,' said James at last.

'That,' said Peter, 'is the charitable explanation.'

'We were fortunate to find it out in time.'

'We were!'

'We mustn't run a risk like that again.'

'Never again!'

'I think we had better take up golf really seriously. It will keep us out of mischief.'

'You're quite right. We ought to do our four rounds a day regularly.'

'In spring, summer, and autumn. And in winter it would be rash not to practise most of the day at one of those indoor schools.'

'We ought to be safe that way.'

'Peter, old man,' said James, 'I've been meaning to speak to you about it for some time. I've got Sandy MacBean's new book, and I think you ought to read it. It is full of helpful hints.'

'James!'

'Peter!'

Silently the two men clasped hands. James Todd and Peter Willard were themselves again.

*

And so (said the Oldest Member) we come back to our original starting-point – to wit, that, while there is nothing to be said definitely against love, your golfer should be extremely careful how he indulges in it. It may improve his game or it may not. But, if he finds that there is any danger that it may not – if the object of his affections is not the kind of girl who will listen to him with cheerful sympathy through the long evenings, while he tells her, illustrating stance and grip and swing with the kitchen poker, each detail of the day's round – then, I say unhesitatingly, he had better leave it alone. Love has had a lot of press-agenting from the oldest times; but there are higher, nobler things than love. A woman is only a woman, but a hefty drive is a slosh.

'ORDEAL BY GOLF'

A pleasant breeze played among the trees on the terrace outside the Marvis Bay Golf and Country Club. It ruffled the leaves and cooled the forehead of the Oldest Member, who, as was his custom of a Saturday afternoon, sat in the shade on a rocking-chair, observing the younger generation as it hooked and sliced in the valley below. The eye of the Oldest Member was thoughtful and reflective. When it looked into yours you saw in it that perfect peace, that peace beyond understanding, which comes at its maximum only to the man who has given up golf.

The Oldest Member has not played golf since the rubber-cored ball superseded the old dignified gutty. But as a spectator and philosopher he still finds pleasure in the pastime. He is watching it now with keen interest. His gaze, passing from the lemonade which he is sucking through a straw, rests upon the Saturday foursome which is struggling raggedly up the hill to the ninth green. Like all Saturday foursomes, it is in difficulties. One of the patients is zigzagging about the fairway like a liner pursued by submarines. Two others seem to be digging for buried treasure, unless – it is too far off to be certain – they are killing snakes. The remaining cripple, who has just foozled a mashie-shot, is blaming his caddie. His voice, as he upbraids the innocent child for breathing during his up-swing, comes clearly up the hill.

The Oldest Member sighs. His lemonade gives a sympathetic gurgle. He puts it down on the table.

How few men, says the Oldest Member, possess the proper golfing temperament! How few indeed, judging by the sights I see here on Saturday afternoons, possess any qualification at all for golf except a pair of baggy knickerbockers and enough money to enable them to pay for the drinks at the end of the round. The ideal golfer never loses his temper. When I played, I never lost my temper. Sometimes, it is true, I may, after missing a shot, have broken my club across my knees; but I did it in a calm and judicial spirit, because the club was obviously no good and I was going to get another one anyway. To lose one's temper at golf is foolish. It gets you nothing, not even relief. Imitate the spirit of Marcus Aurelius. 'Whatever may befall thee,' says that great man in his 'Meditations', 'it was preordained for thee from everlasting. Nothing happens to anybody which he is not fitted by nature to bear.' I like to think that this noble thought came to him after he had sliced a couple of new balls into the woods, and that he jotted it down on the back of his score-card. For there can be no doubt that the man was a golfer, and a bad golfer at that. Nobody who had not had a short putt stop on the edge of the hole could possibly have written the words: 'That which makes the man no worse than he was makes life no worse. It has no power to harm, without or within.' Yes, Marcus Aurelius undoubtedly played golf, and all the evidence seems to indicate that he rarely went round in under a hundred and twenty. The niblick was his club.

Speaking of Marcus Aurelius and the golfing temperament recalls to my mind the case of young Mitchell Holmes. Mitchell, when I knew him first, was a promising young man with a future before him in the Paterson Dyeing and Refining Company, of which my old friend, Alexander Paterson, was the president. He had many engaging qualities – among them an unquestioned ability to imitate a bulldog quarrelling with a Pekingese in a way which had to be heard to be believed. It was a gift which made him much in demand at social gatherings in the neighbourhood, marking him off from other young men who could only almost play the mandolin or recite bits of Gunga Din; and no doubt it was this talent of his which first sowed the seeds of love in the heart of Millicent Boyd. Women are essentially hero-worshippers, and when a warm-hearted girl like Millicent has heard a personable young man imitating a bulldog and a Pekingese to the applause of a crowded drawing-room, and has been able to detect the exact point at which the Pekingese leaves off and the bulldog begins, she can never feel quite the same to other men. In short, Mitchell and Millicent were engaged, and were only waiting to be married till the former could bite the Dyeing and Refining Company's ear for a bit of extra salary.

Mitchell Holmes had only one fault. He lost his temper when playing golf. He seldom played a round without becoming piqued, peeved, or – in many cases – chagrined. The caddies on our links, it was said, could always worst other small boys in verbal argument by calling them some of the things they had heard Mitchell call his ball on discovering it in a cuppy lie. He had a great gift of language, and he used it unsparingly. I will admit that there was some excuse for the man. He had the makings of a brilliant golfer, but a combination of bad luck and inconsistent play invariably robbed him of the fruits of his skill. He was the sort of player who does the first two holes in one under bogey and then takes an eleven at the third. The least thing upset him on the links. He missed short putts because of the uproar of the butterflies in the adjoining meadows.

It seemed hardly likely that this one kink in an otherwise admirable character would ever seriously affect his working or professional life, but it did. One evening, as I was sitting in my garden, Alexander Paterson was announced. A glance at his face told me that he had come to ask my advice. Rightly or wrongly, he regarded me as one capable of giving advice. It was I who had changed the whole current of his life by counselling him to leave the wood in his bag and take a driving-iron off the tee; and in one or two other matters, like the choice of a putter (so much more important than the choice of a wife), I had been of assistance to him.

Alexander sat down and fanned himself with his hat, for the evening was warm. Perplexity was written upon his fine face.

'I don't know what to do,' he said.

'Keep the head still – slow back – don't press,' I said, gravely. There is no better rule for a happy and successful life.

'It's nothing to do with golf this time,' he said. 'It's about the treasurership of my company. Old Smithers retires next week, and I've got to find a man to fill his place.'

'That should be easy. You have simply to select the most deserving from among your other employees.'

'But which *is* the most deserving? That's the point. There are two men who are capable of holding the job quite adequately. But then I realise how little I know of their real characters. It is the treasurership, you understand, which has to be filled. Now, a man who was quite good at another job might easily get wrong ideas into his head when he became a treasurer. He would have the handling of large sums of money. In other words, a man who in ordinary circumstances had never been conscious of any desire to visit the more distant portions of South America might feel the urge, so to speak, shortly after he became a treasurer. That is my difficulty. Of course, one always takes a sporting chance with any treasurer; but how am I to find out which of these two men would give me the more reasonable opportunity of keeping some of my money?'

I did not hesitate a moment. I held strong views on the subject of character-testing.

'The only way,' I said to Alexander, 'of really finding out a man's true character is to play golf with him. In no other walk of life does the cloven hoof so quickly display itself. I employed a lawyer for years, until one day I saw him kick his ball out of a heel-mark. I removed my business from his charge next morning. He has not yet run off with any trust-funds, but there is a nasty gleam in his eye, and I am convinced that it is only a question of time. Golf, my dear fellow, is the infallible test. The man who can go into a patch of rough alone, with the knowledge that only God is watching him, and play his ball where it lies, is the man who will serve you faithfully and well. The man who can smile bravely when his putt is diverted by one of those beastly wormcasts is pure gold right through. But the man who is hasty, unbalanced, and violent on the links will display the same qualities in the wider field of everyday life. You don't want an unbalanced treasurer do you?'

'Not if his books are likely to catch the complaint.'

'They are sure to. Statisticians estimate that the average of crime among good golfers is lower than in any class of the community except possibly bishops. Since Willie Park won the first championship at Prestwick in the year 1860 there has, I believe, been no instance of an Open Champion spending a day in prison. Whereas the bad golfers – and by bad I do not mean incompetent, but black-souled – the men who fail to count a stroke when they miss the globe; the men who never replace a divot; the men who talk while their opponent is driving; and the men who let their angry passions rise – these are in and out of Wormwood Scrubbs all the time. They find it hardly worth while to get their hair cut in their brief intervals of liberty.'

Alexander was visibly impressed.

'That sounds sensible, by George!' he said.

'It is sensible.'

'I'll do it! Honestly, I can't see any other way of deciding between Holmes and Dixon.'

I started.

'Holmes? Not Mitchell Holmes?'

'Yes. Of course you must know him? He lives here, I believe.'

'And by Dixon do you mean Rupert Dixon?'

'That's the man. Another neighbour of yours.'

I confess that my heart sank. It was as if my ball had fallen into the pit which my niblick had digged. I wished heartily that I had thought of waiting to ascertain the names of the two rivals before offering my scheme. I was extremely fond of Mitchell Holmes and of the girl to whom he was engaged to be married. Indeed, it was I who had sketched out a few rough notes for the lad to use when proposing; and results had shown that he had put my stuff across well. And I had listened many a time with a sympathetic ear to his hopes in the matter of securing a rise of salary which would enable him to get married. Somehow, when Alexander was talking, it had not occurred to me that young Holmes might be in the running for so important an office as the treasurership. I had ruined the boy's chances. Ordeal by golf was the one test which he could not possibly undergo with success. Only a miracle could keep him from losing his temper, and I had expressly warned Alexander against such a man.

When I thought of his rival my heart sank still more. Rupert Dixon was rather an unpleasant young man, but the worst of his enemies could not accuse him of not possessing the golfing temperament. From the drive off the tee to the holing of the final putt he was uniformly suave.

When Alexander had gone, I sat in thought for some time. I was faced with a problem. Strictly speaking, no doubt, I had no right to take sides; and, though secrecy had not been enjoined upon me in so many words, I was very well aware that Alexander was under the impression that I would keep the thing under my hat and not reveal to either party the test that awaited him. Each candidate was, of course, to remain ignorant that he was taking part in anything but a friendly game.

But when I thought of the young couple whose future depended on this ordeal, I hesitated no longer. I put on my hat and went round to Miss Boyd's house, where I knew that Mitchell was to be found at this hour.

The young couple were out in the porch, looking at the moon. They greeted me heartily, but their heartiness had rather a tinny sound, and I could see that on the whole they regarded me as one of those things which should not happen. But when I told my story their attitude changed. They began to look on me in the pleasanter light of a guardian, philosopher, and friend.

'Wherever did Mr Paterson get such a silly idea?' said Miss Boyd, indignantly. I had – from the best motives – concealed the source of the scheme. 'It's ridiculous!'

'Oh, I don't know,' said Mitchell. 'The old boy's crazy about golf. It's just the sort of scheme he would cook up. Well, it dishes *me!*'

'Oh, come!' I said.

'It's no good saying "Oh, come!" You know perfectly well that I'm a frank, outspoken golfer. When my ball goes off nor'-nor'-east when I want it to go due west I can't help expressing an opinion about it. It is a curious phenomenon which calls for comment, and I give it. Similarly, when I top my drive, I have to go on record as saying that I did not do it intentionally. And it's just these trifles, as far as I can make out, that are going to decide the thing.'

'Couldn't you learn to control yourself on the links, Mitchell, darling?' asked Millicent. 'After all, golf is only a game!'

Mitchell's eyes met mine, and I have no doubt that mine showed just the same look of horror which I saw in his. Women say these things without thinking. It does not mean that there is any kink in their character. They simply don't realise what they are saying.

'Hush!' said Mitchell, huskily, patting her hand and overcoming his emotion with a strong effort. 'Hush, dearest!'

Two or three days later I met Millicent coming from the post-office. There was a new light of happiness in her eyes, and her face was glowing.

'Such a splendid thing has happened,' she said. 'After Mitchell left that night I happened to be glancing through a magazine, and I came across a wonderful advertisement. It began by saying that all the great men in history owed their success to being able to control themselves, and that Napoleon wouldn't have amounted to anything if he had not curbed his fiery nature, and then it said that we can all be like Napoleon if we fill in the accompanying blank order-form for Professor Orlando Rollitt's wonderful book, "Are You Your Own Master?" absolutely free for five days and then seven shillings, but you must write at once because the demand is enormous and pretty soon it may be too late. I wrote at once, and luckily I was in time, because Professor Rollitt did have a copy left, and it's just arrived. I've been looking through it, and it seems splendid.'

She held out a small volume. I glanced at it. There was a frontispiece showing a signed photograph of Professor Orlando Rollitt controlling himself in spite of having long white whiskers, and then some reading matter, printed between wide margins. One look at the book told me the professor's methods. To be brief, he had simply swiped Marcus Aurelius's best stuff, the copyright having expired some two thousand years ago, and was retailing it as his own. I did not mention this to Millicent. It was no affair of mine. Presumably, however obscure the necessity, Professor Rollitt had to live.

'I'm going to start Mitchell on it today. Don't you think this is good? "Thou seest how few be the things which if a man has at his command his life flows gently on and is divine." I think it will be wonderful if Mitchell's life flows gently on and is divine for seven shillings, don't you?'

At the club-house that evening I encountered Rupert Dixon. He was emerging from a shower-bath, and looked as pleased with himself as usual.

'Just been going round with old Paterson,' he said. 'He was asking after you. He's gone back to town in his car.'

I was thrilled. So the test had begun!

'How did you come out?' I asked.

Rupert Dixon smirked. A smirking man, wrapped in a bath towel, with a wisp of wet hair over one eye, is a repellent sight.

'Oh, pretty well. I won by six and five. In spite of having poisonous luck.'

I felt a gleam of hope at these last words.

'Oh, you had bad luck?'

'The worst. I over-shot the green at the third with the best brassey-shot I've ever made in my life – and that's saying a lot – and lost my ball in the rough beyond it.'

'And I suppose you let yourself go, eh?'

'Let myself go?'

'I take it that you made some sort of demonstration?'

'Oh, no. Losing your temper doesn't get you anywhere at golf. It only spoils your next shot.'

I went away heavy-hearted. Dixon had plainly come through the ordeal as well as any man could have done. I expected to hear every day that the vacant treasurership had been filled, and that Mitchell had not even been called upon to play his test round. I suppose, however, that Alexander Paterson felt that it would be unfair to the other competitor not to give him his chance, for the next I heard of the matter was when Mitchell Holmes rang me up on the Friday and asked me if I would accompany him round the links next day in the match he was playing with Alexander, and give him my moral support.

'I shall need it,' he said. 'I don't mind telling you I'm pretty nervous. I wish I had had longer to get the stranglehold on that "Are You Your Own Master?" stuff. I can see, of course, that it is the real tabasco from start to finish, and absolutely as mother makes it, but the trouble is I've only had a few days to soak it into my system. It's like trying to patch up a motor-car with string. You never know when the thing will break down. Heaven knows what will happen if I sink a ball at the water-hole. And something seems to tell me I am going to do it.'

There was a silence for a moment.

'Do you believe in dreams?' asked Mitchell.

'Believe in what?'

'Dreams.'

'What about them?'

'I said, "Do you believe in dreams?" Because last night I dreamed that I was playing in the final of the Open Championship, and I got into the rough, and there was a cow there, and the cow looked at me in a sad sort of way and said, "Why don't you use the two-V grip instead of the interlocking?" At the time it seemed an odd sort of thing to happen, but I've been thinking it over and I wonder if there isn't something in it. These things must be sent to us for a purpose.'

'You can't change your grip on the day of an important match.'

'I suppose not. The fact is, I'm a bit jumpy, or I wouldn't have mentioned it. Oh, well! See you tomorrow at two.'

The day was bright and sunny, but a tricky cross-wind was blowing when I reached the club-house. Alexander Paterson was there, practising swings on the first tee; and almost immediately Mitchell Holmes arrived, accompanied by Millicent.

'Perhaps,' said Alexander, 'we had better be getting under way. Shall I take the honour?'

'Certainly,' said Mitchell.

Alexander teed up his ball.

Alexander Paterson has always been a careful rather than a dashing player. It is his custom, a sort of ritual, to take two measured practice-swings before addressing the ball, even on the putting-green. When he does address the ball he shuffles his feet for a moment or two, then pauses, and scans the horizon in a suspicious sort of way, as if he had been expecting it to play some sort of a trick on him when he was not looking. A careful inspection seems to convince him of the horizon's *bona fides*, and he turns his attention to the ball again. He shuffles his feet once more, then raises his club. He waggles the club smartly over the ball three times, then lays it behind the globule. At this point he suddenly peers at the horizon again, in the apparent hope of catching it off its guard. This done, he raises his club very slowly, brings it back very slowly till it almost touches the ball, raises it again, brings it down again, raises it once more, and brings it down for the third time. He then stands motionless, wrapped in thought, like some Indian fakir contemplating the infinite. Then he raises his club again and replaces it behind the ball. Finally he quivers all over, swings very slowly back, and drives the ball for about a hundred and fifty yards in a dead straight line.

It is a method of procedure which proves sometimes a little exasperating to the highly strung, and I watched Mitchell's face anxiously to see how he was taking his first introduction to it. The unhappy lad had blenched visibly. He turned to me with the air of one in pain.

'Does he always do that?' he whispered.

'Always,' I replied.

'Then I'm done for! No human being could play golf against a one-ring circus like that without blowing up!'

I said nothing. It was, I feared, only too true. Well-poised as I am, I had long since been compelled to give up playing with Alexander Paterson, much as I esteemed him. It was a choice between that and resigning from the Baptist Church.

At this moment Millicent spoke. There was an open book in her hand. I recognised it as the life-work of Professor Rollitt.

'Think on this doctrine,' she said, in her soft, modulated voice, 'that to be patient is a branch of justice, and that men sin without intending it.'

Mitchell nodded briefly, and walked to the tee with a firm step.

'Before you drive, darling,' said Millicent, 'remember this. Let no act be done at haphazard, nor otherwise than according to the finished rules that govern its kind.'

The next moment Mitchell's ball was shooting through the air, to come to rest two hundred yards down the course. It was a magnificent drive. He had followed the counsel of Marcus Aurelius to the letter.

An admirable iron-shot put him in reasonable proximity to the pin, and he holed out in one under bogey with one of the nicest putts I have ever beheld. And when at the next hole, the dangerous water-hole, his ball soared over the pond and lay safe, giving him bogey for the hole, I began for the first time to breathe freely. Every golfer has his day, and this was plainly Mitchell's. He was playing faultless golf. If he could continue in this vein, his unfortunate failing would have no chance to show itself.

The third hole is long and tricky. You drive over a ravine – or possibly into it. In the latter event you breathe a prayer and call for your niblick. But, once over the ravine, there is nothing to disturb the equanimity. Bogey is five, and a good drive, followed by a brassey-shot, will put you within easy mashie-distance of the green.

Mitchell cleared the ravine by a hundred and twenty yards. He strolled back to me, and watched Alexander go through his ritual with an indulgent smile. I knew just how he was feeling. Never does the world seem so sweet and fair and the foibles of our fellow human beings so little irritating as when we have just swatted the pill right on the spot.

'I can't see why he does it,' said Mitchell, eyeing Alexander with a toleration that almost amounted to affection. 'If I did all those Swedish exercises before I drove, I should forget what I had come out for and go home.' Alexander concluded the movements, and landed a bare three yards on the other side of the ravine. 'He's what you would call a steady performer, isn't he? Never varies!'

Mitchell won the hole comfortably. There was a jauntiness about his stance on the fourth tee which made me a little uneasy. Overconfidence at golf is almost as bad as timidity.

My apprehensions were justified. Mitchell topped his ball. It rolled twenty yards into the rough, and nestled under a dock-leaf. His mouth opened, then closed with a snap. He came over to where Millicent and I were standing.

'I didn't say it!' he said. 'What on earth happened then?'

'Search men's governing principles,' said Millicent, 'and consider the wise, what they shun and what they cleave to.'

'Exactly,' I said. 'You swayed your body.'

'And now I've got to go and look for that infernal ball.'

'Never mind, darling,' said Millicent. 'Nothing has such power to broaden the mind as the ability to investigate systematically and truly all that comes under thy observation in life.'

'Besides,' I said, 'you're three up.'

'I sha'n't be after this hole.'

He was right. Alexander won it in five, one above bogey, and regained the honour.

Mitchell was a trifle shaken. His play no longer had its first careless vigour. He lost the next hole, halved the sixth, lost the short seventh, and then, rallying, halved the eighth.

The ninth hole, like so many on our links, can be a perfectly simple four, although the rolling nature of the green makes bogey always a somewhat doubtful feat; but, on the other hand, if you foozle your drive, you can easily achieve double figures. The tee is on the farther side of the pond, beyond the bridge, where the water narrows almost to the dimensions of a brook. You drive across this water and over a tangle of trees and under-growth on the other bank. The distance to the fairway cannot be more than sixty yards, for the hazard is purely a mental one, and yet how many fair hopes have been wrecked there!

Alexander cleared the obstacles comfortably with his customary short, straight drive, and Mitchell advanced to the tee.

I think the loss of the honour had been preying on his mind. He seemed nervous. His up-swing was shaky, and he swayed back perceptibly. He made a lunge at the ball, sliced it, and it struck a tree on the other side of the water and fell in the long grass. We crossed the bridge to look for it; and it was here that the effect of Professor Rollitt began definitely to wane.

'Why on earth don't they mow this darned stuff?' demanded Mitchell, querulously, as he beat about the grass with his niblick.

'You have to have rough on a course,' I ventured.

'Whatever happens at all,' said Millicent, 'happens as it should. Thou wilt find this true if thou shouldst watch narrowly.'

'That's all very well,' said Mitchell, watching narrowly in a clump of weeds but seeming unconvinced. 'I believe the Greens Committee run this bally club purely in the interests of the caddies. I believe they encourage lost balls, and go halves with the little beasts when they find them and sell them!'

Millicent and I exchanged glances. There were tears in her eyes.

'Oh, Mitchell! Remember Napoleon!'

'Napoleon! What's Napoleon got to do with it? Napoleon never was expected to drive through a primeval forest. Besides, what did Napoleon ever do? Where did Napoleon get off, swanking round as if he amounted to something? Poor fish! All he ever did was to get hammered at Waterloo!'

Alexander re-joined us. He had walked on to where his ball lay.

'Can't find it, eh? Nasty bit of rough, this!'

'No, I can't find it. But tomorrow some miserable, chinless, half-witted reptile of a caddie with pop eyes and eight hundred and thirty-seven pimples will find it, and will sell it to someone for sixpence! No, it was a brand-new ball. He'll probably get a shilling for it. That'll be sixpence for himself and sixpence for the Greens Committee. No wonder they're buying cars quicker than the makers can supply them. No wonder you see their wives going about in mink coats and pearl necklaces. Oh, dash it! I'll drop another!'

'In that case,' Alexander pointed out, 'you will, of course, under the rules governing match-play, lose the hole.'

'All right, then. I'll give up the hole.'

'Then that, I think, makes me one up on the first nine,' said Alexander. 'Excellent! A very pleasant, even game.'

'Pleasant! On second thoughts I don't believe the Greens Committee let the wretched caddies get any of the loot. They hang round behind trees till the deal's concluded, and then sneak out and choke it out of them!'

I saw Alexander raise his eyebrows. He walked up the hill to the next tee with me.

'Rather a quick-tempered young fellow, Holmes!' he said, thoughtfully. 'I should never have suspected it. It just shows how little one can know of a man, only meeting him in business hours.'

I tried to defend the poor lad.

'He has an excellent heart, Alexander. But the fact is – we are such old friends that I know you will forgive my mentioning it – your style of play gets, I fancy, a little on his nerves.'

'My style of play? What's wrong with my style of play?'

'Nothing is actually wrong with it, but to a young and ardent spirit there is apt to be something a trifle upsetting in being, compelled to watch a man play quite so slowly as you do. Come now, Alexander, as one friend to another, is it necessary to take two practice-swings before you putt?'

'Dear, dear!' said Alexander. 'You really mean to say that that upsets him? Well, I'm afraid I am too old to change my methods now.'

I had nothing more to say.

As we reached the tenth tee, I saw that we were in for a few minutes' wait. Suddenly I felt a hand on my arm. Millicent was standing beside me, dejection written on her face. Alexander and young Mitchell were some distance away from us.

'Mitchell doesn't want me to come round the rest of the way with him,' she said, despondently. 'He says I make him nervous.'

I shook my head.

'That's bad! I was looking on you as a steadying influence.'

'I thought I was, too. But Mitchell says no. He says my being there keeps him from concentrating.'

'Then perhaps it would be better for you to remain in the clubhouse till we return. There is, I fear, dirty work ahead.'

A choking sob escaped the unhappy girl.

'I'm afraid so. There is an apple tree near the thirteenth hole, and Mitchell's caddie is sure to start eating apples. I am thinking of what Mitchell will do when he hears the crunching when he is addressing his ball.'

'That is true.'

'Our only hope,' she said, holding out Professor Rollitt's book, 'is this. Will you please read him extracts when you see him getting nervous? We went through the book last night and marked all the passages in blue pencil which might prove helpful. You will see notes against them in the margin, showing when each is supposed to be used.'

It was a small favour to ask. I took the book and gripped her hand silently. Then I joined Alexander and Mitchell on the tenth tee.

Mitchell was still continuing his speculations regarding the Greens Committee.

'The hole after this one,' he said, 'used to be a short hole. There was no chance of losing a ball. Then, one day, the wife of one of the Greens Committee happened to mention that the baby needed new shoes, so now they've tacked on another hundred and fifty yards to it. You have to drive over the brow of a hill, and if you slice an eighth of an inch you get into a sort of No Man's Land, full of rocks and bushes and crevices and old pots and pans. The Greens Committee practically live there in the summer. You see them prowling round in groups, encouraging each other with merry cries as they fill their sacks. Well, I'm going to fool them today. I'm going to drive an old ball which is just hanging together by a thread. It'll come to pieces when they pick it up.'

Golf, however, is a curious game – a game of fluctuations. One might have supposed that Mitchell, in such a frame of mind, would have continued to come to grief. But at the beginning of the second nine he once more found his form. A perfect drive put him in position to reach the tenth green with an iron-shot, and, though the ball was several yards from the hole, he laid it dead with his approach-putt and holed his second for a bogey four. Alexander could only achieve a five, so that they were all square again.

The eleventh, the subject of Mitchell's recent criticism, is certainly a tricky hole, and it is true that a slice does land the player in grave difficulties. Today, however, both men kept their drives straight, and found no difficulty in securing fours.

'A little more of this,' said Mitchell, beaming, 'and the Greens Committee will have to give up piracy and go back to work.'

The twelfth is a long, dog-leg hole, bogey five. Alexander plugged steadily round the bend, holing out in six, and Mitchell, whose second shot had landed him in some long grass, was obliged to use his niblick. He contrived, however, to halve the hole with a nicely-judged mashie-shot to the edge of the green.

Alexander won the thirteenth. It is a three hundred and sixty yard hole, free from bunkers. It took Alexander three strokes to reach the green, but his third laid the ball dead; while Mitchell, who was on in two, required three putts.

'That reminds me,' said Alexander, chattily, 'of a story I heard. Friend calls out to a beginner, 'How are you getting on, old man?' and the beginner says, 'Splendidly. I just made three perfect putts on the last green!''

Mitchell did not appear amused. I watched his face anxiously. He had made no remark, but the missed putt which would have saved the hole had been very short, and I feared the worst. There was a brooding look in his eye as we walked to the fourteenth tee.

There are few more picturesque spots in the whole of the countryside than the neighbourhood of the fourteenth tee. It is a sight to charm the nature-lover's heart.

But, if golf has a defect, it is that it prevents a man being a whole-hearted lover of nature. Where the layman sees waving grass and romantic tangles of undergrowth, your golfer beholds nothing but a nasty patch of rough from which he must divert his ball. The cry of the birds, wheeling against the sky, is to the golfer merely something that may put him off his putt. As a spectator, I am fond of the ravine at the bottom of the slope. It pleases the eye. But, as a golfer, I have frequently found it the very devil.

The last hole had given Alexander the honour again. He drove even more deliberately than before. For quite half a minute he stood over his ball, pawing at it with his driving-iron like a cat investigating a tortoise. Finally he despatched it to one of the few safe spots on the hillside. The drive from this tee has to be carefully calculated, for, if it be too straight, it will catch the slope and roll down into the ravine.

Mitchell addressed his ball. He swung up, and then, from immediately behind him came a sudden sharp crunching sound. I looked quickly in the direction whence it came. Mitchell's caddie, with a glassy look in his eyes, was gnawing a large apple. And even as I breathed a silent prayer, down came the driver, and the ball, with a terrible slice on it, hit the side of the hill and bounded into the ravine.

There was a pause – a pause in which the world stood still. Mitchell dropped his club and turned. His face was working horribly.

'Mitchell!' I cried. 'My boy! Reflect! Be calm!'

'Calm! What's the use of being calm when people are chewing apples in thousands all round you? What *is* this, anyway – a golf match or a pleasant day's outing for the children of the poor? Apples! Go on, my boy, take another bite. Take several. Enjoy yourself! Never mind if it seems to cause me a fleeting annoyance. Go on with your lunch! You probably had a light breakfast, eh, and are feeling a little peckish, yes? If you will wait here, I will run to the club-house and get you a sandwich and a bottle of ginger-ale. Make yourself quite at home, you lovable little fellow! Sit down and have a good time!'

I turned the pages of Professor Rollitt's book feverishly. I could not find a passage that had been marked in blue pencil to meet this emergency. I selected one at random.

'Mitchell,' I said, 'one moment. How much time he gains who does not look to see what his neighbour says or does, but only at what he does himself, to make it just and holy.'

'Well, look what I've done myself! I'm somewhere down at the bottom of that dashed ravine, and it'll take me a dozen strokes to get out. Do you call that just and holy? Here, give me that book for a moment!'

He snatched the little volume out of my hands. For an instant he looked at it with a curious expression of loathing, then he placed it gently on the ground and jumped on it a few times. Then he hit it with his driver. Finally, as if feeling that the time for half measures had passed, he took a little run and kicked it strongly into the long grass.

He turned to Alexander, who had been an impassive spectator of the scene.

'I'm through!' he said. 'I concede the match. Good-bye. You'll find me in the bay!'

'Going swimming?'

'No. Drowning myself.'

A gentle smile broke out over my old friend's usually grave face. He patted Mitchell's shoulder affectionately.

'Don't do that, my boy,' he said. 'I was hoping you would stick around the office awhile as treasurer of the company.'

Mitchell tottered. He grasped my arm for support. Everything was very still. Nothing broke the stillness but the humming of the bees, the murmur of the distant wavelets, and the sound of Mitchell's caddie going on with his apple.

'What!' cried Mitchell.

'The position,' said Alexander, 'will be falling vacant very shortly, as no doubt you know. It is yours, if you care to accept it.'

'You mean – you mean – you're going to give me the job?'

'You have interpreted me exactly.'

Mitchell gulped. So did his caddie. One from a spiritual, the other from a physical cause.

'If you don't mind excusing me,' said Mitchell, huskily, 'I think I'll be popping back to the club-house. Someone I want to see.'

He disappeared through the trees, running strongly. I turned to Alexander.

'What does this mean?' I asked. 'I am delighted, but what becomes of the test?'

My old friend smiled gently.

'The test,' he replied, 'has been eminently satisfactory. Circumstances, perhaps, have compelled me to modify the original idea of it, but nevertheless it has been a completely successful test. Since we started out, I have been doing a good deal of thinking, and I have come to the conclusion that what the Paterson Dyeing and Refining Company really needs is a treasurer whom I can beat at golf. And I have discovered the ideal man. Why,' he went on, a look of holy enthusiasm on his fine old face, 'do you realise that I can always lick the stuffing out of that boy, good player as he is, simply by taking a little trouble? I can make him get the wind up every time, simply by taking one or two extra practice-swings! That is the sort of man I need for a responsible post in my office.'

'But what about Rupert Dixon?' I asked.

He gave a gesture of distaste.

'I wouldn't trust that man. Why, when I played with him, everything went wrong, and he just smiled and didn't say a word. A man who can do that is not the man to trust with the control of large sums of money. It wouldn't be safe. Why, the fellow isn't honest! He can't be.' He paused for a moment. 'Besides,' he added, thoughtfully, 'he beat me by six and five. What's the good of a treasurer who beats the boss by six and five?'

'SUNDERED HEARTS'

In the smoking-room of the club-house a cheerful fire was burning, and the Oldest Member glanced from time to time out of the window into the gathering dusk. Snow was falling lightly on the links. From where he sat, the Oldest Member had a good view of the ninth green; and presently, out of the greyness of the December evening, there appeared over the brow of the hill a golf-ball. It trickled across the green, and stopped within a yard of the hole. The Oldest Member nodded approvingly. A good approach-shot.

A young man in a tweed suit clambered on to the green, holed out with easy confidence, and, shouldering his bag, made his way to the club-house. A few moments later he entered the smoking-room, and uttered an exclamation of rapture at the sight of the fire.

'I'm frozen stiff!'

He rang for a waiter and ordered a hot drink. The Oldest Member gave a gracious assent to the suggestion that he should join him.

'I like playing in winter,' said the young man. 'You get the course to yourself, for the world is full of slackers who only turn out when the weather suits them. I cannot understand where they get the nerve to call themselves golfers.'

'Not everyone is as keen as you are, my boy,' said the Sage, dipping gratefully into his hot drink. 'If they were, the world would be a better place, and we should hear less of all this modern unrest.'

'I *am* pretty keen,' admitted the young man.

'I have only encountered one man whom I could describe as keener. I allude to Mortimer Sturgis.'

'The fellow who took up golf at thirty-eight and let the girl he was engaged to marry go off with someone else because he hadn't the time to combine golf with courtship? I remember. You were telling me about him the other day.'

'There is a sequel to that story, if you would care to hear it,' said the Oldest Member.

'You have the honour,' said the young man. 'Go ahead!'

*

Some people (began the Oldest Member) considered that Mortimer Sturgis was too wrapped up in golf, and blamed him for it. I could never see eye to eye with them. In the days of King Arthur nobody thought the worse of a young knight if he suspended all his social and business engagements in favour of a search for the Holy Grail. In the Middle Ages a man could devote his whole life to the Crusades, and the public fawned upon him. Why, then, blame the man of today for a zealous attention to the modern equivalent, the Quest of Scratch! Mortimer Sturgis never became a scratch player, but he did eventually get his handicap down to nine, and I honour him for it.

The story which I am about to tell begins in what might be called the middle period of Sturgis's career. He had reached the stage when his handicap was a wobbly twelve; and, as you are no doubt aware, it is then that a man really begins to golf in the true sense of the word.

Mortimer's fondness for the game until then had been merely tepid compared with what it became now. He had played a little before, but now he really buckled to and got down to it. It was at this point, too, that he began once more to entertain thoughts of marriage. A profound statistician in this one department, he had discovered that practically all the finest exponents of the art are married men; and the thought that there might be something in the holy state which improved a man's game, and that he was missing a good thing, troubled him a great deal.

Moreover, the paternal instinct had awakened in him. As he justly pointed out, whether marriage improved your game or not, it was to Old Tom Morris's marriage that the existence of young Tommy Morris, winner of the British Open Championship four times in succession, could be directly traced. In fact, at the age of forty-two, Mortimer Sturgis was in just the frame of mind to take some nice girl aside and ask her to become a step-mother to his eleven drivers, his baffy, his twenty-eight putters, and the rest of the ninety-four clubs which he had accumulated in the course of his golfing career. The sole stipulation, of course, which he made when dreaming his daydreams was that the future Mrs Sturgis must be a golfer. I can still recall the horror in his face when one girl, admirable in other respects, said that she had never heard of Harry Vardon, and didn't he mean Dolly Vardon? She has since proved an excellent wife and mother, but Mortimer Sturgis never spoke to her again.

With the coming of January, it was Mortimer's practice to leave England and go to the South of France, where there was sunshine and crisp dry turf. He pursued his usual custom this year. With his suit-case and his ninety-four clubs he went off to Saint Brule, staying as he always did at the Hotel Superbe, where they knew him, and treated with an amiable tolerance his habit of practising chip-shots in his bedroom. On the first evening, after breaking a statuette of the Infant Samuel in Prayer, he dressed and went down to dinner. And the first thing he saw was Her.

Mortimer Sturgis, as you know, had been engaged before, but Betty Weston had never inspired the tumultuous rush of emotion which the mere sight of this girl had set loose in him. He told me later that just to watch her holing out her soup gave him a sort of feeling you get when your drive collides with a rock in the middle of a tangle of rough and kicks back into the middle of the fairway. If golf had come late in life to Mortimer Sturgis, love came later still, and just as the golf, attacking him in middle life, had been some golf, so was the love considerable love. Mortimer finished his dinner in a trance, which is the best way to do it at some hotels, and then scoured the place for someone who would introduce him. He found such a person eventually and the meeting took place.

*

She was a small and rather fragile-looking girl, with big blue eyes and a cloud of golden hair. She had a sweet expression, and her left wrist was in a sling. She looked up at Mortimer as if she had at last found something that amounted to Something. I am inclined to think it was a case of love at first sight on both sides.

'Fine weather we're having,' said Mortimer, who was a capital conversationalist.

'Yes,' said the girl.

'I like fine weather.'

'So do I.'

'There's something about fine weather!'

'Yes.'

'It's – it's – well, fine weather's so much finer than weather that isn't fine,' said Mortimer.

He looked at the girl a little anxiously, fearing he might be taking her out of her depth, but she seemed to have followed his train of thought perfectly.

'Yes, isn't it?' she said. 'It's so – so fine.'

'That's just what I meant,' said Mortimer. 'So fine. You've just hit it.'

He was charmed. The combination of beauty with intelligence is so rare.

'I see you've hurt your wrist,' he went on, pointing to the sling.

'Yes. I strained it a little playing in the championship.'

'The championship?' Mortimer was interested. 'It's awfully rude of me,' he said, apologetically, 'but I didn't catch your name just now.'

'My name is Somerset.'

Mortimer had been bending forward solicitously. He overbalanced and nearly fell off his chair. The shock had been stunning. Even before he had met and spoken to her, he had told himself that he loved this girl with the stored-up love of a lifetime. And she was Mary Somerset! The hotel lobby danced before Mortimer's eyes.

The name will, of course, be familiar to you. In the early rounds of the Ladies' Open Golf Championship of that year nobody had paid much attention to Mary Somerset. She had survived her first two matches, but her opponents had been nonentities like herself. And then, in the third round, she had met and defeated the champion. From that point on, her name was on everybody's lips. She became favourite. And she justified the public confidence by sailing into the final and winning easily. And here she was, talking to him like an ordinary person, and, if he could read the message in her eyes, not altogether indifferent to his charms, if you could call them that.

'Golly!' said Mortimer, awed.

*

Their friendship ripened rapidly, as friendships do in the South of France. In that favoured clime, you find the girl and Nature does the rest. On the second morning of their acquaintance Mortimer invited her to walk round the links with him and watch him play. He did it a little diffidently, for his golf was not of the calibre that would be likely to extort admiration from a champion. On the other hand, one should never let slip the opportunity of acquiring wrinkles on the game, and he thought that Miss Somerset, if she watched one or two of his shots, might tell him just what he ought to do. And sure enough, the opening arrived on the fourth hole, where Mortimer, after a drive which surprised even himself, found his ball in a nasty cuppy lie.

He turned to the girl.

'What ought I to do here?' he asked.

Miss Somerset looked at the ball. She seemed to be weighing the matter in her mind.

'Give it a good hard knock,' she said.

Mortimer knew what she meant. She was advocating a full iron. The only trouble was that, when he tried anything more ambitious than a half-swing, except off the tee, he almost invariably topped. However, he could not fail this wonderful girl, so he swung well back and took a chance. His enterprise was rewarded. The ball flew out of the indentation in the turf as cleanly as though John Henry Taylor had been behind it, and rolled, looking neither to left nor to right, straight for the pin. A few moments later Mortimer Sturgis had holed out one under bogey, and it was only the fear that, having

known him for so short a time, she might be startled and refuse
him that kept him from proposing then and there. This exhibition
of golfing generalship on her part had removed his last doubts. He
knew that, if he lived for ever, there could be no other girl in the
world for him. With her at his side, what might he not do? He
might get his handicap down to six – to three – to scratch – to
plus something! Good heavens, why, even the Amateur Championship was not outside the range of possibility. Mortimer Sturgis
shook his putter solemnly in the air, and vowed a silent vow that
he would win this pearl among women.

Now, when a man feels like that, it is impossible to restrain him
long. For a week Mortimer Sturgis's soul sizzled within him: then
he could contain himself no longer. One night, at one of the informal dances at the hotel, he drew the girl out on to the moonlit
terrace.

'Miss Somerset –' he began, stuttering with emotion like an
imperfectly-corked bottle of ginger-beer. 'Miss Somerset – may I
call you Mary?'

The girl looked at him with eyes that shone softly in the dim
light.

'Mary?' she repeated. 'Why, of course, if you like—'

'If I like!' cried Mortimer. 'Don't you know that it is my dearest
wish? Don't you know that I would rather be permitted to call you
Mary than do the first hole at Muirfield in two? Oh, Mary, how
I have longed for this moment! I love you! I love you! Ever since
I met you I have known that you were the one girl in this vast
world whom I would die to win! Mary, will you be mine? Shall
we go round together? Will you fix up a match with me on the
links of life which shall end only when the Grim Reaper lays us
both a stymie?'

She drooped towards him.

'Mortimer!' she murmured.

He held out his arms, then drew back. His face had grown suddenly tense, and there were lines of pain about his mouth.

'Wait!' he said, in a strained voice. 'Mary, I love you dearly, and because I love you so dearly I cannot let you trust your sweet life to me blindly. I have a confession to make, I am not – I have not always been' – he paused – 'a good man,' he said, in a low voice.

She started indignantly.

'How can you say that? You are the best, the kindest, the bravest man I have ever met! Who but a good man would have risked his life to save me from drowning?'

'Drowning?' Mortimer's voice seemed perplexed. 'You? What do you mean?'

'Have you forgotten the time when I fell in the sea last week, and you jumped in with all your clothes on—'

'Of course, yes,' said Mortimer. 'I remember now. It was the day I did the long seventh in five. I got off a good tee-shot straight down the fairway, took a baffy for my second, and – But that is not the point. It is sweet and generous of you to think so highly of what was the merest commonplace act of ordinary politeness, but I must repeat, that judged by the standards of your snowy purity, I am not a good man. I do not come to you clean and spotless as a young girl should expect her husband to come to her. Once, playing in a foursome, my ball fell in some long grass. Nobody was near me. We had no caddies, and the others were on the fairway. God knows – ' His voice shook. 'God knows I struggled against the temptation. But I fell. I kicked the ball on to a little bare mound, from which it was an easy task with a nice half-mashie to reach the green for a snappy seven. Mary, there have been times when, going round by myself, I have allowed myself ten-foot putts on three holes in succession, simply in order to be able to say I had done the course in under a hundred. Ah! you shrink from me! You are disgusted!'

'I'm not disgusted! And I don't shrink! I only shivered because it is rather cold.'

'Then you can love me in spite of my past?'

'Mortimer!'

She fell into his arms.

'My dearest,' he said presently, 'what a happy life ours will be. That is, if you do not find that you have made a mistake.'

'A mistake!' she cried, scornfully.

'Well, my handicap is twelve, you know, and not so darned twelve at that. There are days when I play my second from the fairway of the next hole but one, days when I couldn't putt into a coal-hole with 'Welcome!' written over it. And you are a Ladies' Open Champion. Still, if you think it's all right – . Oh, Mary, you little know how I have dreamed of some day marrying a really first-class golfer! Yes, that was my vision – of walking up the aisle with some sweet plus two girl on my arm. You shivered again. You are catching cold.'

'It is a little cold,' said the girl. She spoke in a small voice.

'Let me take you in, sweetheart,' said Mortimer. 'I'll just put you in a comfortable chair with a nice cup of coffee, and then I think I really must come out again and tramp about and think how perfectly splendid everything is.'

*

They were married a few weeks later, very quietly, in the little village church of Saint Brule. The secretary of the local golf-club acted as best man for Mortimer, and a girl from the hotel was the only bridesmaid. The whole business was rather a disappointment to Mortimer, who had planned out a somewhat florid ceremony at St. George's, Hanover Square, with the Vicar of Tooting (a scratch player excellent at short approach shots) officiating, and 'The Voice That Breathed O'er St. Andrews' boomed from the organ. He had even had the idea of copying the military wedding and escorting his bride out of the church under an arch of crossed cleeks. But she would have none of this pomp. She insisted on a quiet wedding, and for the honeymoon trip preferred a tour through Italy. Mortimer, who had wanted to go to Scotland to visit the birthplace of James Braid, yielded amiably, for he loved her dearly. But he did not think much of Italy. In Rome, the great monuments of the past left him cold. Of the Temple of Vespasian, all he thought was that it would be a devil of a place to be bunkered behind. The Colosseum aroused a faint spark of interest in him, as he speculated whether Abe Mitchell would use a full brassey to carry it. In Florence, the view over the Tuscan Hills from the Torre Rosa, Fiesole, over which his bride waxed enthusiastic, seemed to him merely a nasty bit of rough which would take a deal of getting out of.

And so, in the fullness of time, they came home to Mortimer's cosy little house adjoining the links.

*

Mortimer was so busy polishing his ninety-four clubs on the evening of their arrival that he failed to notice that his wife was preoccupied. A less busy man would have perceived at a glance that she was distinctly nervous. She started at sudden noises, and once, when he tried the newest of his mashie-niblicks and broke one of the drawing-room windows, she screamed sharply. In short her manner was strange, and, if Edgar Allen Poe had put her into 'The Fall Of the House of Usher', she would have fitted it like the paper on the wall. She had the air of one waiting tensely for the approach of some imminent doom. Mortimer, humming gaily to himself as he sand-papered the blade of his twenty-second putter, observed none of this. He was thinking of the morrow's play.

'Your wrist's quite well again now, darling, isn't it?' he said.

'Yes. Yes, quite well.'

'Fine!' said Mortimer. 'We'll breakfast early – say at half-past seven – and then we'll be able to get in a couple of rounds before lunch. A couple more in the afternoon will about see us through. One doesn't want to over-golf oneself the first day.' He swung the putter joyfully. 'How had we better play do you think? We might start with you giving me a half.'

She did not speak. She was very pale. She clutched the arm of her chair tightly till the knuckles showed white under the skin.

To anybody but Mortimer her nervousness would have been even more obvious on the following morning, as they reached the first tee. Her eyes were dull and heavy, and she started when a grasshopper chirruped.

But Mortimer was too occupied with thinking how jolly it was having the course to themselves to notice anything.

He scooped some sand out of the box, and took a ball out of her bag. His wedding present to her had been a brand-new golf-bag, six dozen balls, and a full set of the most expensive clubs, all born in Scotland.

'Do you like a high tee?' he asked.

'Oh, no,' she replied, coming with a start out of her thoughts. 'Doctors say it's indigestible.'

Mortimer laughed merrily.

'Deuced good!' he chuckled. 'Is that your own or did you read it in a comic paper? There you are!' He placed the ball on a little hill of sand, and got up. 'Now let's see some of that championship form of yours!'

She burst into tears.

'My darling!'

Mortimer ran to her and put his arms round her. She tried weakly to push him away.

'My angel! What is it?'

She sobbed brokenly. Then, with an effort, she spoke.

'Mortimer, I have deceived you!'

'Deceived me?'

'I have never played golf in my life! I don't even know how to hold the caddie!'

Mortimer's heart stood still. This sounded like the gibberings of an unbalanced mind, and no man likes his wife to begin gibbering immediately after the honeymoon.

'My precious! You are not yourself!'

'I am! That's the whole trouble! I'm myself and not the girl you thought I was!'

Mortimer stared at her, puzzled. He was thinking that it was a little difficult and that, to work it out properly, he would need a pencil and a bit of paper.

'My name is not Mary!'

'But you said it was.'

'I didn't. You asked if you could call me Mary, and I said you might, because I loved you too much to deny your smallest whim. I was going on to say that it wasn't my name, but you interrupted me.'

'Not Mary!' The horrid truth was coming home to Mortimer. 'You were not Mary Somerset?'

'Mary is my cousin. My name is Mabel.'

'But you said you had sprained your wrist playing in the championship.'

'So I had. The mallet slipped in my hand.'

'The mallet!' Mortimer clutched at his forehead. 'You didn't say "the mallet"?'

'Yes, Mortimer! The mallet!'

A faint blush of shame mantled her cheek, and into her blue eyes there came a look of pain, but she faced him bravely.

'I am the Ladies' Open Croquet Champion!' she whispered.

Mortimer Sturgis cried aloud, a cry that was like the shriek of some wounded animal.

'Croquet!' He gulped, and stared at her with unseeing eyes. He was no prude, but he had those decent prejudices of which no self-respecting man can wholly rid himself, however broad-minded he may try to be.

'Croquet!'

There was a long silence. The light breeze sang in the pines above them. The grasshoppers chirruped at their feet.

She began to speak again in a low, monotonous voice.

'I blame myself! I should have told you before, while there was yet time for you to withdraw. I should have confessed this to you that night on the terrace in the moonlight. But you swept me off my feet, and I was in your arms before I realised what you would think of me. It was only then that I understood what my supposed skill at golf meant to you, and then it was too late. I loved you too much to let you go! I could not bear the thought of you recoiling from me. Oh, I was mad – mad! I knew that I could not keep up the deception for ever, that you must find me out in time. But I had a wild hope that by then we should be so close to one another that you might find it in your heart to forgive. But I was wrong. I see it now. There are some things that no man can forgive. Some things,' she repeated, dully, 'which no man can forgive.'

She turned away. Mortimer awoke from his trance.

'Stop!' he cried. 'Don't go!'

'I must go.'

'I want to talk this over.'

She shook her head sadly and started to walk slowly across the sunlit grass. Mortimer watched her, his brain in a whirl of chaotic thoughts.

She disappeared through the trees.

Mortimer sat down on the tee-box, and buried his face in his hands. For a time he could think of nothing but the cruel blow he had received. This was the end of those rainbow visions of himself and her going through life side by side, she lovingly criticising his stance and his back-swing, he learning wisdom from her. A croquet-player! He was married to a woman who hit coloured balls through hoops. Mortimer Sturgis writhed in torment. A strong man's agony.

The mood passed. How long it had lasted, he did not know. But suddenly, as he sat there, he became once more aware of the glow of the sunshine and the singing of the birds. It was as if a shadow had lifted. Hope and optimism crept into his heart.

He loved her. He loved her still. She was part of him, and nothing that she could do had power to alter that. She had deceived him, yes. But why had she deceived him? Because she loved him so much that she could not bear to lose him. Dash it all, it was a bit of a compliment.

And, after all, poor girl, was it her fault? Was it not rather the fault of her upbringing? Probably she had been taught to play croquet when a mere child, hardly able to distinguish right from wrong. No steps had been taken to eradicate the virus from her system, and the thing had become chronic. Could she be blamed? Was she not more to be pitied than censured?

Mortimer rose to his feet, his heart swelling with generous forgiveness. The black horror had passed from him. The future seemed once more bright. It was not too late. She was still young, many years younger than he himself had been when he took up golf, and surely, if she put herself into the hands of a good specialist and practised every day, she might still hope to become a fair player. He reached the house and ran in, calling her name.

No answer came. He sped from room to room, but all were empty.

She had gone. The house was there. The furniture was there. The canary sang in its cage, the cook in the kitchen. The pictures still hung on the walls. But she had gone. Everything was at home except his wife.

Finally, propped up against the cup he had once won in a handicap competition, he saw a letter. With a sinking heart he tore open the envelope.

It was a pathetic, a tragic letter, the letter of a woman endeavouring to express all the anguish of a torn heart with one of those fountain-pens which suspend the flow of ink about twice in every three words. The gist of it was that she felt she had wronged him; that, though he might forgive, he could never forget; and that she was going away, away out into the world alone.

Mortimer sank into a chair, and stared blankly before him. She had scratched the match.

*

I am not a married man myself, so have had no experience of how it feels to have one's wife whizz off silently into the unknown; but I should imagine that it must be something like taking a full swing with a brassey and missing the ball. Something, I take it, of the same sense of mingled shock, chagrin, and the feeling that nobody loves one, which attacks a man in such circumstances, must come to the bereaved husband. And one can readily understand how terribly the incident must have shaken Mortimer Sturgis. I was away at the time, but I am told by those who saw him that his game went all to pieces.

He had never shown much indication of becoming anything in the nature of a first-class golfer, but he had managed to acquire one or two decent shots. His work with the light iron was not at all bad, and he was a fairly steady putter. But now, under the shadow of this tragedy, he dropped right back to the form of his earliest period. It was a pitiful sight to see this gaunt, haggard man with the look of dumb anguish behind his spectacles taking as many as three shots sometimes to get past the ladies' tee. His slice, of which he had almost cured himself, returned with such virulence that in the list of ordinary hazards he had now to include the tee-box. And, when he was not slicing, he was pulling. I have heard that he was known, when driving at the sixth, to get bunkered in his own caddie, who had taken up his position directly behind him. As for the deep sand-trap in front of the seventh green, he spent so much of his time in it that there was some informal talk among the members of the committee of charging him a small weekly rent.

A man of comfortable independent means, he lived during these days on next to nothing. Golf-balls cost him a certain amount, but the bulk of his income he spent in efforts to discover his wife's whereabouts. He advertised in all the papers. He employed private detectives. He even, much as it revolted his finer instincts, took to travelling about the country, watching croquet matches. But she was never among the players. I am not sure that he did not find a melancholy comfort in this, for it seemed to show that, whatever his wife might be and whatever she might be doing, she had not gone right under.

Summer passed. Autumn came and went. Winter arrived. The days grew bleak and chill, and an early fall of snow, heavier than had been known at that time of the year for a long while, put an end to golf. Mortimer spent his days indoors, staring gloomily through the window at the white mantle that covered the earth.

It was Christmas Eve.

The young man shifted uneasily on his seat. His face was long and sombre.

'All this is very depressing,' he said.

'These soul tragedies,' agreed the Oldest Member, 'are never very cheery.'

'Look here,' said the young man, firmly, 'tell me one thing frankly, as man to man. Did Mortimer find her dead in the snow, covered except for her face, on which still lingered that faint, sweet smile which he remembered so well? Because, if he did, I'm going home.'

'No, no,' protested the Oldest Member. 'Nothing of that kind.'

'You're sure? You aren't going to spring it on me suddenly?'

'No, no!'

The young man breathed a relieved sigh.

'It was your saying that about the white mantle covering the earth that made me suspicious.'

The Sage resumed.

It was Christmas Eve. All day the snow had been falling, and now it lay thick and deep over the countryside. Mortimer Sturgis, his frugal dinner concluded – what with losing his wife and not being able to get any golf, he had little appetite these days – was sitting in his drawing-room, moodily polishing the blade of his jigger. Soon wearying of this once congenial task, he laid down the club and went to the front door to see if there was any chance of a thaw. But no. It was freezing. The snow, as he tested it with his shoe, crackled crisply. The sky above was black and full of cold stars. It seemed to Mortimer that the sooner he packed up and went to the South of France, the better. He was just about to close the door, when suddenly he thought he heard his own name called.

'Mortimer!'

Had he been mistaken? The voice had sounded faint and far away.

'Mortimer!'

He thrilled from head to foot. This time there could be no mistake. It was the voice he knew so well, his wife's voice, and it had come from somewhere down near the garden-gate. It is difficult to judge distance where sounds are concerned, but Mortimer estimated that the voice had spoken about a short mashie-niblick and an easy putt from where he stood.

The next moment he was racing down the snow-covered path. And then his heart stood still. What was that dark something on the ground just inside the gate? He leaped towards it. He passed his hands over it. It was a human body. Quivering, he struck a match. It went out. He struck another. That went out, too. He struck a third, and it burnt with a steady flame; and, stooping, he saw that it was his wife who lay there, cold and stiff. Her eyes were closed, and on her face still lingered that faint, sweet smile which he remembered so well.

The young man rose with a set face. He reached for his golf-bag.

'I call that a dirty trick,' he said, 'after you promised—'

The Sage waved him back to his seat.

'Have no fear! She had only fainted.'

'You said she was cold.'

'Wouldn't you be cold if you were lying in the snow?'

'And stiff.'

'Mrs Sturgis was stiff because the train-service was bad, it being the holiday-season, and she had had to walk all the way from the junction, a distance of eight miles. Sit down and allow me to proceed.'

Tenderly, reverently Mortimer Sturgis picked her up and began to bear her into the house. Half-way there, his foot slipped on a piece of ice and he fell heavily, barking his shin and shooting his lovely burden out on to the snow.

The fall brought her to. She opened her eyes.

'Mortimer, darling!' she said.

Mortimer had just been going to say something else, but he checked himself.

'Are you alive?' he asked.

'Yes,' she replied.

'Thank God!' said Mortimer, scooping some of the snow out of the back of his collar.

Together they went into the house, and into the drawing-room. Wife gazed at husband, husband at wife. There was a silence.

'Rotten weather!' said Mortimer.

'Yes, isn't it!'

The spell was broken. They fell into each other's arms. And presently they were sitting side by side on the sofa, holding hands, just as if that awful parting had been but a dream.

It was Mortimer who made the first reference to it.

'I say, you know,' he said, 'you oughtn't to have nipped away like that!'

'I thought you hated me!'

'Hated *you*! I love you better than life itself! I would sooner have smashed my pet driver than have had you leave me!'

She thrilled at the words.

'Darling!'

Mortimer fondled her hand.

'I was just coming back to tell you that I loved you still. I was going to suggest that you took lessons from some good professional. And I found you gone!'

'I wasn't worthy of you, Mortimer!'

'My angel!' He pressed his lips to her hair, and spoke solemnly. 'All this has taught me a lesson, dearest. I knew all along, and I know it more than ever now, that it is you – you that I want. Just you! I don't care if you don't play golf. I don't care—' He hesitated, then went on manfully. 'I don't care even if you play croquet, so long as you are with me!'

For a moment her face showed rapture that made it almost angelic. She uttered a low moan of ecstasy. She kissed him. Then she rose.

'Mortimer, look!'

'What at?'

'Me. Just look!'

The jigger which he had been polishing lay on a chair close by. She took it up. From the bowl of golf-balls on the mantelpiece she selected a brand new one. She placed it on the carpet. She addressed it. Then, with a merry cry of 'Fore!' she drove it hard and straight through the glass of the china-cupboard.

'Good God!' cried Mortimer, astounded. It had been a bird of a shot.

She turned to him, her whole face alight with that beautiful smile.

'When I left you, Mortie,' she said, 'I had but one aim in life, somehow to make myself worthy of you. I saw your advertisements in the papers, and I longed to answer them, but I was not ready. All this long, weary while I have been in the village of Auchter-muchtie, in Scotland, studying under Tamms McMickle.'

'Not the Tamms McMickle who finished fourth in the Open Championship of 1911, and had the best ball in the foursome in 1912 with Jock McHaggis, Andy McHeather, and Sandy McHoots!'

'Yes, Mortimer, the very same. Oh, it was difficult at first. I missed my mallet, and long to steady the ball with my foot and use the toe of the club. Wherever there was a direction post I aimed at it automatically. But I conquered my weakness. I practised steadily. And now Mr McMickle says my handicap would be a good twenty-four on any links.' She smiled apologetically. 'Of course, that doesn't sound much to you! You were a twelve when I left you, and now I suppose you are down to eight or something.'

Mortimer shook his head.

'Alas, no!' he replied, gravely. 'My game went right off for some reason or other, and I'm twenty-four, too.'

'For some reason or other!' She uttered a cry. 'Oh, I know what the reason was! How can I ever forgive myself! I have ruined your game!'

The brightness came back to Mortimer's eyes. He embraced her fondly.

'Do not reproach yourself, dearest,' he murmured. 'It is the best thing that could have happened. From now on, we start level, two hearts that beat as one, two drivers that drive as one. I could not wish it otherwise. By George! It's just like that thing of Tennyson's.'

He recited the lines softly:

> *My bride,*
> *My wife, my life. Oh, we will walk the links*
> *Yoked in all exercise of noble end,*
> *And so thro' those dark bunkers off the course*
> *That no man knows. Indeed, I love thee: come,*
> *Yield thyself up: our handicaps are one;*
> *Accomplish thou my manhood and thyself;*
> *Lay thy sweet hands in mine and trust to me.*

She laid her hands in his.

'And now, Mortie, darling,' she said, 'I want to tell you all about how I did the long twelfth at Auchtermuchtie in one under bogey.'

'THE SALVATION
OF
GEORGE MACKINTOSH'

The young man came into the club-house. There was a frown on his usually cheerful face, and he ordered a ginger-ale in the sort of voice which an ancient Greek would have used when asking the executioner to bring on the hemlock.

Sunk in the recesses of his favourite settee the Oldest Member had watched him with silent sympathy.

'How did you get on?' he inquired.

'He beat me.'

The Oldest Member nodded his venerable head.

'You have had a trying time, if I am not mistaken. I feared as much when I saw you go out with Pobsley. How many a young man have I seen go out with Herbert Pobsley exulting in his youth, and crawl back at eventide looking like a toad under the harrow! He talked?'

'All the time, confound it! Put me right off my stroke.'

The Oldest Member sighed.

'The talking golfer is undeniably the most pronounced pest of our complex modern civilization,' he said, 'and the most difficult to deal with. It is a melancholy thought that the noblest of games should have produced such a scourge. I have frequently marked Herbert Pobsley in action. As the crackling of thorns under a pot … He is almost as bad as poor George Mackintosh in his worst period. Did I ever tell you about George Mackintosh?'

'I don't think so.'

'His,' said the Sage, 'is the only case of golfing garrulity I have ever known where a permanent cure was effected. If you would care to hear about it − ?'

George Mackintosh (said the Oldest Member), when I first knew him, was one of the most admirable young fellows I have ever met. A handsome, well-set-up man, with no vices except a tendency to use the mashie for shots which should have been made with the light iron. And as for his positive virtues, they were too numerous to mention. He never swayed his body, moved his head, or pressed. He was always ready to utter a tactful grunt when his opponent foozled. And when he himself achieved a glaring fluke, his self-reproachful click of the tongue was music to his adversary's bruised soul. But of all his virtues the one that most endeared him to me and to all thinking men was the fact that, from the start of a round to the finish, he never spoke a word except when absolutely compelled to do so by the exigencies of the game. And it was this man who subsequently, for a black period which lives in the memory of all his contemporaries, was known as Gabby George and became a shade less popular than the germ of Spanish Influenza. Truly, *corruptio optimi pessima!*

One of the things that sadden a man as he grows older and reviews his life is the reflection that his most devastating deeds were generally the ones which he did with the best motives. The thought is disheartening. I can honestly say that, when George Mackintosh came to me and told me his troubles, my sole desire was to ameliorate his lot. That I might be starting on the downward path a man whom I liked and respected never once occurred to me.

One night after dinner when George Mackintosh came in, I could see at once that there was something on his mind, but what this could be I was at a loss to imagine, for I had been playing with him myself all the afternoon, and he had done an eighty-one and a seventy-nine. And, as I had not left the links till dusk was beginning to fall, it was practically impossible that he could have gone out again and done badly. The idea of financial trouble seemed equally out of the question. George had a good job with the old-established legal firm of Peabody, Peabody, Peabody, Peabody, Cootes, Toots, and Peabody. The third alternative, that he might be in love, I rejected at once. In all the time I had known him I had never seen a sign that George Mackintosh gave a thought to the opposite sex.

Yet this, bizarre as it seemed, was the true solution. Scarcely had he seated himself and lit a cigar when he blurted out his confession.

'What would you do in a case like this?' he said.

'Like what?'

'Well—' He choked, and a rich blush permeated his surface. 'Well, it seems a silly thing to say and all that, but I'm in love with Miss Tennant, you know!'

'You are in love with Celia Tennant?'

'Of course I am. I've got eyes, haven't I? Who else is there that any sane man could possibly be in love with? That,' he went on, moodily, 'is the whole trouble. There's a field of about twenty-nine, and I should think my place in the betting is about thirty-three to one.'

'I cannot agree with you there,' I said. 'You have every advantage, it appears to me. You are young, amiable, good-looking, comfortably off, scratch—'

'But I can't talk, confound it!' he burst out. 'And how is a man to get anywhere at this sort of game without talking?'

'You are talking perfectly fluently now.'

'Yes, to you. But put me in front of Celia Tennant, and I simply make a sort of gurgling noise like a sheep with the botts. It kills my chances stone dead. You know these other men. I can give Claude Mainwaring a third and beat him. I can give Eustace Brinkley a stroke a hole and simply trample on his corpse. But when it comes to talking to a girl, I'm not in their class.'

'You must not be diffident.'

'But I *am* diffident. What's the good of saying I mustn't be diffident when I'm the man who wrote the words and music, when Diffidence is my middle name and my telegraphic address? I can't help being diffident.'

'Surely you could overcome it?'

'But how? It was in the hope that you might be able to suggest something that I came round tonight.'

And this was where I did the fatal thing. It happened that, just before I took up 'Braid on the Push-Shot', I had been dipping into the current number of a magazine, and one of the advertisements, I chanced to remember, might have been framed with a special eye to George's unfortunate case. It was that one, which I have no doubt you have seen, which treats of 'How to Become a Convincing Talker'. I picked up this magazine now and handed it to George.

He studied it for a few minutes in thoughtful silence. He looked at the picture of the Man who had taken the course being fawned upon by lovely women, while the man who had let this opportunity slip stood outside the group gazing with a wistful envy.

'They never do that to me,' said George.

'Do what, my boy?'

'Cluster round, clinging cooingly.'

'I gather from the letterpress that they will if you write for the booklet.'

'You think there is really something in it?'

'I see no reason why eloquence should not be taught by mail. One seems to be able to acquire every other desirable quality in that manner nowadays.'

'I might try it. After all, it's not expensive. There's no doubt about it,' he murmured, returning to his perusal, 'that fellow does look popular. Of course, the evening dress may have something to do with it.'

'Not at all. The other man, you will notice, is also wearing evening dress, and yet he is merely among those on the outskirts. It is simply a question of writing for the booklet.'

'Sent post free.'

'Sent, as you say, post free.'

'I've a good mind to try it.'

'I see no reason why you should not.'

'I will, by Duncan!' He tore the page out of the magazine and put it in his pocket. 'I'll tell you what I'll do. I'll give this thing a trial for a week or two, and at the end of that time I'll go to the boss and see how he reacts when I ask for a rise of salary. If he crawls, it'll show there's something in this. If he flings me out, it will prove the thing's no good.'

We left it at that, and I am bound to say – owing, no doubt, to my not having written for the booklet of the Memory Training Course advertised on the adjoining page of the magazine – the matter slipped from my mind. When, therefore, a few weeks later, I received a telegram from young Mackintosh which ran:

Worked like magic,

I confess I was intensely puzzled. It was only a quarter of an hour before George himself arrived that I solved the problem of its meaning.

'So the boss crawled?' I said, as he came in.

He gave a light, confident laugh. I had not seen him, as I say, for some time, and I was struck by the alteration in his appearance. In what exactly this alteration consisted I could not at first have said; but gradually it began to impress itself on me that his eye was brighter, his jaw squarer, his carriage a trifle more upright than it had been. But it was his eye that struck me most forcibly. The George Mackintosh I had known had had a pleasing gaze, but, though frank and agreeable, it had never been more dynamic than a fried egg. This new George had an eye that was a combination of a gimlet and a searchlight. Coleridge's Ancient Mariner, I imagine, must have been somewhat similarly equipped. The Ancient Mariner stopped a wedding guest on his way to a wedding; George Mackintosh gave me the impression that he could have stopped the Cornish Riviera express on its way to Penzance. Self-confidence – aye, and more than self-confidence – a sort of sinful, overbearing swank seemed to exude from his very pores.

'Crawled?' he said. 'Well, he didn't actually lick my boots, because I saw him coming and side-stepped; but he did everything short of that. I hadn't been talking an hour when—'

'An hour!' I gasped. 'Did you talk for an hour?'

'Certainly. You wouldn't have had me be abrupt, would you? I went into his private office and found him alone. I think at first he would have been just as well pleased if I had retired. In fact, he said as much. But I soon adjusted that outlook. I took a seat and a cigarette, and then I started to sketch out for him the history of my connection with the firm. He began to wilt before the end of the first ten minutes. At the quarter of an hour mark he was looking at me like a lost dog that's just found its owner. By the half-hour he was making little bleating noises and massaging my coat-sleeve. And when, after perhaps an hour and a half, I came to my peroration and suggested a rise, he choked back a sob, gave me double what I had asked, and invited me to dine at his club next Tuesday. I'm a little sorry now I cut the thing so short. A few minutes more, and I fancy he would have given me his sock-suspenders and made over his life-insurance in my favour.'

'Well,' I said, as soon as I could speak, for I was finding my young friend a trifle overpowering, 'this is most satisfactory.'

'So-so,' said George. 'Not un-so-so. A man wants an addition to his income when he is going to get married.'

'Ah!' I said. 'That, of course, will be the real test.'

'What do you mean?'

'Why, when you propose to Celia Tennant. You remember you were saying when we spoke of this before—'

'Oh, that!' said George, carelessly. 'I've arranged all that.'

'What!'

'Oh, yes. On my way up from the station. I looked in on Celia about an hour ago, and it's all settled.'

'Amazing!'

'Well, I don't know. I just put the thing to her, and she seemed to see it.'

'I congratulate you. So now, like Alexander, you have no more worlds to conquer.'

'Well, I don't know so much about that,' said George. 'The way it looks to me is that I'm just starting. This eloquence is a thing that rather grows on one. You didn't hear about my after-dinner speech at the anniversary banquet of the firm, I suppose? My dear fellow, a riot! A positive stampede. Had 'em laughing and then crying and then laughing again and then crying once more till six of 'em had to be led out and the rest down with hiccoughs. Napkins waving ... three tables broken ... waiters in hysterics. I tell you, I played on them as on a stringed instrument ... '

'Can you play on a stringed instrument?'

'As it happens, no. But as I would have played on a stringed instrument if I could play on a stringed instrument. Wonderful sense of power it gives you. I mean to go in pretty largely for that sort of thing in future.'

'You must not let it interfere with your golf.'

He gave a laugh which turned my blood cold.

'Golf!' he said. 'After all, what is golf? Just pushing a small ball into a hole. A child could do it. Indeed, children have done it with great success. I see an infant of fourteen has just won some sort of championship. Could that stripling convulse a roomful of banqueters? I think not! To sway your fellow-men with a word, to hold them with a gesture ... that is the real salt of life. I don't suppose I shall play much more golf now. I'm making arrangements for a lecturing-tour, and I'm booked up for fifteen lunches already.'

Those were his words. A man who had once done the lake-hole in one. A man whom the committee were grooming for the amateur championship. I am no weakling, but I confess they sent a chill shiver down my spine.

George Mackintosh did not, I am glad to say, carry out his mad project to the letter. He did not altogether sever himself from golf. He was still to be seen occasionally on the links. But now – and I know of nothing more tragic that can befall a man – he found himself gradually shunned, he who in the days of his sanity had been besieged with more offers of games than he could manage to accept. Men simply would not stand his incessant flow of talk. One by one they dropped off, until the only person he could find to go round with him was old Major Moseby, whose hearing completely petered out as long ago as the year '98. And, of course, Celia Tennant would play with him occasionally; but it seemed to me that even she, greatly as no doubt she loved him, was beginning to crack under the strain.

So surely had I read the pallor of her face and the wild look of dumb agony in her eyes that I was not surprised when, as I sat one morning in my garden reading 'Ray on Taking Turf', my man announced her name. I had been half expecting her to come to me for advice and consolation, for I had known her ever since she was a child. It was I who had given her her first driver and taught her infant lips to lisp 'Fore!' It is not easy to lisp the word 'Fore!' but I had taught her to do it, and this constituted a bond between us which had been strengthened rather than weakened by the passage of time.

She sat down on the grass beside my chair, and looked up at my face in silent pain. We had known each other so long that I know that it was not my face that pained her, but rather some unspoken *malaise* of the soul. I waited for her to speak, and suddenly she burst out impetuously as though she could hold back her sorrow no longer.

'Oh, I can't stand it! I can't stand it!'

'You mean ... ?' I said, though I knew only too well.

'This horrible obsession of poor George's,' she cried passionately. 'I don't think he has stopped talking once since we have been engaged.'

'He *is* chatty,' I agreed. 'Has he told you the story about the Irishman?'

'Half a dozen times. And the one about the Swede oftener than that. But I would not mind an occasional anecdote. Women have to learn to bear anecdotes from the men they love. It is the curse of Eve. It is his incessant easy flow of chatter on all topics that is undermining even my devotion.'

'But surely, when he proposed to you, he must have given you an inkling of the truth. He only hinted at it when he spoke to me, but I gather that he was eloquent.'

'When he proposed,' said Celia dreamily, 'he was wonderful. He spoke for twenty minutes without stopping. He said I was the essence of his every hope, the tree on which the fruit of his life grew; his Present, his Future, his Past ... oh, and all that sort of thing. If he would only confine his conversation now to remarks of a similar nature, I could listen to him all day long. But he doesn't. He talks politics and statistics and philosophy and ... oh, and everything. He makes my head ache.'

'And your heart also, I fear,' I said gravely.

'I love him!' she replied simply. 'In spite of everything, I love him dearly. But what to do? What to do? I have an awful fear that when we are getting married instead of answering 'I will,' he will go into the pulpit and deliver an address on Marriage Ceremonies of All Ages. The world to him is a vast lecture-platform. He looks on life as one long after-dinner, with himself as the principal speaker of the evening. It is breaking my heart. I see him shunned by his former friends. Shunned! They run a mile when they see him coming. The mere sound of his voice outside the club-house is enough to send brave men diving for safety beneath the sofas. Can you wonder that I am in despair? What have I to live for?'

'There is always golf.'

'Yes, there is always golf,' she whispered bravely.

'Come and have a round this afternoon.'

'I had promised to go for a walk ... ' She shuddered, then pulled herself together, ' ... for a walk with George.'

I hesitated for a moment.

'Bring him along,' I said, and patted her hand. 'It may be that together we shall find an opportunity of reasoning with him.'

She shook her head.

'You can't reason with George. He never stops talking long enough to give you time.'

'Nevertheless, there is no harm in trying. I have an idea that this malady of his is not permanent and incurable. The very violence with which the germ of loquacity has attacked him gives me hope. You must remember that before this seizure he was rather a notice-ably silent man. Sometimes I think that it is just Nature's way of restoring the average, and that soon the fever may burn itself out. Or it may be that a sudden shock ... At any rate, have courage.'

'I will try to be brave.'

'Capital! At half-past two on the first tee, then.'

'You will have to give me a stroke on the third, ninth, twelfth, fifteenth, sixteenth and eighteenth,' she said, with a quaver in her voice. 'My golf has fallen off rather lately.'

I patted her hand again.

'I understand,' I said gently. 'I understand.'

The steady drone of a baritone voice as I alighted from my car and approached the first tee told me that George had not forgotten the tryst. He was sitting on the stone seat under the chestnut-tree, speaking a few well-chosen words on the Labour Movement.

'To what conclusion, then, do we come?' he was saying. 'We come to the foregone and inevitable conclusion that ... '

'Good afternoon, George,' I said.

He nodded briefly, but without verbal salutation. He seemed to regard my remark as he would have regarded the unmannerly heckling of someone at the back of the hall. He proceeded evenly with his speech, and was still talking when Celia addressed her ball and drove off. Her drive, coinciding with a sharp rhetorical question from George, wavered in mid-air, and the ball trickled off into the rough half-way down the hill. I can see the poor girl's tortured face even now. But she breathed no word of reproach. Such is the miracle of women's love.

'Where you went wrong there,' said George, breaking off his remarks on Labour, 'was that you have not studied the dynamics of golf sufficiently. You did not pivot properly. You allowed your left heel to point down the course when you were at the top of your swing. This makes for instability and loss of distance. The fundamental law of the dynamics of golf is that the left foot shall be solidly on the ground at the moment of impact. If you allow your heel to point down the course, it is almost impossible to bring it back in time to make the foot a solid fulcrum.'

I drove, and managed to clear the rough and reach the fairway. But it was not one of my best drives. George Mackintosh, I confess, had unnerved me. The feeling he gave me resembled the self-conscious panic which I used to experience in my childhood when informed that there was One Awful Eye that watched my every movement and saw my every act. It was only the fact that poor Celia appeared even more affected by his espionage that enabled me to win the first hole in seven.

On the way to the second tee George discoursed on the beauties of Nature, pointing out at considerable length how exquisitely the silver glitter of the lake harmonised with the vivid emerald turf near the hole and the duller green of the rough beyond it. As Celia teed up her ball, he directed her attention to the golden glory of the sand-pit to the left of the flag. It was not the spirit in which to approach the lake-hole, and I was not surprised when the unfortunate girl's ball fell with a sickening plop half-way across the water.

'Where you went wrong there,' said George, 'was that you made the stroke a sudden heave instead of a smooth, snappy flick of the wrists. Pressing is always bad, but with the mashie—'

'I think I will give you this hole,' said Celia to me, for my shot had cleared the water and was lying on the edge of the green. 'I wish I hadn't used a new ball.'

'The price of golf-balls,' said George, as we started to round the lake, 'is a matter to which economists should give some attention. I am credibly informed that rubber at the present time is exceptionally cheap. Yet we see no decrease in the price of golf-balls, which, as I need scarcely inform you, are rubber-cored. Why should this be so? You will say that the wages of skilled labour have gone up. True. But—'

'One moment, George, while I drive,' I said. For we had now arrived at the third tee.

'A curious thing, concentration,' said George, 'and why certain phenomena should prevent us from focusing our attention – This brings me to the vexed question of sleep. Why is it that we are able to sleep through some vast convulsion of Nature when a dripping tap is enough to keep us awake? I am told that there were people who slumbered peacefully through the San Francisco earthquake, merely stirring drowsily from time to time to tell an imaginary person to leave it on the mat. Yet these same people—'

Celia's drive bounded into the deep ravine which yawns some fifty yards from the tee. A low moan escaped her.

'Where you went wrong there—' said George.

'I know,' said Celia. 'I lifted my head.'

I had never heard her speak so abruptly before. Her manner, in a girl less noticeably pretty, might almost have been called snappish. George, however, did not appear to have noticed anything amiss. He filled his pipe and followed her into the ravine.

'Remarkable,' he said, 'how fundamental a principle of golf is this keeping the head still. You will hear professionals tell their pupils to keep their eye on the ball. Keeping the eye on the ball is only a secondary matter. What they really mean is that the head should be kept rigid, as otherwise it is impossible to—'

His voice died away. I had sliced my drive into the woods on the right, and after playing another had gone off to try to find my ball, leaving Celia and George in the ravine behind me. My last glimpse of them showed me that her ball had fallen into a stone-studded cavity in the side of the hill, and she was drawing her niblick from her bag as I passed out of sight. George's voice, blurred by distance to a monotonous murmur, followed me until I was out of earshot.

I was just about to give up the hunt for my ball in despair, when I heard Celia's voice calling to me from the edge of the under-growth. There was a sharp note in it which startled me.

I came out, trailing a portion of some unknown shrub which had twined itself about my ankle.

'Yes?' I said, picking twigs out of my hair.

'I want your advice,' said Celia.

'Certainly. What is the trouble? By the way,' I said, looking round, 'where is your *fiancé*?'

'I have no *fiancé*,' she said, in a dull, hard voice.

'You have broken off the engagement?'

'Not exactly. And yet – well, I suppose it amounts to that.'

'I don't quite understand.'

'Well, the fact is,' said Celia, in a burst of girlish frankness, 'I rather think I've killed George.'

'Killed him, eh?'

It was a solution that had not occurred to me, but now that it was presented for my inspection I could see its merits. In these days of national effort, when we are all working together to try to make our beloved land fit for heroes to live in, it was astonishing that nobody before had thought of a simple, obvious thing like killing George Mackintosh. George Mackintosh was undoubtedly better dead, but it had taken a woman's intuition to see it.

'I killed him with my niblick,' said Celia.

I nodded. If the thing was to be done at all, it was unquestion-ably a niblick shot.

'I had just made my eleventh attempt to get out of that ravine,' the girl went on, 'with George talking all the time about the recent excavations in Egypt, when suddenly – you know what it is when something seems to snap –'

'I had the experience with my shoe-lace only this morning.'

'Yes, it was like that. Sharp – sudden – happening all in a moment. I suppose I must have said something, for George stopped talking about Egypt and said that he was reminded by a remark of the last speaker's of a certain Irishman—'

I pressed her hand.

'Don't go on if it hurts you,' I said, gently.

'Well, there is very little more to tell. He bent his head to light his pipe, and well – the temptation was too much for me. That's all.'

'You were quite right.'

'You really think so?'

'I certainly do. A rather similar action, under far less provocation, once made Jael the wife of Heber the most popular woman in Israel.'

'I wish I could think so too,' she murmured. 'At the moment, you know, I was conscious of nothing but an awful elation. But – but – oh, he was such a darling before he got this dreadful affliction. I can't help thinking of G-George as he used to be.'

She burst into a torrent of sobs.

'Would you care for me to view the remains?' I said.

'Perhaps it would be as well.'

She led me silently into the ravine. George Mackintosh was lying on his back where he had fallen.

'There!' said Celia.

And, as she spoke, George Mackintosh gave a kind of snorting groan and sat up. Celia uttered a sharp shriek and sank on her knees before him. George blinked once or twice and looked about him dazedly.

'Save the women and children!' he cried. 'I can swim.'

'Oh, George!' said Celia.

'Feeling a little better?' I asked.

'A little. How many people were hurt?'

'Hurt?'

'When the express ran into us.' He cast another glance around him. 'Why, how did I get here?'

'You were here all the time,' I said.

'Do you mean after the roof fell in or before?'

Celia was crying quietly down the back of his neck.

'Oh, George!' she said, again.

He groped out feebly for her hand and patted it.

'Brave little woman!' he said. 'Brave little woman! She stuck by me all through. Tell me – I am strong enough to bear it – what caused the explosion?'

It seemed to me a case where much unpleasant explanation might be avoided by the exercise of a little tact.

'Well, some say one thing and some another,' I said. 'Whether it was a spark from a cigarette—'

Celia interrupted me. The woman in her made her revolt against this well-intentioned subterfuge.

'I hit you, George!'

'Hit me?' he repeated, curiously. 'What with? The Eiffel Tower?'

'With my niblick.'

'You hit me with your niblick? But why?'

She hesitated. Then she faced him bravely.

'Because you wouldn't stop talking.'

He gaped.

'Me!' he said. '*I* wouldn't stop talking! But I hardly talk at all. I'm noted for it.'

Celia's eyes met mine in agonised inquiry. But I saw what had happened. The blow, the sudden shock, had operated on George's brain-cells in such a way as to effect a complete cure. I have not the technical knowledge to be able to explain it, but the facts were plain.

'Lately, my dear fellow,' I assured him, 'you have dropped into the habit of talking rather a good deal. Ever since we started out this afternoon you have kept up an incessant flow of conversation!'

'Me! On the links! It isn't possible.'

'It is only too true, I fear. And that is why this brave girl hit you with her niblick. You started to tell her a funny story just as she was making her eleventh shot to get her ball out of this ravine, and she took what she considered the necessary steps.'

'Can you ever forgive me, George?' cried Celia.

George Mackintosh stared at me. Then a crimson blush mantled his face.

'So I did! It's all beginning to come back to me. Oh, heavens!'

'*Can* you forgive me, George?' cried Celia again.

He took her hand in his.

'Forgive you?' he muttered. 'Can *you* forgive *me?* Me – a tee-talker, a green-gabbler, a prattler on the links, the lowest form of life known to science! I am unclean, unclean!'

'It's only a little mud, dearest,' said Celia, looking at the sleeve of his coat. 'It will brush off when it's dry.'

'How can you link your lot with a man who talks when people are making their shots?'

'You will never do it again.'

'But I have done it. And you stuck to me all through! Oh, Celia!'

'I loved you, George!'

The man seemed to swell with a sudden emotion. His eye lit up, and he thrust one hand into the breast of his coat while he raised the other in a sweeping gesture. For an instant he appeared on the verge of a flood of eloquence. And then, as if he had been made sharply aware of what it was that he intended to do, he suddenly sagged. The gleam died out of his eyes. He lowered his hand.

'Well, I must say that was rather decent of you,' he said.

A lame speech, but one that brought an infinite joy to both his hearers. For it showed that George Mackintosh was cured beyond possibility of relapse.

'Yes, I must say you are rather a corker,' he added.

'George!' cried Celia.

I said nothing, but I clasped his hand; and then, taking my clubs, I retired. When I looked round she was still in his arms. I left them there, alone together in the great silence.

And so (concluded the Oldest Member) you see that a cure is possible, though it needs a woman's gentle hand to bring it about. And how few women are capable of doing what Celia Tennant did. Apart from the difficulty of summoning up the necessary resolution, an act like hers requires a straight eye and a pair of strong and supple wrists. It seems to me that for the ordinary talking golfer there is no hope. And the race seems to be getting more numerous every day. Yet the finest golfers are always the least loquacious. It is related of the illustrious Sandy McHoots that when, on the occasion of his winning the British Open Championship, he was interviewed by reporters from the leading daily papers as to his views on Tariff Reform, Bimetallism, the Trial by Jury System, and the Modern Craze for Dancing, all they could extract from him was the single word 'Mphm!' Having uttered which, he shouldered his bag and went home to tea. A great man. I wish there were more like him.

'THE CLICKING OF CUTHBERT'

'I play nothing but golf,' wrote Wodehouse from Long Island to his great friend William Townend in February 1920. 'Greatest game on earth. You must take it up. It beats everything else.' Once he found the sweet spot for his humour in a golfing context, Wodehouse turned out new fairway-set stories with ease. In the same letter to Townend, he remarked: 'I have just finished an eight thousand word golf story in two days!! Darned good, too. It just came pouring out.' Sophie Ratcliffe, editor of P. G. Wodehouse: A life in Letters, *advises us that the story in question was the one you are about to read.*

The young man came into the smoking-room of the club-house, and flung his bag with a clatter on the floor. He sank moodily into an arm-chair and pressed the bell.

'Waiter!'

'Sir?'

The young man pointed at the bag with every evidence of distaste.

'You may have these clubs,' he said. 'Take them away. If you don't want them yourself, give them to one of the caddies.'

Across the room the Oldest Member gazed at him with a grave sadness through the smoke of his pipe. His eye was deep and dreamy – the eye of a man who, as the poet says, has seen Golf steadily and seen it whole.

'You are giving up golf?' he said.

He was not altogether unprepared for such an attitude on the young man's part: for from his eyrie on the terrace above the ninth green he had observed him start out on the afternoon's round and had seen him lose a couple of balls in the lake at the second hole after taking seven strokes at the first.

'Yes!' cried the young man fiercely. 'For ever, dammit! Footling game! Blanked infernal fat-headed silly ass of a game! Nothing but a waste of time.'

The Sage winced.

'Don't say that, my boy.'

'But I do say it. What earthly good is golf? Life is stern and life is earnest. We live in a practical age. All round us we see foreign competition making itself unpleasant. And we spend our time playing golf! What do we get out of it? Is golf any *use*? That's what I'm asking you. Can you name me a single case where devotion to this pestilential pastime has done a man any practical good?'

The Sage smiled gently.

'I could name a thousand.'

'One will do.'

'I will select,' said the Sage, 'from the innumerable memories that rush to my mind, the story of Cuthbert Banks.'

'Never heard of him.'

'Be of good cheer,' said the Oldest Member. 'You are going to hear of him now.'

*

It was in the picturesque little settlement of Wood Hills (said the Oldest Member) that the incidents occurred which I am about to relate. Even if you have never been in Wood Hills, that suburban paradise is probably familiar to you by name. Situated at a convenient distance from the city, it combines in a notable manner the advantages of town life with the pleasant surroundings and healthful air of the country.

Its inhabitants live in commodious houses, standing in their own grounds, and enjoy so many luxuries – such as gravel soil, main drainage, electric light, telephone, baths (h. and c.), and company's own water, that you might be pardoned for imagining life to be so ideal for them that no possible improvement could be added to their lot. Mrs Willoughby Smethurst was under no such delusion. What Wood Hills needed to make it perfect, she realised, was Culture. Material comforts are all very well, but, if the *summum bonum* is to be achieved, the Soul also demands a look in, and it was Mrs Smethurst's unfaltering resolve that never while she had her strength should the Soul be handed the loser's end. It was her intention to make Wood Hills a centre of all that was most cultivated and refined, and, golly! how she had succeeded. Under her presidency the Wood Hills Literary and Debating Society had tripled its membership.

But there is always a fly in the ointment, a caterpillar in the salad. The local golf club, an institution to which Mrs Smethurst strongly objected, had also tripled its membership; and the division of the community into two rival camps, the Golfers and the Cultured, had become more marked than ever. This division, always acute, had attained now to the dimensions of a Schism. The rival sects treated one another with a cold hostility.

Unfortunate episodes came to widen the breach. Mrs Smethurst's house adjoined the links, standing to the right of the fourth tee: and, as the Literary Society was in the habit of entertaining visiting lecturers, many a golfer had foozled his drive owing to sudden loud outbursts of applause coinciding with his down-swing. And not long before this story opens a sliced ball, whizzing in at the open window, had come within an ace of incapacitating Raymond Parsloe Devine, the rising young novelist (who rose at that moment a clear foot and a half) from any further exercise of his art. Two inches, indeed, to the right and Raymond must inevitably have handed in his dinner-pail.

To make matters worse, a ring at the front-door bell followed almost immediately, and the maid ushered in a young man of pleasing appearance in a sweater and baggy knickerbockers who apologetically but firmly insisted on playing his ball where it lay, and, what with the shock of the lecturer's narrow escape and the spectacle of the intruder standing on the table and working away with a niblick, the afternoon's session had to be classed as a complete frost. Mr Devine's determination, from which no argument could swerve him, to deliver the rest of his lecture in the coal-cellar gave the meeting a jolt from which it never recovered.

I have dwelt upon this incident, because it was the means of introducing Cuthbert Banks to Mrs Smethurst's niece, Adeline. As Cuthbert, for it was he who had so nearly reduced the muster-roll of rising novelists by one, hopped down from the table after his stroke, he was suddenly aware that a beautiful girl was looking at him intently. As a matter of fact, everyone in the room was looking at him intently, none more so than Raymond Parsloe Devine, but none of the others were beautiful girls. Long as the members of Wood Hills Literary Society were on brain, they were short on looks, and, to Cuthbert's excited eye, Adeline Smethurst stood out like a jewel in a pile of coke.

He had never seen her before, for she had only arrived at her aunt's house on the previous day, but he was perfectly certain that life, even when lived in the midst of gravel soil, main drainage, and company's own water, was going to be a pretty poor affair if he did not see her again. Yes, Cuthbert was in love: and it is interesting to record, as showing the effect of the tender emotion on a man's game, that twenty minutes after he had met Adeline he did the short eleventh in one, and as near as a toucher got a three on the four-hundred-yard twelfth.

I will skip lightly over the intermediate stages of Cuthbert's courtship and come to the moment when – at the annual ball in aid of the local Cottage Hospital, the only occasion during the year on which the lion, so to speak, lay down with the lamb, and the Golfers and the Cultured met on terms of easy comradeship, their differences temporarily laid aside – he proposed to Adeline and was badly stymied.

That fair, soulful girl could not see him with a spy-glass.

'Mr Banks,' she said, 'I will speak frankly.'

'Charge right ahead,' assented Cuthbert.

'Deeply sensible as I am of—'

'I know. Of the honour and the compliment and all that. But, passing lightly over all that guff, what seems to be the trouble? I love you to distraction—'

'Love is not everything.'

'You're wrong,' said Cuthbert, earnestly. 'You're right off it. Love—' And he was about to dilate on the theme when she interrupted him.

'I am a girl of ambition.'

'And very nice, too,' said Cuthbert.

'I am a girl of ambition,' repeated Adeline, 'and I realise that the fulfilment of my ambitions must come through my husband. I am very ordinary myself—'

'What!' cried Cuthbert. 'You ordinary? Why, you are a pearl among women, the queen of your sex. You can't have been looking in a glass lately. You stand alone. Simply alone. You make the rest look like battered repaints.'

'Well,' said Adeline, softening a trifle, 'I believe I am fairly good-looking—'

'Anybody who was content to call you fairly good-looking would describe the Taj Mahal as a pretty nifty tomb.'

'But that is not the point. What I mean is, if I marry a nonentity I shall be a nonentity myself for ever. And I would sooner die than be a nonentity.'

'And, if I follow your reasoning, you think that that lets *me* out?'

'Well, really, Mr Banks, *have* you done anything, or are you likely ever to do anything worth while?'

Cuthbert hesitated.

'It's true,' he said, 'I didn't finish in the first ten in the Open, and I was knocked out in the semi-final of the Amateur, but I won the French Open last year.'

'The – what?'

'The French Open Championship. Golf, you know.'

'Golf! You waste all your time playing golf. I admire a man who is more spiritual, more intellectual.'

A pang of jealousy rent Cuthbert's bosom.

'Like What's-his-name Devine?' he said, sullenly.

'Mr Devine,' replied Adeline, blushing faintly, 'is going to be a great man. Already he has achieved much. The critics say that he is more Russian than any other young English writer.'

'And is that good?'

'Of course it's good.'

'I should have thought the wheeze would be to be more English than any other young English writer.'

'Nonsense! Who wants an English writer to be English? You've got to be Russian or Spanish or something to be a real success. The mantle of the great Russians has descended on Mr Devine.'

'From what I've heard of Russians, I should hate to have that happen to *me*.'

'There is no danger of that,' said Adeline scornfully.

'Oh! Well, let me tell you that there is a lot more in me than you think.'

'That might easily be so.'

'You think I'm not spiritual and intellectual,' said Cuthbert, deeply moved. 'Very well. Tomorrow I join the Literary Society.'

Even as he spoke the words his leg was itching to kick himself for being such a chump, but the sudden expression of pleasure on Adeline's face soothed him; and he went home that night with the feeling that he had taken on something rather attractive. It was only in the cold, grey light of the morning that he realised what he had let himself in for.

I do not know if you have had any experience of suburban literary societies, but the one that flourished under the eye of Mrs Willoughby Smethurst at Wood Hills was rather more so than the average. With my feeble powers of narrative, I cannot hope to make clear to you all that Cuthbert Banks endured in the next few weeks. And, even if I could, I doubt if I should do so. It is all very well to excite pity and terror, as Aristotle recommends, but there are limits. In the ancient Greek tragedies it was an ironclad rule that all the real rough stuff should take place off-stage, and I shall follow this admirable principle. It will suffice if I say merely that J. Cuthbert Banks had a thin time.

After attending eleven debates and fourteen lectures on *vers libre* Poetry, the Seventeenth-Century Essayists, the Neo-Scandinavian Movement in Portuguese Literature, and other subjects of a similar nature, he grew so enfeebled that, on the rare occasions when he had time for a visit to the links, he had to take a full iron for his mashie shots.

It was not simply the oppressive nature of the debates and lectures that sapped his vitality. What really got right in amongst him was the torture of seeing Adeline's adoration of Raymond Parsloe

Devine. The man seemed to have made the deepest possible impression upon her plastic emotions. When he spoke, she leaned forward with parted lips and looked at him. When he was not speaking – which was seldom – she leaned back and looked at him. And when he happened to take the next seat to her, she leaned sideways and looked at him. One glance at Mr Devine would have been more than enough for Cuthbert; but Adeline found him a spectacle that never palled. She could not have gazed at him with a more rapturous intensity if she had been a small child and he a saucer of ice-cream. All this Cuthbert had to witness while still endeavouring to retain the possession of his faculties sufficiently to enable him to duck and back away if somebody suddenly asked him what he thought of the sombre realism of Vladimir Brusiloff. It is little wonder that he tossed in bed, picking at the coverlet, through sleepless nights, and had to have all his waistcoats taken in three inches to keep them from sagging.

This Vladimir Brusiloff to whom I have referred was the famous Russian novelist, and, owing to the fact of his being in the country on a lecturing tour at the moment, there had been something of a boom in his works. The Wood Hills Literary Society had been studying them for weeks, and never since his first entrance into intellectual circles had Cuthbert Banks come nearer to throwing in the towel. Vladimir specialised in grey studies of hopeless misery, where nothing happened till page three hundred and eighty, when the moujik decided to commit suicide. It was tough going for a man whose deepest reading hitherto had been Vardon on the Push-Shot, and there can be no greater proof of the magic of love than the fact that Cuthbert stuck it without a cry.

But the strain was terrible and I am inclined to think that he must have cracked, had it not been for the daily reports in the papers of the internecine strife which was proceeding so briskly in Russia.

Cuthbert was an optimist at heart, and it seemed to him that, at the rate at which the inhabitants of that interesting country were murdering one another, the supply of Russian novelists must eventually give out.

One morning, as he tottered down the road for the short walk which was now almost the only exercise to which he was equal, Cuthbert met Adeline. A spasm of anguish flitted through all his nerve-centres as he saw that she was accompanied by Raymond Parsloe Devine.

'Good morning, Mr Banks,' said Adeline.

'Good morning,' said Cuthbert hollowly.

'Such good news about Vladimir Brusiloff.'

'Dead?' said Cuthbert, with a touch of hope.

'Dead? Of course not. Why should he be? No, Aunt Emily met his manager after his lecture at Queen's Hall yesterday, and he has promised that Mr Brusiloff shall come to her next Wednesday reception.'

'Oh, ah!' said Cuthbert, dully.

'I don't know how she managed it. I think she must have told him that Mr Devine would be there to meet him.'

'But you said he was coming,' argued Cuthbert.

'I shall be very glad,' said Raymond Devine, 'of the opportunity of meeting Brusiloff.'

'I'm sure,' said Adeline, 'he will be very glad of the opportunity of meeting you.'

'Possibly,' said Mr Devine. 'Possibly. Competent critics have said that my work closely resembles that of the great Russian Masters.'

'Your psychology is so deep.'

'Yes, yes.'

'And your atmosphere.'

'Quite.'

Cuthbert in a perfect agony of spirit prepared to withdraw from this love-feast. The sun was shining brightly, but the world was black to him. Birds sang in the tree-tops, but he did not hear them. He might have been a moujik for all the pleasure he found in life.

'You will be there, Mr Banks?' said Adeline, as he turned away.

'Oh, all right,' said Cuthbert.

When Cuthbert had entered the drawing-room on the following Wednesday and had taken his usual place in a distant corner where, while able to feast his gaze on Adeline, he had a sporting chance of being overlooked or mistaken for a piece of furniture, he perceived the great Russian thinker seated in the midst of a circle of admiring females. Raymond Parsloe Devine had not yet arrived.

His first glance at the novelist surprised Cuthbert. Doubtless with the best motives, Vladimir Brusiloff had permitted his face to become almost entirely concealed behind a dense zareba of hair, but his eyes were visible through the undergrowth, and it seemed to Cuthbert that there was an expression in them not unlike that of a cat in a strange backyard surrounded by small boys. The man looked forlorn and hopeless, and Cuthbert wondered whether he had had bad news from home.

This was not the case. The latest news which Vladimir Brusiloff had had from Russia had been particularly cheering. Three of his principal creditors had perished in the last massacre of the *bourgeoisie*, and a man whom he owed for five years for a samovar and a pair of overshoes had fled the country, and had not been heard of since. It was not bad news from home that was depressing Vladimir. What was wrong with him was the fact that this was the eighty-second suburban literary reception he had been compelled to attend since he had landed in the country on his lecturing tour, and he was sick to death of it. When his agent had first suggested the trip, he had signed on the dotted line without an instant's hesitation. Worked out in roubles, the fees offered had seemed just about right. But now, as he peered through the brushwood at the faces round him, and realised that eight out of ten of those present had manuscripts of some sort concealed on their persons, and were only waiting for an opportunity to whip them out and start reading, he wished that he had stayed at his quiet home in Nijni-Novgorod, where the worst thing that could happen to a fellow was a brace of bombs coming in through the window and mixing themselves up with his breakfast egg.

At this point in his meditations he was aware that his hostess was looming up before him with a pale young man in horn-rimmed spectacles at her side. There was in Mrs Smethurst's demeanour something of the unction of the master-of-ceremonies at the big fight who introduces the earnest gentleman who wishes to challenge the winner.

'Oh, Mr Brusiloff,' said Mrs Smethurst, 'I do so want you to meet Mr Raymond Parsloe Devine, whose work I expect you know. He is one of our younger novelists.'

The distinguished visitor peered in a wary and defensive manner through the shrubbery, but did not speak. Inwardly he was thinking how exactly like Mr Devine was to the eighty-one other younger novelists to whom he had been introduced at various hamlets throughout the country.

Raymond Parsloe Devine bowed courteously, while Cuthbert, wedged into his corner, glowered at him.

'The critics,' said Mr Devine, 'have been kind enough to say that my poor efforts contain a good deal of the Russian spirit. I owe much to the great Russians. I have been greatly influenced by Sovietski.'

Down in the forest something stirred. It was Vladimir Brusiloff's mouth opening, as he prepared to speak. He was not a man who prattled readily, especially in a foreign tongue. He gave the impression that each word was excavated from his interior by some up-to-date process of mining. He glared bleakly at Mr Devine, and allowed three words to drop out of him.

'Sovietski no good!'

He paused for a moment, set the machinery working again, and delivered five more at the pithead.

'I spit me of Sovietski!'

There was a painful sensation. The lot of a popular idol is in many ways an enviable one, but it has the drawback of uncertainty. Here today and gone tomorrow. Until this moment Raymond Parsloe Devine's stock had stood at something considerably over par in Wood Hills intellectual circles, but now there was a rapid slump. Hitherto he had been greatly admired for being influenced by Sovietski, but it appeared now that this was not a good thing to be. It was evidently a rotten thing to be. The law could not touch you for being influenced by Sovietski, but there is an ethical as well as a legal code, and this it was obvious that Raymond Parsloe Devine had transgressed. Women drew away from him slightly, holding their skirts. Men looked at him censoriously. Adeline Smethurst started violently, and dropped a tea-cup. And Cuthbert Banks, doing his popular imitation of a sardine in his corner, felt for the first time that life held something of sunshine.

Raymond Parsloe Devine was plainly shaken, but he made an adroit attempt to recover his lost prestige.

'When I say I have been influenced by Sovietski, I mean, of course, that I was once under his spell. A young writer commits many follies. I have long since passed through that phase. The false glamour of Sovietski has ceased to dazzle me. I now belong wholeheartedly to the school of Nastikoff.'

There was a reaction. People nodded at one another sympathetically. After all, we cannot expect old heads on young shoulders, and a lapse at the outset of one's career should not be held against one who has eventually seen the light.

'Nastikoff no good,' said Vladimir Brusiloff, coldly. He paused, listening to the machinery. 'Nastikoff worse than Sovietski.' He paused again. 'I spit me of Nastikoff!' he said.

This time there was no doubt about it. The bottom had dropped out of the market, and Raymond Parsloe Devine Preferred were down in the cellar with no takers. It was clear to the entire assembled company that they had been all wrong about Raymond Parsloe Devine. They had allowed him to play on their innocence and sell them a pup. They had taken him at his own valuation, and had been cheated into admiring him as a man who amounted to something, and all the while he had belonged to the school of Nastikoff. You never can tell. Mrs Smethurst's guests were well-bred, and there was consequently no violent demonstration, but you could see by their faces what they felt. Those nearest Raymond Parsloe jostled to get further away. Mrs Smethurst eyed him stonily through a raised lorgnette. One or two low hisses were heard, and over at the other end of the room somebody opened the window in a marked manner.

Raymond Parsloe Devine hesitated for a moment, then, realising his situation, turned and slunk to the door. There was an audible sigh of relief as it closed behind him.

Vladimir Brusiloff proceeded to sum up.

'No novelists any good except me. Sovietski – yah! Nastikoff – bah! I spit me of zem all. No novelists anywhere any good except me. P. G. Wodehouse and Tolstoi not bad. Not good, but not bad. No novelists any good except me.'

And, having uttered this dictum, he removed a slab of cake from a near-by plate, steered it through the jungle, and began to champ.

It is too much to say that there was a dead silence. There could never be that in any room in which Vladimir Brusiloff was eating cake. But certainly what you might call the general chit-chat was pretty well down and out. Nobody liked to be the first to speak.

The members of the Wood Hills Literary Society looked at one another timidly. Cuthbert, for his part, gazed at Adeline; and Adeline gazed into space. It was plain that the girl was deeply stirred. Her eyes were opened wide, a faint flush crimsoned her cheeks, and her breath was coming quickly.

Adeline's mind was in a whirl. She felt as if she had been walking gaily along a pleasant path and had stopped suddenly on the very brink of a precipice. It would be idle to deny that Raymond Parsloe Devine had attracted her extraordinarily. She had taken him at his own valuation as an extremely hot potato, and her hero-worship had gradually been turning into love. And now her hero had been shown to have feet of clay. It was hard, I consider, on Raymond Parsloe Devine, but that is how it goes in this world. You get a following as a celebrity, and then you run up against another bigger celebrity and your admirers desert you. One could moralise on this at considerable length, but better not, perhaps. Enough to say that the glamour of Raymond Devine ceased abruptly in that moment for Adeline, and her most coherent thought at this juncture was the resolve, as soon as she got up to her room, to burn the three signed photographs he had sent her and to give the autographed presentation set of his books to the grocer's boy.

Mrs Smethurst, meanwhile, having rallied somewhat, was endeavouring to set the feast of reason and flow of soul going again.

'And how do you like England, Mr Brusiloff?' she asked.

The celebrity paused in the act of lowering another segment of cake.

'Dam good,' he replied, cordially.

'I suppose you have travelled all over the country by this time?'

'You said it,' agreed the Thinker.

'Have you met many of our great public men?'

'Yais – Yais – Quite a few of the nibs – Lloyid Gorge, I meet him. But—' Beneath the matting a discontented expression came into his face, and his voice took on a peevish note. 'But I not meet your real great men – your Arbmishel, your Arreevadon – I not meet them. That's what gives me the pipovitch. Have *you* ever met Arbmishel and Arreevadon?'

A strained, anguished look came into Mrs Smethurst's face and was reflected in the faces of the other members of the circle. The eminent Russian had sprung two entirely new ones on them, and they felt that their ignorance was about to be exposed. What would Vladimir Brusiloff think of the Wood Hills Literary Society? The reputation of the Wood Hills Literary Society was at stake, trembling in the balance, and coming up for the third time. In dumb agony Mrs Smethurst rolled her eyes about the room searching for someone capable of coming to the rescue. She drew blank.

And then, from a distant corner, there sounded a deprecating, cough, and those nearest Cuthbert Banks saw that he had stopped twisting his right foot round his left ankle and his left foot round his right ankle and was sitting up with a light of almost human intelligence in his eyes.

'Er – ' said Cuthbert, blushing as every eye in the room seemed to fix itself on him, 'I think he means Abe Mitchell and Harry Vardon.'

'Abe Mitchell and Harry Vardon?' repeated Mrs Smethurst, blankly. 'I never heard of—'

'Yais! Yais! Most! Very!' shouted Vladimir Brusiloff, enthusiastically. 'Arbmishel and Arreevadon. You know them, yes, what, no, perhaps?'

'I've played with Abe Mitchell often, and I was partnered with Harry Vardon in last year's Open.'

The great Russian uttered a cry that shook the chandelier.

'You play in ze Open? Why,' he demanded reproachfully of Mrs Smethurst, 'was I not been introduced to this young man who play in opens?'

'Well, really,' faltered Mrs Smethurst. 'Well, the fact is, Mr Brusiloff—'

She broke off. She was unequal to the task of explaining, without hurting anyone's feelings, that she had always regarded Cuthbert as a piece of cheese and a blot on the landscape.

'Introduce me!' thundered the Celebrity.

'Why, certainly, certainly, of course. This is Mr—'

She looked appealingly at Cuthbert.

'Banks,' prompted Cuthbert.

'Banks!' cried Vladimir Brusiloff. 'Not Cootaboot Banks?'

'*Is* your name Cootaboot?' asked Mrs Smethurst, faintly.

'Well, it's Cuthbert.'

'Yais! Yais! Cootaboot!' There was a rush and swirl, as the effervescent Muscovite burst his way through the throng and rushed to where Cuthbert sat. He stood for a moment eyeing him excitedly, then, stooping swiftly, kissed him on both cheeks before Cuthbert could get his guard up. 'My dear young man, I saw you win ze French Open. Great! Great! Grand! Superb! Hot stuff, and you can say I said so! Will you permit one who is but eighteen at Nijni-Novgorod to salute you once more?'

And he kissed Cuthbert again. Then, brushing aside one or two intellectuals who were in the way, he dragged up a chair and sat down.

'You are a great man!' he said.

'Oh, no,' said Cuthbert modestly.

'Yais! Great. Most! Very! The way you lay your approach-putts dead from anywhere!'

'Oh, I don't know.'

Mr Brusiloff drew his chair closer.

'Let me tell you one vairy funny story about putting. It was one day I play at Nijni-Novgorod with the pro. against Lenin and Trotsky, and Trotsky had a two-inch putt for the hole. But, just as he addresses the ball, someone in the crowd he tries to assassinate Lenin with a rewolwer – you know that is our great national sport, trying to assassinate Lenin with rewolwers – and the bang puts Trotsky off his stroke and he goes five yards past the hole, and then Lenin, who is rather shaken, you understand, he misses again himself, and we win the hole and match and I clean up three hundred and ninety-six thousand roubles, or fifteen shillings in your money. Some gameovitch! And now let me tell you one other vairy funny story—'

Desultory conversation had begun in murmurs over the rest of the room, as the Wood Hills intellectuals politely endeavoured to conceal the fact that they realised that they were about as much out of it at this re-union of twin souls as cats at a dog-show. From time to time they started as Vladimir Brusiloff's laugh boomed out. Perhaps it was a consolation to them to know that he was enjoying himself.

As for Adeline, how shall I describe her emotions? She was stunned. Before her very eyes the stone which the builders had rejected had become the main thing, the hundred-to-one shot had walked away with the race. A rush of tender admiration for Cuthbert Banks flooded her heart.

She saw that she had been all wrong. Cuthbert, whom she had always treated with a patronising superiority, was really a man to be looked up to and worshipped. A deep, dreamy sigh shook Adeline's fragile form.

Half an hour later Vladimir and Cuthbert Banks rose.

'Goot-a-bye, Mrs Smet-thirst,' said the Celebrity. 'Zank you for a most charming visit. My friend Cootaboot and me we go now to shoot a few holes. You will lend me clobs, friend Cootaboot?'

'Any you want.'

'The niblicksky is what I use most. Goot-a-bye, Mrs Smet-thirst.'

They were moving to the door, when Cuthbert felt a light touch on his arm. Adeline was looking up at him tenderly.

'May I come, too, and walk round with you?'

Cuthbert's bosom heaved.

'Oh,' he said, with a tremor in his voice, 'that you would walk round with me for life!'

Her eyes met his.

'Perhaps,' she whispered, softly, 'it could be arranged.'

*

'And so,' (concluded the Oldest Member), 'you see that golf can be of the greatest practical assistance to a man in Life's struggle. Raymond Parsloe Devine, who was no player, had to move out of the neighbourhood immediately, and is now, I believe, writing scenarios out in California for the Flicker Film Company. Adeline is married to Cuthbert, and it was only his earnest pleading which prevented her from having their eldest son christened Abe Mitchell Ribbed-Faced Mashie Banks, for she is now as keen a devotee of the great game as her husband. Those who know them say that theirs is a union so devoted, so—'

*

The Sage broke off abruptly, for the young man had rushed to the door and out into the passage. Through the open door he could hear him crying passionately to the waiter to bring back his clubs.

'THE MAGIC PLUS
FOURS'

In May 1923 Wodehouse felt moved to record a great leap forward, into the golden age of his golf game: he wrote to Denis Mackail with the news that he had 'improved my golf beyond my wildest dreams. You will scarcely credit it, but I now go round almost habitually in the 80s – generally 85 – and once did a 79.' What spurs a golfer – or any sportsperson – to such notable improvement? In the words of the great Severiano Ballesteros: 'To give yourself the best possible chance of playing to your potential, you must prepare for every eventuality. That means practice.' And over the preceding winter of 1922–23 Wodehouse had indeed been playing eighteen holes near enough daily.

That said, accounts of diligent practice leading to successful execution don't make for very lively storytelling; whereas the influence of the dark arts, of black magic ... that is another matter entirely, and broached here in one of Wodehouse's rare forays into the twilight zone.

'After all,' said the young man, 'golf is only a game.'

He spoke bitterly and with the air of one who has been following a train of thought. He had come into the smoking-room of the club-house in low spirits at the dusky close of a November evening, and for some minutes had been sitting, silent and moody, staring at the log fire.

'Merely a pastime,' said the young man.

The Oldest Member, nodding in his arm-chair, stiffened with horror, and glanced quickly over his shoulder to make sure that none of the waiters had heard these terrible words.

'Can this be George William Pennefather speaking! ' he said, reproachfully. 'My boy, you are not yourself.'

The young man flushed a little beneath his tan: for he had had a good upbringing and was not bad at heart.

'Perhaps I ought not to have gone quite so far as that,' he admitted. 'I was only thinking that a fellow's got no right, just because he happens to have come on a bit in his form lately, to treat a fellow as if a fellow was a leper or something.'

The Oldest Member's face cleared, and he breathed a relieved sigh.

'Ah! I see,' he said. 'You spoke hastily and in a sudden fit of pique because something upset you out on the links today. Tell me all. Let me see, you were playing with Nathaniel Frisby this afternoon, were you not? I gather that he beat you.'

'Yes, he did. Giving me a third. But it isn't being beaten that I mind. What I object to is having the blighter behave as if he were a sort of champion condescending to a mere mortal. Dash it, it seemed to bore him playing with me! Every time I sliced off the tee he looked at me as if I were a painful ordeal. Twice when I was having a bit of trouble in the bushes I caught him yawning. And after we had finished he started talking about what a good game croquet was, and he wondered more people didn't take it up. And it's only a month or so ago that I could play the man level!'

The Oldest Member shook his snowy head sadly.

'There is nothing to be done about it,' he said. 'We can only hope that the poison will in time work its way out of the man's system. Sudden success at golf is like the sudden acquisition of wealth. It is apt to unsettle and deteriorate the character. And, as it comes almost miraculously, so only a miracle can effect a cure. The best advice I can give you is to refrain from playing with Nathaniel Frisby till you can keep your tee-shots straight.'

'Oh, but don't run away with the idea that I wasn't pretty good off the tee this afternoon!' said the young man. 'I should like to describe to you the shot I did on the—'

'Meanwhile,' proceeded the Oldest Member, 'I will relate to you a little story which bears on what I have been saying.'

'From the very moment I addressed the ball—'

'It is the story of two loving hearts temporarily estranged owing to the sudden and unforeseen proficiency of one of the couple—'

'I waggled quickly and strongly, like Duncan. Then, swinging smoothly back, rather in the Vardon manner—'

'But as I see,' said the Oldest Member, 'that you are all impatience for me to begin, I will do so without further preamble.'

To the philosophical student of golf like myself (said the Oldest Member) perhaps the most outstanding virtue of this noble pursuit is the fact that it is a medicine for the soul. Its great service to humanity is that it teaches human beings that, whatever petty triumphs they may have achieved in other walks of life, they are after all merely human. It acts as a corrective against sinful pride. I attribute the insane arrogance of the later Roman emperors almost entirely to the fact that, never having played golf, they never knew that strange chastening humility which is engendered by a topped chip-shot. If Cleopatra had been outed in the first round of the Ladies' Singles, we should have heard a lot less of her proud imperiousness. And, coming down to modern times, it was undoubtedly his rotten golf that kept Wallace Chesney the nice unspoiled fellow he was. For in every other respect he had everything in the world calculated to make a man conceited and arrogant. He was the best-looking man for miles around; his health was perfect; and, in addition to this, he was rich; danced, rode, played bridge and polo with equal skill; and was engaged to be married to Charlotte Dix. And when you saw Charlotte Dix you realised that being engaged to her would by itself have been quite enough luck for any one man.

But Wallace, as I say, despite all his advantages, was a thoroughly nice, modest young fellow. And I attribute this to the fact that, while one of the keenest golfers in the club, he was also one of the worst players. Indeed, Charlotte Dix used to say to me in his presence that she could not understand why people paid money to go to the circus when by merely walking over the brow of a hill they could watch Wallace Chesney trying to get out of the bunker by the eleventh green. And Wallace took the gibe with perfect good humour, for there was a delightful camaraderie between them which robbed it of any sting. Often at lunch in the club-house I used to hear him and Charlotte planning the handicapping details of a proposed match between Wallace and a non-existent cripple whom Charlotte claimed to have discovered in the village – it being agreed finally that he should accept seven bisques from the cripple, but that, if the latter ever recovered the use of his arms, Wallace should get a stroke a hole.

In short, a thoroughly happy and united young couple. Two hearts, if I may coin an expression, that beat as one.

I would not have you misjudge Wallace Chesney. I may have given you the impression that his attitude towards golf was light and frivolous, but such was not the case. As I have said, he was one of the keenest members of the club. Love made him receive the joshing of his *fiancée* in the kindly spirit in which it was meant, but at heart he was as earnest as you could wish. He practised early and late; he bought golf books; and the mere sight of a patent club of any description acted on him like catnip on a cat. I remember remonstrating with him on the occasion of his purchasing a wooden-faced driving-mashie which weighed about two pounds, and was, taking it for all in all, as foul an instrument as ever came out of the workshop of a club-maker who had been dropped on the head by his nurse when a baby.

'I know, I know,' he said, when I had finished indicating some of the weapon's more obvious defects. 'But the point is, I believe in it. It gives me confidence. I don't believe you could slice with a thing like that if you tried.'

Confidence! That was what Wallace Chesney lacked, and that, as he saw it, was the prime grand secret of golf. Like an alchemist on the track of the Philosopher's Stone, he was for ever seeking for something which would really give him confidence. I recollect that he even tried repeating to himself fifty times every morning the words, 'Every day in every way I grow better and better.' This, however, proved such a black lie that he gave it up. The fact is, the man was a visionary, and it is to auto-hypnosis of some kind that I attribute the extraordinary change that came over him at the beginning of his third season.

You may have noticed in your perambulations about the City a shop bearing above its door and upon its windows the legend :

COHEN BROS.,
Second-hand Clothiers

a statement which is borne out by endless vistas seen through the door of every variety of what is technically known as Gents' Wear. But the Brothers Cohen, though their main stock-in-trade is garments which have been rejected by their owners for one reason or another, do not confine their dealings to Gents' Wear. The place is a museum of derelict goods of every description. You can get a second-hand revolver there, or a second-hand sword, or a second-hand umbrella. You can do a cheap deal in field-glasses, trunks, dog collars, canes, photograph frames, attaché cases, and bowls for goldfish. And on the bright spring morning when Wallace Chesney happened to pass by there was exhibited in the window a putter of such pre-eminently lunatic design that he stopped dead as if he had run into an invisible wall, and then, panting like an overwrought fish, charged in through the door.

The shop was full of the Cohen family, sombre-eyed, smileless men with purposeful expressions; and two of these, instantly descending upon Wallace Chesney like leopards, began in swift silence to thrust him into a suit of yellow tweed. Having worked the coat over his shoulders with a shoe-horn, they stood back to watch the effect.

'A beautiful fit,' announced Isidore Cohen.

'A little snug under the arms,' said his brother Irving. 'But that'll give.'

'The warmth of the body will make it give,' said Isidore.

'Or maybe you'll lose weight in the summer,' said Irving.

Wallace, when he had struggled out of the coat and was able to breathe, said that he had come in to buy a putter. Isidore thereupon sold him the putter, a dog collar, and a set of studs, and Irving sold him a fireman's helmet: and he was about to leave when their elder brother Lou, who had just finished fitting out another customer, who had come in to buy a cap, with two pairs of trousers and a miniature aquarium for keeping newts in, saw that business was in progress and strolled up. His fathomless eye rested on Wallace, who was toying feebly with the putter.

'You play golf?' asked Lou. 'Then looka here!'

He dived into an alleyway of dead clothing, dug for a moment, and emerged with something at the sight of which Wallace Chesney, hardened golfer that he was, blenched and threw up an arm defensively.

'No, no!' he cried.

The object which Lou Cohen was waving insinuatingly before his eyes was a pair of those golfing breeches which are technically known as Plus Fours. A player of two years' standing, Wallace Chesney was not unfamiliar with Plus Fours – all the club cracks wore them – but he had never seen Plus Fours like these. What might be termed the main motif of the fabric was a curious vivid pink, and with this to work on the architect had let his imagination run free, and had produced so much variety in the way of chessboard squares of white, yellow, violet, and green that the eye swam as it looked upon them.

'These were made to measure for Sandy McHoots, the Open Champion,' said Lou, stroking the left leg lovingly. 'But he sent 'em back for some reason or other.'

'Perhaps they frightened the children,' said Wallace, recollecting having heard that Mr McHoots was a married man.

'They'll fit you nice,' said Lou.

'Sure they'll fit him nice,' said Isidore, warmly.

'Why, just take a look at yourself in the glass,' said Irving, 'and see if they don't fit you nice.'

And, as one who wakes from a trance, Wallace discovered that his lower limbs were now encased in the prismatic garment. At what point in the proceedings the brethren had slipped them on him, he could not have said. But he was undeniably in.

Wallace looked in the glass. For a moment, as he eyed his reflection, sheer horror gripped him. Then suddenly, as he gazed, he became aware that his first feelings were changing. The initial shock over, he was becoming calmer. He waggled his right leg with a certain sang-froid.

There is a certain passage in the works of the poet Pope with which you may be familiar. It runs as follows:

> 'Vice is a monster of so frightful mien
> As to be hated needs but to be seen :
> Yet seen too oft, familiar with her face,
> We first endure, then pity, then embrace.'

Even so was it with Wallace Chesney and these Plus Fours. At first he had recoiled from them as any decent-minded man would have done. Then, after a while, almost abruptly he found himself in the grip of a new emotion. After an unsuccessful attempt to analyse this, he suddenly got it.

Amazing as it may seem, it was pleasure that he felt. He caught his eye in the mirror, and it was smirking. Now that the things were actually on, by Hutchinson, they didn't look half bad. By Braid, they didn't. There was a sort of something about them. Take away that expanse of bare leg with its unsightly sock-suspender and substitute a woolly stocking, and you would have the lower section of a golfer. For the first time in his life, he thought, he looked like a man who could play golf.

There came to him an odd sensation of masterfulness. He was still holding the putter, and now he swung it up above his shoulder. A fine swing, all lissomness and supple grace, quite different from any swing he had ever done before.

Wallace Chesney gasped. He knew that at last he had discovered that prime grand secret of golf for which he had searched so long. It was the costume that did it. All you had to do was wear Plus Fours. He had always hitherto played in grey flannel trousers. Naturally he had not been able to do himself justice. Golf required an easy dash, and how could you be easily dashing in concertina-shaped trousers with a patch on the knee? He saw now – what he had never seen before – that it was not because they were crack players that crack players wore Plus Fours: it was because they wore Plus Fours that they were crack players.

And these Plus Fours had been the property of an Open Champion. Wallace Chesney's bosom swelled, and he was filled, as by some strange gas, with joy – with excitement – with confidence. Yes, for the first time in his golfing life, he felt really confident.

True, the things might have been a shade less gaudy: they might perhaps have hit the eye with a slightly less violent punch: but what of that? True, again, he could scarcely hope to avoid the censure of his club-mates when he appeared like this on the links: but what of that? His club-mates must set their teeth and learn to bear these Plus Fours like men. That was what Wallace Chesney thought about it. If they did not like his Plus Fours, let them go and play golf somewhere else.

'How much?' he muttered, thickly. And the Brothers Cohen clustered grimly round with notebooks and pencils.

In predicting a stormy reception for his new apparel, Wallace Chesney had not been unduly pessimistic. The moment he entered the club-house Disaffection reared its ugly head. Friends of years' standing called loudly for the committee, and there was a small and vehement party of the left wing, headed by Raymond Gandle, who was an artist by profession, and consequently had a sensitive eye, which advocated the tearing off and public burial of the obnoxious garment. But, prepared as he had been for some such demonstration on the part of the coarser-minded, Wallace had hoped for better things when he should meet Charlotte Dix, the girl who loved him. Charlotte, he had supposed, would understand and sympathise.

Instead of which, she uttered a piercing cry and staggered to a bench, whence a moment later she delivered her ultimatum.

'Quick!' she said. 'Before I have to look again.'

'What do you mean?'

'Pop straight back into the changing-room while I've got my eyes shut, and remove the fancy-dress.'

'What's wrong with them?'

'Darling,' said Charlotte, 'I think it's sweet and patriotic of you to be proud of your cycling club colours or whatever they are, but you mustn't wear them on the links. It will unsettle the caddies.'

'They *are* a trifle on the bright side,' admitted Wallace. 'But it helps my game, wearing them. I was trying a few practice-shots just now, and I couldn't go wrong. Slammed the ball on the meat every time. They inspire me, if you know what I mean. Come on, let's be starting.'

Charlotte opened her eyes incredulously.

'You can't seriously mean that you're really going to *play* in – those? It's against the rules. There must be a rule somewhere in the book against coming out looking like a sunset. Won't you go and burn them for my sake?'

'But I tell you they give me confidence. I sort of squint down at them when I'm addressing the ball, and I feel like a pro'

'Then the only thing to do is for me to play you for them. Come on, Wally, be a sportsman. I'll give you a half and play you for the whole outfit – the breeches, the red jacket, the little cap, and the belt with the snake's-head buckle. I'm sure all those things must have gone with the breeches. Is it a bargain?'

Strolling on the club-house terrace some two hours later, Raymond Gandle encountered Charlotte and Wallace coming up from the eighteenth green.

'Just the girl I wanted to see,' said Raymond. 'Miss Dix, I represent a select committee of my fellow-members, and I have come to ask you on their behalf to use the influence of a good woman to induce Wally to destroy those Plus Fours of his, which we all consider nothing short of Bolshevik propaganda and a menace to the public weal. May I rely on you?'

'You may not,' retorted Charlotte. 'They are the poor boy's mascot. You've no idea how they have improved his game. He has just beaten me hollow. I am going to try to learn to bear them, so you must. Really, you've no notion how he has come on. My cripple won't be able to give him more than a couple of bisques if he keeps up this form.'

'It's something about the things,' said Wallace. 'They give me confidence.'

'They give *me* a pain in the neck,' said Raymond Gandle.

To the thinking man nothing is more remarkable in this life than the way in which Humanity adjusts itself to conditions which at their outset might well have appeared intolerable. Some great cataclysm occurs, some storm or earthquake, shaking the community to its foundations; and after the first pardonable consternation one finds the sufferers resuming their ordinary pursuits as if nothing had happened. There have been few more striking examples of this adaptability than the behaviour of the members of our golf-club under the impact of Wallace Chesney's Plus Fours. For the first few days it is not too much to say that they were stunned. Nervous players sent their caddies on in front of them at blind holes, so that they might be warned in time of Wallace's presence ahead and not have him happening to them all of a sudden. And even the pro. was not unaffected. Brought up in Scotland in an atmosphere of tartan kilts, he nevertheless winced, and a startled 'Hoots!' was forced from his lips when Wallace Chesney suddenly appeared in the valley as he was about to drive from the fifth tee.

But in about a week conditions were back to normalcy. Within ten days the Plus Fours became a familiar feature of the landscape, and were accepted as such without comment. They were pointed out to strangers together with the waterfall, the Lovers' Leap, and the view from the eighth green as things you ought not to miss when visiting the course; but apart from that one might almost say they were ignored. And meanwhile Wallace Chesney continued day by day to make the most extraordinary progress in his play.

As I said before, and I think you will agree with me when I have told you what happened subsequently, it was probably a case of auto-hypnosis. There is no other sphere in which a belief in oneself has such immediate effects as it has in golf. And Wallace, having acquired self-confidence, went on from strength to strength. In under a week he had ploughed his way through the Unfortunate Incidents – of which class Peter Willard was the best example – and was challenging the fellows who kept three shots in five somewhere on the fairway. A month later he was holding his own with ten-handicap men. And by the middle of the summer he was so far advanced that his name occasionally cropped up in speculative talks on the subject of the July medal. One might have been excused for supposing that, as far as Wallace Chesney was concerned, all was for the best in the best of all possible worlds.

And yet –

The first inkling I received that anything was wrong came through a chance meeting with Raymond Gandle, who happened to pass my gate on his way back from the links just as I drove up in my taxi; for I had been away from home for many weeks on a pro-tracted business tour. I welcomed Gandle's advent and invited him in to smoke a pipe and put me abreast of local gossip. He came readily enough – and seemed, indeed, to have something on his mind and to be glad of the opportunity of revealing it to a sym-pathetic auditor.

'And how,' I asked him, when we were comfortably settled, 'did your game this afternoon come out?'

'Oh, he beat me,' said Gandle, and it seemed to me that there was a note of bitterness in his voice.

'Then He, whoever he was, must have been an extremely competent performer? ' I replied, courteously, for Gandle was one of the finest players in the club. 'Unless, of course, you were giving him some impossible handicap.'

'No; we played level.'

'Indeed! Who was your opponent?'

'Chesney.'

'Wallace Chesney! And he beat you, playing level! This is the most amazing thing I have ever heard.'

'He's improved out of all knowledge.'

'He must have done. Do you think he would ever beat you again?'

'No. Because he won't have the chance.'

'You surely do not mean that you will not play him because you are afraid of being beaten?'

'It isn't being beaten I mind.'

And if I omit to report the remainder of his speech it is not merely because it contained expressions with which I am reluctant to sully my lips, but because, omitting these expletives, what he said was almost word for word what you were saying to me just now about Nathaniel Frisby. It was, it seemed, Wallace Chesney's manner, his arrogance, his attitude of belonging to some superior order of being that had so wounded Raymond Gandle. Wallace Chesney had, it appeared, criticised Gandle's mashie-play in no friendly spirit; had hung up the game on the fourteenth tee in order to show him how to place his feet; and on the way back to the club-house had said that the beauty of golf was that the best player could enjoy a round even with a dud, because, though there might be no interest in the match, he could always amuse himself by playing for his medal score.

I was profoundly shaken.

'Wallace Chesney!' I exclaimed. 'Was it really Wallace Chesney who behaved in the manner you describe?'

'Unless he's got a twin brother of the same name, it was.'

'Wallace Chesney a victim to swelled head! I can hardly credit it.'

'Well, you needn't take my word for it unless you want to. Ask anybody. It isn't often he can get anyone to play with him now.'

'You horrify me!'

Raymond Gandle smoked awhile in brooding silence.

'You've heard about his engagement?' he said at length.

'I have heard nothing, nothing. What about his engagement?'

'Charlotte Dix has broken it off.'

'No!'

'Yes. Couldn't stand him any longer.'

I got rid of Gandle as soon as I could. I made my way as quickly as possible to the house where Charlotte lived with her aunt. I was determined to sift this matter to the bottom and to do all that lay in my power to heal the breach between two young people for whom I had a great affection.

'I have just heard the news,' I said, when the aunt had retired to some secret lair, as aunts do, and Charlotte and I were alone.

'What news?' said Charlotte, dully. I thought she looked pale and ill, and she had certainly grown thinner.

'This dreadful news about your engagement to Wallace Chesney. Tell me, why did you do this thing? Is there no hope of a reconciliation?'

'Not unless Wally becomes his old self again.'

'But I had always regarded you two as ideally suited to one another.'

'Wally has completely changed in the last few weeks. Haven't you heard?'

'Only sketchily, from Raymond Gandle.'

'I refuse,' said Charlotte, proudly, all the woman in her leaping to her eyes, 'to marry a man who treats me as if I were a kronen at the present rate of exchange, merely because I slice an occasional tee-shot. The afternoon I broke off the engagement' – her voice shook, and I could see that her indifference was but a mask – 'the afternoon I broke off the en-gug-gug-gagement, he t-told me I ought to use an iron off the tee instead of a dud-dud-driver.'

And the stricken girl burst into an uncontrollable fit of sobbing. And realising that, if matters had gone as far as that, there was little I could do, I pressed her hand silently and left her.

But though it seemed hopeless I decided to persevere. I turned my steps towards Wallace Chesney's bungalow, resolved to make one appeal to the man's better feelings. He was in his sitting-room when I arrived, polishing a putter; and it seemed significant to me even, in that tense moment, that the putter was quite an ordinary one, such as any capable player might use. In the brave old happy days of his dudhood, the only putters you ever found in the society of Wallace Chesney were patent self-adjusting things that looked like croquet mallets that had taken the wrong turning in childhood.

'Well, Wallace, my boy,' I said.

'Hallo!' said Wallace Chesney. 'So you're back?'

We fell into conversation, and I had not been in the room two minutes before I realised that what I had been told about the change in him was nothing more than the truth. The man's bearing and his every remark were insufferably bumptious. He spoke of his prospects in the July medal competition as if the issue were already settled. He scoffed at his rivals.

I had some little difficulty in bringing the talk round to the matter which I had come to discuss.

'My boy,' I said at length, 'I have just heard the sad news.'

'What sad news?'

'I have been talking to Charlotte.'

'Oh, that!' said Wallace Chesney.

'She was telling me.'

'Perhaps it's all for the best.'

'All for the best? What do you mean?'

'Well,' said Wallace, 'one doesn't wish, of course, to say anything ungallant, but, after all, poor Charlotte's handicap is fourteen and wouldn't appear to have much chance of getting any lower. I mean, there's such a thing as a fellow throwing himself away.'

Was I revolted at these callous words? For a moment, yes. Then it struck me that, though he had uttered them with a light laugh, that laugh had had in it more than a touch of bravado. I looked at him keenly. There was a bored, discontented expression in his eyes, a line of pain about his mouth.

'My boy,' I said, gravely, 'you are not happy.'

For an instant I think he would have denied the imputation. But my visit had coincided with one of those twilight moods in which a man requires, above all else, sympathy. He uttered a weary sigh.

'I'm fed up,' he admitted. 'It's a funny thing. When I was a dud, I used to think how perfect it must be to be scratch. I used to watch the cracks buzzing round the course and envy them. It's all a fraud. The only time when you enjoy golf is when an occasional decent shot is enough to make you happy for the day. I'm plus two, and I'm bored to death. I'm too good. And what's the result? Everybody's jealous of me. Everybody's got it in for me. Nobody loves me.'

His voice rose in a note of anguish, and at the sound his terrier, which had been sleeping on the rug, crept forward and licked his hand.

'The dog loves you,' I said, gently, for I was touched.

'Yes, but I don't love the dog,' said Wallace Chesney.

'Now come, Wallace,' I said. 'Be reasonable, my boy. It is only your unfortunate manner on the links which has made you perhaps a little unpopular at the moment. Why not pull yourself up? Why ruin your whole life with this arrogance? All that you need is a little tact, a little forbearance. Charlotte, I am sure, is just as fond of you as ever, but you have wounded her pride. Why must you be unkind about her tee-shots?'

Wallace Chesney shook his head despondently.

'I can't help it,' he said. 'It exasperates me to see anyone foozling, and I have to say so.'

'Then there is nothing to be done,' I said, sadly.

All the medal competitions at our club are, as you know, important events; but, as you are also aware, none of them is looked forward to so keenly or contested so hotly as the one in July. At the beginning of the year of which I am speaking, Raymond Gandle had been considered the probable winner of the fixture; but as the season progressed and Wallace Chesney's skill developed to such a remarkable extent most of us were reluctantly inclined to put our money on the latter. Reluctantly, because Wallace's unpopularity was now so general that the thought of his winning was distasteful to all. It grieved me to see how cold his fellow-members were towards him. He drove off from the first tee without a solitary hand-clap; and, though the drive was of admirable quality and nearly carried the green, there was not a single cheer. I noticed Charlotte Dix among the spectators. The poor girl was looking sad and wan.

In the draw for partners Wallace had had Peter Willard allotted to him; and he muttered to me in a quite audible voice that it was as bad as handicapping him half-a-dozen strokes to make him play with such a hopeless performer. I do not think Peter heard, but it would not have made much difference to him if he had, for I doubt if anything could have had much effect for the worse on his game. Peter Willard always entered for the medal competition, because he said that competition-play was good for the nerves.

On this occasion he topped his ball badly, and Wallace lit his pipe with the exaggeratedly patient air of an irritated man. When Peter topped his second also, Wallace was moved to speech.

'For goodness' sake,' he snapped, 'what's the good of playing at all if you insist on lifting your head? Keep it down, man, keep it down. You don't need to watch to see where the ball is going. It isn't likely to go as far as all that. Make up your mind to count three before you look up.'

'Thanks,' said Peter, meekly. There was no pride in Peter to be wounded. He knew the sort of player he was.

The couples were now moving off with smooth rapidity, and the course was dotted with the figures of players and their accompanying spectators. A fair proportion of these latter had decided to follow the fortunes of Raymond Gandle, but by far the larger number were sticking to Wallace, who right from the start showed that Gandle or anyone else would have to return a very fine card to beat him. He was out in thirty-seven, two above bogey, and with the assistance of a superb second, which landed the ball within a foot of the pin, got a three on the tenth, where a four is considered good. I mention this to show that by the time he arrived at the short lake-hole Wallace Chesney was at the top of his form. Not even the fact that he had been obliged to let the next couple through owing to Peter Willard losing his ball had been enough to upset him.

The course has been rearranged since, but at that time the lake-hole, which is now the second, was the eleventh, and was generally looked on as the crucial hole in a medal round. Wallace no doubt realised this, but the knowledge did not seem to affect him. He lit his pipe with the utmost coolness: and, having replaced the match-box in his hip-pocket, stood smoking nonchalantly as he waited for the couple in front to get off the green.

They holed out eventually, and Wallace walked to the tee. As he did so, he was startled to receive a resounding smack.

'Sorry,' said Peter Willard, apologetically. 'Hope I didn't hurt you. A wasp.' And he pointed to the corpse, which was lying in a used-up attitude on the ground.

'Afraid it would sting you,' said Peter.

'Oh, thanks,' said Wallace.

He spoke a little stiffly, for Peter Willard had a large, hard, flat hand, the impact of which had shaken him up considerably. Also, there had been laughter in the crowd. He was fuming as he bent to address his ball, and his annoyance became acute when, just as he reached the top of his swing, Peter Willard suddenly spoke.

'Just a second, old man,' said Peter. Wallace spun round, outraged.

'What is it? I do wish you would wait till I've made my shot.'

'Just as you like,' said Peter, humbly.

'There is no greater crime that a man can commit on the links than to speak to a fellow when he's making his stroke.'

'Of course, of course,' acquiesced Peter, crushed.

Wallace turned to his ball once more. He was vaguely conscious of a discomfort to which he could not at the moment give a name. At first he thought that he was having a spasm of lumbago, and this surprised him, for he had never in his life been subject to even a suspicion of that malady. A moment later he realised that this diagnosis had been wrong.

'Good heavens!' he cried, leaping nimbly some two feet into the air. 'I'm on fire!'

'Yes,' said Peter, delighted at his ready grasp of the situation. 'That's what I wanted to mention just now.'

Wallace slapped vigorously at the seat of his Plus Fours.

'It must have been when I killed that wasp,' said Peter, beginning to see clearly into the matter. 'You had a match-box in your pocket.'

Wallace was in no mood to stop and discuss first causes. He was springing up and down on his pyre, beating at the flames.

'Do you know what I should do if I were you?' said Peter Willard. 'I should jump into the lake.'

One of the cardinal rules of golf is that a player shall accept no advice from anyone but his own caddie; but the warmth about his lower limbs had now become so generous that Wallace was prepared to stretch a point. He took three rapid strides and entered the water with a splash.

The lake, though muddy, is not deep, and presently Wallace was to be observed standing up to his waist some few feet from the shore.

'That ought to have put it out,' said Peter Willard. 'It was a bit of luck that it happened at this hole.' He stretched out a hand to the bather. 'Catch hold, old man, and I'll pull you out.'

'No!' said Wallace Chesney.

'Why not?'

'Never mind!' said Wallace, austerely.

He bent as near to Peter as he was able.

'Send a caddie up to the club-house to fetch my grey flannel trousers from my locker,' he whispered, tensely.

'Oh, ah!' said Peter.

It was some little time before Wallace, encircled by a group of male spectators, was enabled to change his costume; and during the interval he continued to stand waist-deep in the water, to the chagrin of various couples who came to the tee in the course of their round and complained with not a little bitterness that his presence there added a mental hazard to an already difficult hole. Eventually, however, he found himself back ashore, his ball before him, his mashie in his hand.

'Carry on,' said Peter Willard, as the couple in front left the green. 'All clear now.'

Wallace Chesney addressed his ball. And, even as he did so, he was suddenly aware that an odd psychological change had taken place in himself. He was aware of a strange weakness. The charred remains of the Plus Fours were lying under an adjacent bush; and, clad in the old grey flannels of his early golfing days, Wallace felt diffident, feeble, uncertain of himself. It was as though virtue had gone out of him, as if some indispensable adjunct to good play had been removed. His corrugated trouser-leg caught his eye as he waggled, and all at once he became acutely alive to the fact that many eyes were watching him. The audience seemed to press on him like a blanket. He felt as he had been wont to feel in the old days when he had had to drive off the first tee in front of a terrace-full of scoffing critics.

The next moment his ball had bounded weakly over the intervening patch of turf and was in the water.

'Hard luck!' said Peter Willard, ever a generous foe. And the words seemed to touch some almost atrophied chord in Wallace's breast. A sudden love for his species flooded over him. Dashed decent of Peter, he thought, to sympathise. Peter was a good chap. So were the spectators good chaps. So was everybody, even his caddie.

Peter Willard, as if resolved to make his sympathy practical, also rolled his ball into the lake.

'Hard luck!' said Wallace Chesney, and started as he said it; for many weeks had passed since he had commiserated with an opponent. He felt a changed man. A better, sweeter, kindlier man. It was as if a curse had fallen from him.

He teed up another ball, and swung.

'Hard luck!' said Peter.

'Hard luck!' said Wallace, a moment later.

'Hard luck!' said Peter, a moment after that.

Wallace Chesney stood on the tee watching the spot in the water where his third ball had fallen. The crowd was now openly amused, and, as he listened to their happy laughter, it was borne in upon Wallace that he, too, was amused and happy. A weird, almost effervescent exhilaration filled him. He turned and beamed upon the spectators. He waved his mashie cheerily at them. This, he felt, was something like golf. This was golf as it should be – not the dull, mechanical thing which had bored him during all these past weeks of his perfection, but a gay, rollicking adventure. That was the soul of golf, the thing that made it the wonderful pursuit it was – that speculative-ness, that not knowing where the dickens your ball was going when you hit it, that eternal hoping for the best, that never-failing chanciness. It is better to travel hopefully than to arrive, and at last this great truth had come home to Wallace Chesney. He realised now why pros were all grave, silent men who seemed to struggle manfully against some secret sorrow. It was because they were too darned good. Golf had no surprises for them, no gallant spirit of adventure.

'I'm going to get a ball over if I stay here all night,' cried Wallace Chesney, gaily, and the crowd echoed his mirth. On the face of Charlotte Dix was the look of a mother whose prodigal son has rolled into the old home once more. She caught Wallace's eye and gesticulated to him blithely.

'The cripple says he'll give you a stroke a hole, Wally!' she shouted.

'I'm ready for him!' bellowed Wallace.

'Hard *luck!*' said Peter Willard.

Under their bush the Plus Fours, charred and dripping, lurked unnoticed. But Wallace Chesney saw them. They caught his eye as he sliced his eleventh into the marshes on the right. It seemed to him that they looked sullen. Disappointed. Baffled.

Wallace Chesney was himself again.

'THE AWAKENING
OF ROLLO PODMARSH'

Down on the new bowling-green behind the club-house some sort of competition was in progress. The seats about the smooth strip of turf were crowded, and the weak-minded yapping of the patients made itself plainly audible to the Oldest Member as he sat in his favourite chair in the smoking-room. He shifted restlessly, and a frown marred the placidity of his venerable brow. To the Oldest Member a golf-club was a golf-club, and he resented the introduction of any alien element. He had opposed the institution of tennis-courts; and the suggestion of a bowling-green had stirred him to his depths.

A young man in spectacles came into the smoking-room. His high forehead was aglow, and he lapped up a ginger-ale with the air of one who considers that he has earned it.

'Capital exercise!' he said, beaming upon the Oldest Member.

The Oldest Member laid down his *Vardon On Casual Water*, and peered suspiciously at his companion.

'What did you go round in?' he asked.

'Oh, I wasn't playing golf,' said the young man. 'Bowls.'

'A nauseous pursuit!' said the Oldest Member, coldly, and resumed his reading.

The young man seemed nettled.

'I don't know why you should say that,' he retorted. 'It's a splendid game.'

'I rank it,' said the Oldest Member, 'with the juvenile pastime of marbles.'

The young man pondered for some moments.

'Well, anyway,' he said at length, 'it was good enough for Drake.'

'As I have not the pleasure of the acquaintance of your friend Drake, I am unable to estimate the value of his endorsement.'

'*The* Drake. The Spanish Armada Drake. He was playing bowls on Plymouth Hoe when they told him that the Armada was in sight. "There is time to finish the game," he replied. That's what Drake thought of bowls.'

'If he had been a golfer he would have ignored the Armada altogether.'

'It's easy enough to say that,' said the young man, with spirit, 'but can the history of golf show a parallel case?'

'A million, I should imagine.'

'But you've forgotten them, eh?' said the young man, satirically.

'On the contrary,' said the Oldest Member. 'As a typical instance, neither more nor less remarkable than a hundred others, I will select the story of Rollo Podmarsh.' He settled himself comfortably in his chair, and placed the tips of his fingers together. 'This Rollo Podmarsh—'

'No, I say!' protested the young man, looking at his watch.

'This Rollo Podmarsh—'

'Yes, but—'

This Rollo Podmarsh (said the Oldest Member) was the only son of his mother, and she was a widow; and like other young men in that position he had rather allowed a mother's tender care to take the edge off what you might call his rugged manliness. Not to put too fine a point on it, he had permitted his parent to coddle him ever since he had been in the nursery; and now, in his twenty-eighth year, he invariably wore flannel next his skin, changed his shoes the moment they got wet, and – from September to May, inclusive – never went to bed without partaking of a bowl of hot arrowroot. Not, you would say, the stuff of which heroes are made. But you would be wrong. Rollo Podmarsh was a golfer, and consequently pure gold at heart; and in his hour of crisis all the good in him came to the surface.

In giving you this character-sketch of Rollo, I have been at pains to make it crisp, for I observe that you are wriggling in a restless manner and you persist in pulling out that watch of yours and gazing at it. Let me tell you that, if a mere skeleton outline of the man has this effect upon you, I am glad for your sake that you never met his mother. Mrs Podmarsh could talk with enjoyment for hours on end about her son's character and habits. And, on the September evening on which I introduce her to you, though she had, as a fact, been speaking only for some ten minutes, it had seemed like hours to the girl, Mary Kent, who was the party of the second part to the conversation.

Mary Kent was the daughter of an old school-friend of Mrs Podmarsh, and she had come to spend the autumn and winter with her while her parents were abroad. The scheme had never looked particularly good to Mary, and after ten minutes of her hostess on the subject of Rollo she was beginning to weave dreams of knotted sheets and a swift getaway through the bedroom window in the dark of the night.

'He is a strict teetotaller,' said Mrs Podmarsh.

'Really?'

'And has never smoked in his life.'

'Fancy that!'

'But here is the dear boy now,' said Mrs Podmarsh, fondly.

Down the road towards them was coming a tall, well-knit figure in a Norfolk coat and grey flannel trousers. Over his broad shoulders was suspended a bag of golf-clubs.

'Is that Mr Podmarsh?' exclaimed Mary.

She was surprised. After all she had been listening to about the arrowroot and the flannel next the skin and the rest of it, she had pictured the son of the house as a far weedier specimen. She had been expecting to meet a small, slender young man with an eyebrow moustache, and pince-nez; and this person approaching might have stepped straight out of Jack Dempsey's training-camp.

'Does he play golf?' asked Mary, herself an enthusiast.

'Oh yes,' said Mrs Podmarsh. 'He makes a point of going out on the links once a day. He says the fresh air gives him such an appetite.'

Mary, who had taken a violent dislike to Rollo on the evidence of his mother's description of his habits, had softened towards him on discovering that he was a golfer. She now reverted to her previous opinion. A man who could play the noble game from such ignoble motives was beyond the pale.

'Rollo is exceedingly good at golf,' proceeded Mrs Podmarsh. 'He scores more than a hundred and twenty every time, while Mr Burns, who is supposed to be one of the best players in the club, seldom manages to reach eighty. But Rollo is very modest – modesty is one of his best qualities – and you would never guess he was so skilful unless you were told.'

'Well, Rollo darling, did you have a nice game? You didn't get your feet wet, I hope? This is Mary Kent, dear.'

Rollo Podmarsh shook hands with Mary. And at her touch the strange dizzy feeling which had come over him at the sight of her suddenly became increased a thousand-fold. As I see that you are consulting your watch once more, I will not describe his emotions as exhaustively as I might. I will merely say that he had never felt anything resembling this sensation of dazed ecstasy since the occasion when a twenty-foot putt of his, which had been going well off the line, as his putts generally did, had hit a worm-cast sou'-sou'-east of the hole and popped in, giving him a snappy six. Rollo Podmarsh, as you will have divined, was in love at first sight. Which makes it all the sadder to think Mary at the moment was regarding him as an outcast and a blister.

Mrs Podmarsh, having enfolded her son in a vehement embrace, drew back with a startled exclamation, sniffing.

'Rollo!' she cried. 'You smell of tobacco-smoke.'

Rollo looked embarrassed.

'Well, the fact is, mother—'

A hard protuberance in his coat-pocket attracted Mrs Podmarsh's notice. She swooped and drew out a big-bowled pipe.

'Rollo!' she exclaimed, aghast.

'Well, the fact is, mother—'

'Don't you know,' cried Mrs Podmarsh, 'that smoking is poisonous, and injurious to the health?'

'Yes. But the fact is, mother—'

'It causes nervous dyspepsia, sleeplessness, gnawing of the stomach, headache, weak eyes, red spots on the skin, throat irritation, asthma, bronchitis, heart failure, lung trouble, catarrh, melancholy, neurasthenia, loss of memory, impaired will-power, rheumatism, lumbago, sciatica, neuritis, heartburn, torpid liver, loss of appetite, enervation, lassitude, lack of ambition, and falling out of hair.'

'Yes, I know, mother. But the fact is, Ted Ray smokes all the time he's playing, and I thought it might improve my game.'

And it was at these splendid words that Mary Kent felt for the first time that something might be made of Rollo Podmarsh. That she experienced one-millionth of the fervour which was gnawing at his vitals I will not say. A woman does not fall in love in a flash like a man. But at least she no longer regarded him with loathing. On the contrary, she found herself liking him. There was, she considered, the right stuff in Rollo. And if, as seemed probable from his mother's conversation, it would take a bit of digging to bring it up, well – she liked rescue-work and had plenty of time.

Mr Arnold Bennett, in a recent essay, advises young bachelors to proceed with a certain caution in matters of the heart. They should, he asserts, first decide whether or not they are ready for love; then, whether it is better to marry earlier or later; thirdly, whether their ambitions are such that a wife will prove a hindrance to their career. These romantic preliminaries concluded, they may grab a girl and go to it.

Rollo Podmarsh would have made a tough audience for these precepts. Since the days of Antony and Cleopatra probably no one had ever got more swiftly off the mark. One may say that he was in love before he had come within two yards of the girl. And each day that passed found him more nearly up to his eyebrows in the tender emotion.

He thought of Mary when he was changing his wet shoes; he dreamed of her while putting flannel next his skin; he yearned for her over the evening arrowroot. Why, the man was such a slave to his devotion that he actually went to the length of purloining small articles belonging to her. Two days after Mary's arrival Rollo Podmarsh was driving off the first tee with one of her handkerchiefs, a powder-puff, and a dozen hairpins secreted in his left breast-pocket. When dressing for dinner he used to take them out and look at them, and at night he slept with them under his pillow. Heavens, how he loved that girl!

One evening when they had gone out into the garden together to look at the new room – Rollo, by his mother's advice, wearing a woollen scarf to protect his throat – he endeavoured to bring the conversation round to the important subject. Mary's last remark had been about earwigs. Considered as a cue, it lacked a subtle something; but Rollo was not the man to be discouraged by that.

'Talking of earwigs. Miss Kent,' he said, in a low musical voice, 'have you ever been in love?'

Mary was silent for a moment before replying.

'Yes, once. When I was eleven. With a conjurer who came to perform at my birthday-party. He took a rabbit and two eggs out of my hair, and life seemed one grand sweet song.'

'Never since then?'

'Never.'

'Suppose – just for the sake of argument – suppose you ever did love anyone – er – what sort of a man would it be?'

'A hero,' said Mary, promptly.

'A hero?' said Rollo, somewhat taken aback. 'What sort of hero?'

'Any sort. I could only love a really brave man – a man who had done some wonderful heroic action.'

'Shall we go in?' said Rollo, hoarsely. 'The air is a little chilly.'

We have now, therefore, arrived at a period in Rollo Podmarsh's career which might have inspired those lines of Henley's about 'the night that covers me, black as the pit from pole to pole.' What with one thing and another, he was in an almost Job-like condition of despondency. I say 'one thing and another,' for it was not only hopeless love that weighed him down. In addition to being hope-lessly in love, he was greatly depressed about his golf.

On Rollo in his capacity of golfer I have so far not dwelt. You have probably allowed yourself, in spite of the significant episode of the pipe, to dismiss him as one of those placid, contented – shall I say dilettante? – golfers who are so frequent in these degenerate days. Such was not the case. Outwardly placid, Rollo was consumed inwardly by an ever-burning fever of ambition. His aims were not extravagant. He did not want to become amateur champion, nor even to win a monthly medal; but he did, with his whole soul, desire one of these days to go round the course in under a hundred. This feat accomplished, it was his intention to set the seal on his golfing career by playing a real money-match; and already he had selected his opponent, a certain Colonel Bodger, a tottery performer of advanced years who for the last decade had been a martyr to lumbago.

But it began to look as if even the modest goal he had marked out for himself were beyond his powers. Day after day he would step on to the first tee, glowing with zeal and hope, only to crawl home in the quiet evenfall with another hundred and twenty on his card. Little wonder, then, that he began to lose his appetite and would moan feebly at the sight of a poached egg.

With Mrs Podmarsh sedulously watching over her son's health, you might have supposed that this inability on his part to teach the foodstuffs to take a joke would have caused consternation in the home. But it so happened that Rollo's mother had recently been reading a medical treatise in which an eminent physician stated that we all eat too much nowadays, and that the secret of a happy life is to lay off the carbohydrates to some extent. She was, therefore, delighted to observe the young man's moderation in the matter of food, and frequently held him up as an example to be noted and followed by little Lettice Willoughby, her grand-daughter, who was a good and consistent trencherwoman, particularly rough on the puddings. Little Lettice, I should mention, was the daughter of Rollo's sister Enid, who lived in the neighbourhood. Mrs Willoughby had been compelled to go away on a visit a few days before and had left her child with Mrs Podmarsh during her absence.

You can fool some of the people all the time, but Lettice Willoughby was not of the type that is easily deceived. A nice, old-fashioned child would no doubt have accepted without questioning her grandmother's dictum that roly-poly pudding could not fail to hand a devastating wallop to the blood-pressure, and that to take two helpings of it was practically equivalent to walking right into the family vault. A child with less decided opinions of her own would have been impressed by the spectacle of her uncle refusing sustenance, and would have received without demur the statement that he did it because he felt that abstinence was good for his health. Lettice was a modern child and knew better. She had had experience of this loss of appetite and its significance. The first symptom which had preceded the demise of poor old Ponto, who had recently handed in his portfolio after holding office for ten years as the Willoughby family dog, had been this same disinclination to absorb nourishment. Besides, she was an observant child, and had not failed to note the haggard misery in her uncle's eyes. She tackled him squarely on the subject one morning after breakfast. Rollo had retired into the more distant parts of the garden, and was leaning forward, when she found him, with his head buried in his hands.

'Hallo, uncle,' said Lettice.

Rollo looked up wanly.

'Ah, child!' he said. He was fond of his niece.

'Aren't you feeling well, uncle?'

'Far, far from well.'

'It's old age, I expect,' said Lettice.

'I feel old,' admitted Rollo. 'Old and battered. Ah, Lettice, laugh and be gay while you can.'

'All right, uncle.'

'Make the most of your happy, careless, smiling, halcyon childhood.'

'Right-o, uncle.'

'When you get to my age, dear, you will realise that it is a sad, hopeless world. A world where, if you keep your head down, you forget to let the club-head lead: where even if you do happen by a miracle to keep 'em straight with your brassie, you blow up on the green and foozle a six-inch putt.'

Lettice could not quite understand what Uncle Rollo was talking about, but she gathered broadly that she had been correct in supposing him to be in a bad state, and her warm, childish heart was filled with pity for him. She walked thoughtfully away, and Rollo resumed his reverie.

Into each life, as the poet says, some rain must fall. So much had recently been falling into Rollo's that, when Fortune at last sent along a belated sunbeam, it exercised a cheering effect out of all proportion to its size. By this I mean that when, some four days after his conversation with Lettice, Mary Kent asked him to play golf with her, he read into the invitation a significance which only a lover could have seen in it. I will not go so far as to say that Rollo Podmarsh looked on Mary Kent's suggestion that they should have a round together as actually tantamount to a revelation of undying love; but he certainly regarded it as a most encouraging sign. It seemed to him that things were beginning to move, that Rollo Preferred were on a rising market. Gone was the gloom of the past days. He forgot those sad, solitary wanderings of his in the bushes at the bottom of the garden; he forgot that his mother had bought him a new set of winter woollies which felt like horsehair; he forgot that for the last few evenings his arrowroot had tasted rummy. His whole mind was occupied with the astounding fact that she had voluntarily offered to play golf with him, and he walked out on to the first tee filled with a yeasty exhilaration which nearly caused him to burst into song.

'How shall we play?' asked Mary. 'I am a twelve. What is your handicap?'

Rollo was under the disadvantage of not actually possessing a handicap. He had a sort of private system of book-keeping of his own by which he took strokes over if they did not seem to him to be up to sample, and allowed himself five-foot putts at discretion. So he had never actually handed in the three cards necessary for handicapping purposes.

'I don't exactly know,' he said. 'It's my ambition to get round in under a hundred, but I've never managed it yet.'

'Never?'

'Never! It's strange, but something always seems to go wrong.'

'Perhaps you'll manage it today,' said Mary, encouragingly, so encouragingly that it was all that Rollo could do to refrain from flinging himself at her feet and barking like a dog. 'Well, I'll start you two holes up, and we'll see how we get on. Shall I take the honour?'

She drove off one of those fair-to-medium balls which go with a twelve handicap. Not a great length, but nice and straight.

'Splendid!' cried Rollo, devoutly.

'Oh, I don't know,' said Mary. 'I wouldn't call it anything special.'

Titanic emotions were surging in Rollo's bosom as he addressed his ball. He had never felt like this before, especially on the first tee – where as a rule he found himself overcome with a nervous humility.

'Oh, Mary! Mary!' he breathed to himself as he swung.

You who squander your golden youth fooling about on a bowling-green will not understand the magic of those three words. But if you were a golfer, you would realise that in selecting just that invocation to breathe to himself Rollo Podmarsh had hit, by sheer accident, on the ideal method of achieving a fine drive. Let me explain. The first two words, tensely breathed, are just sufficient to take a man with the proper slowness to the top of his swing; the first syllable of the second 'Mary' exactly coincides with the striking of the ball; and the final 'ry!' takes care of the follow-through.

The consequence was that Rollo's ball, instead of hopping down the hill like an embarrassed duck, as was its usual practice, sang off the tee with a scream like a shell, nodded in passing Mary's ball, where it lay some hundred and fifty yards down the course, and, carrying on from there, came to rest within easy distance of the green. For the first time in his golfing life Rollo Podmarsh had hit a nifty.

Mary followed the ball's flight with astonished eyes.

'But this will never do!' she exclaimed. 'I can't possibly start you two up if you're going to do this sort of thing.'

Rollo blushed.

'I shouldn't think it would happen again,' he said. 'I've never done a drive like that before.'

'But it must happen again,' said Mary, firmly. 'This is evidently your day. If you don't get round in under a hundred today, I shall never forgive you.'

Rollo shut his eyes, and his lips moved feverishly. He was registering a vow that, come what might, he would not fail her. A minute later he was holing out in three, one under bogey.

The second hole is the short lake-hole. Bogey is three, and Rollo generally did it in four; for it was his custom not to count any balls he might sink in the water, but to start afresh with one which happened to get over, and then take three putts. But today something seemed to tell him that he would not require the aid of this ingenious system. As he took his mashie from the bag, he knew that his first shot would soar successfully on to the green.

'Ah, Mary!' he breathed as he swung.

These subtleties are wasted on a worm, if you will pardon the expression, like yourself, who, possibly owing to a defective education, is content to spend life's springtime rolling wooden balls across a lawn ; but I will explain that in altering and shortening his soliloquy at this juncture Rollo had done the very thing any good pro. would have recommended. If he had murmured, 'Oh, Mary! Mary!' as before he would have over-swung. 'Ah, Mary!' was exactly right for a half-swing with the mashie. His ball shot up in a beautiful arc, and trickled to within six inches of the hole.

Mary was delighted. There was something about this big, diffident man which had appealed from the first to everything in her that was motherly.

'Marvellous!' she said. 'You'll get a two. Five for the first two holes! Why, you simply must get round in under a hundred now.' She swung, but too lightly; and her ball fell in the water. 'I'll give you this,' she said, without the slightest chagrin, for this girl had a beautiful nature. 'Let's get on to the third. Four up ! Why, you're wonderful! '

And not to weary you with too much detail, I will simply remark that, stimulated by her gentle encouragement, Rollo Podmarsh actually came off the ninth green with a medal score of forty-six for the half-round. A ten on the seventh had spoiled his card to some extent, and a nine on the eighth had not helped, but nevertheless here he was in forty-six, with the easier half of the course before him. He tingled all over – partly because he was wearing the new winter woollies to which I have alluded previously, but principally owing to triumph, elation, and love. He gazed at Mary as Dante might have gazed at Beatrice on one of his particularly sentimental mornings.

Mary uttered an exclamation.

'Oh, I've just remembered,' she exclaimed. 'I promised to write last night to Jane Simpson and give her that new formula for knitting jumpers. I think I'll 'phone her now from the club-house and then it'll be off my mind. You go on to the tenth, and I'll join you there.'

*

Rollo proceeded over the brow of the hill to the tenth tee, and was filling in the time with practice-swings when he heard his name spoken.

'Good gracious, Rollo! I couldn't believe it was you at first.'

He turned to see his sister, Mrs Willoughby, the mother of the child Lettice.

'Hallo! 'he said. 'When did you get back?'

'Late last night. Why, it's extraordinary!'

'Hope you had a good time. What's extraordinary? Listen, Enid. Do you know what I've done? Forty-six for the first nine! Forty-six! And holing out every putt.'

'Oh, then that accounts for it.'

'Accounts for what?'

'Why, your looking so pleased with life. I got an idea from Letty, when she wrote to me, that you were at death's door. Your gloom seems to have made a deep impression on the child. Her letter was full of it.'

Rollo was moved.

'Dear little Letty! She is wonderfully sympathetic.'

'Well, I must be off now,' said Enid Willoughby. 'I'm late. Oh, talking of Letty. Don't children say the funniest things! She wrote in her letter that you were very old and wretched and that she was going to put you out of your misery.'

'Ha ha ha! ' laughed Rollo.

'We had to poison poor old Ponto the other day, you know, and poor little Letty was inconsolable till we explained to her that it was really the kindest thing to do, because he was so old and ill. But just imagine her thinking of wanting to end your sufferings !'

'Ha ha!' laughed Rollo. 'Ha ha h—!'

His voice trailed off into a broken gurgle. Quite suddenly a sinister thought had come to him.

The arrowroot had, tasted rummy!

'Why, what on earth is the matter?' asked Mrs Willoughby, regarding his ashen face.

Rollo could find no words. He stammered speechlessly. Yes, for several nights the arrowroot had tasted very rummy. Rummy! There was no other adjective. Even as he plied the spoon he had said to himself: 'This arrowroot tastes rummy!' And – he uttered a sharp yelp as he remembered – it had been little Lettice who had brought it to him. He recollected being touched at the time by the kindly act.

'What is the matter, Rollo?' demanded Mrs Willoughby, sharply. 'Don't stand there looking like a dying duck.'

'I am a dying duck,' responded Rollo, hoarsely. 'A dying man, I mean. Enid, that infernal child has poisoned me!'

'Don't be ridiculous! And kindly don't speak of her like that!'

'I'm sorry. I shouldn't blame her, I suppose. No doubt her motives were good. But the fact remains.'

'Rollo, you're too absurd.'

'But the arrowroot tasted rummy.'

'I never knew you could be such an idiot,' said his exasperated sister with sisterly outspokenness. 'I thought you would think it quaint. I thought you would roar with laughter.'

'I did – till I remembered about the rumminess of the arrowroot.'

Mrs Willoughby uttered an impatient exclamation and walked away.

Rollo Podmarsh stood on the tenth tee, a volcano of mixed emotions. Mechanically he pulled out his pipe and lit it. But he found that he could not smoke. In this supreme crisis of his life tobacco seemed to have lost its magic. He put the pipe back in his pocket and gave himself up to his thoughts. Now terror gripped him; anon a sort of gentle melancholy. It was so hard that he should be compelled to leave the world just as he had begun to hit 'em right.

And then in the welter of his thoughts there came one of practical value. To wit, that by hurrying to the doctor's without delay he might yet be saved. There might be antidotes.

He turned to go and there was Mary Kent standing beside him with her bright, encouraging smile.

'I'm sorry I kept you so long,' she said. 'It's your honour. Fire away, and remember that you've got to do this nine in fifty-three at the outside.'

Rollo's thoughts flitted wistfully to the snug surgery where Dr Brown was probably sitting at this moment surrounded by the finest antidotes.

'Do you know, I think I ought to—'

'Of course you ought to,' said Mary. 'If you did the first nine in forty-six, you can't possibly take fifty-three coming in.'

For one long moment Rollo continued to hesitate – a moment during which the instinct of self-preservation seemed as if it must win the day. All his life he had been brought up to be nervous about his health, and panic gripped him. But there is a deeper, nobler instinct than that of self-preservation – the instinctive desire of a golfer who is at the top of his form to go on and beat his medal-score record. And little by little this grand impulse began to dominate Rollo. If, he felt, he went off now to take antidotes, the doctor might possibly save his life; but reason told him that never again would he be likely to do the first nine in forty-six. He would have to start all over afresh.

Rollo Podmarsh hesitated no longer. With a pale, set face he teed up his ball and drove.

If I were telling this story to a golfer instead of to an excrescence – I use the word in the kindliest spirit – who spends his time messing about on a bowling-green, nothing would please me better than to describe shot by shot Rollo's progress over the remaining nine holes. Epics have been written with less material. But these details would, I am aware, be wasted on you. Let it suffice that by the time his last approach trickled on to the eighteenth green he had taken exactly fifty shots.

'Three for it !' said Mary Kent. 'Steady now! Take it quite easy and be sure to lay your second dead.'

It was prudent counsel, but Rollo was now thoroughly above himself. He had got his feet wet in a puddle on the sixteenth, but he did not care. His winter woolies seemed to be lined with ants, but he ignored them. All he knew was that he was on the last green in ninety-six, and he meant to finish in style. No tame three putts for him ! His ball was five yards away, but he aimed for the back of the hole and brought his putter down with a whack. Straight and true the ball sped, hit the tin, jumped high in the air, and fell into the hole with a rattle.

'Oo!' cried Mary.

Rollo Podmarsh wiped his forehead and leaned dizzily on his putter. For a moment so intense is the fervour induced by the game of games, all he could think of was that he had gone round in ninety-seven. Then, as one waking from a trance, he began to appreciate his position. The fever passed, and a clammy dismay took possession of him. He had achieved his life's ambition; but what now? Already he was conscious of a curious discomfort within him. He felt as he supposed Italians of the Middle Ages must have felt after dropping in to take pot-luck with the Borgias. It was hard. He had gone round in ninety-seven, but he could never take the next step in the career which he had mapped out in his dreams – the money-match with the lumbago-stricken Colonel Bodger.

Mary Kent was fluttering round him, bubbling congratulations, but Rollo sighed.

'Thanks,' he said. 'Thanks very much. But the trouble is, I'm afraid I'm going to die almost immediately. I've been poisoned!'

'Poisoned!'

'Yes. Nobody is to blame. Everything was done with the best intentions. But there it is.'

'But I don't understand.'

Rollo explained. Mary listened pallidly.

'Are you sure?' she gasped.

'Quite sure,' said Rollo, gravely. 'The arrowroot tasted rummy.'

'But arrowroot always does.'

Rollo shook his head.

'No,' he said. 'It tastes like warm blotting-paper, but not rummy.'

Mary was sniffing.

'Don't cry,' urged Rollo, tenderly. 'Don't cry.'

'But I must. And I've come out without a handkerchief.'

'Permit me,' said Rollo, producing one of her best from his left breast-pocket.

'I wish I had a powder-puff,' said Mary.

'Allow me,' said Rollo. 'And your hair has become a little disordered. If I may –' And from the same reservoir he drew a handful of hairpins.

Mary gazed at these exhibits with astonishment.

'But these are mine,' she said.

'Yes. I sneaked them from time to time.'

'But why?'

'Because I loved you,' said Rollo. And in a few moving sentences which I will not trouble you with he went on to elaborate this theme.

Mary listened with her heart full of surging emotions, which I cannot possibly go into if you persist in looking at that damned watch of yours. The scales had fallen from her eyes. She had thought slightingly of this man because he had been a little over-careful of his health, and all the time he had had within him the potentiality of heroism.

Something seemed to snap inside her.

'Rollo!' she cried, and flung herself into his arms.

'Mary!' muttered Rollo, gathering her up.

'I told you it was all nonsense,' said Mrs Willoughby, coming up at this tense moment and going on with the conversation where she had left off. 'I've just seen Letty, and she said she meant to put you out of your misery but the chemist wouldn't sell her any poison, so she let it go.'

Rollo disentangled himself from Mary.

'What?' he cried.

Mrs Willoughby repeated her remarks.

'You're sure?' he said.

'Of course I'm sure.'

'Then why did the arrowroot taste rummy?'

'I made inquiries about that. It seems that mother was worried about your taking to smoking, and she found an advertisement in one of the magazines about the Tobacco Habit Cured in Three Days by a secret method without the victim's knowledge. It was a gentle, safe, agreeable method of eliminating the nicotine poison from the system, strengthening the weakened membranes, and overcoming the craving; so she put some in your arrowroot every night.'

There was a long silence. To Rollo Podmarsh it seemed as though the sun had suddenly begun to shine, the birds to sing, and the grasshoppers to toot. All Nature was one vast substantial smile. Down in the valley by the second hole he caught sight of Wallace Chesney's Plus Fours gleaming as their owner stooped to play his shot, and it seemed to him that he had never in his life seen anything so lovely.

'Mary,' he said, in a low, vibrant voice, 'will you wait here for me? I want to go into the club-house for a moment.'

'To change your wet shoes?'

'No!' thundered Rollo. 'I'm never going to change my wet shoes again in my life.' He felt in his pocket, and hurled a box of patent pills far into the undergrowth. 'But I *am* going to change my winter woollies. And when I've put those dashed barbed-wire entanglements into the club-house furnace, I'm going to 'phone to old Colonel Bodger. I hear his lumbago's worse than ever. I'm going to fix up a match with him for a shilling a hole. And if I don't lick the boots off him you can break the engagement!'

'My hero!' murmured Mary.

Rollo kissed her, and with long, resolute steps strode to the club-house.

'THE HEART
OF A GOOF'

It was a morning when all Nature shouted 'Fore!' The breeze, as it blew gently up from the valley, seemed to bring a message of hope and cheer, whispering of chip-shots holed and brassies landing squarely on the meat. The fairway, as yet unscarred by the irons of a hundred dubs, smiled greenly up at the azure sky; and the sun, peeping above the trees, looked like a giant golf-ball perfectly lofted by the mashie of some unseen god and about to drop dead by the pin of the eighteenth. It was the day of the opening of the course after the long winter, and a crowd of considerable dimensions had collected at the first tee. Plus fours gleamed in the sunshine, and the air was charged with happy anticipation.

In all that gay throng there was but one sad face. It belonged to the man who was waggling his driver over the new ball perched on its little hill of sand. This man seemed careworn, hopeless. He had the aspect of one who knows that he is shortly about to receive it in the gizzard from a remorseless Fate. He gazed down the fairway, shifted his feet, waggled, gazed down the fairway again, shifted the dogs once more, and waggled afresh. He waggled as Hamlet might have waggled, moodily, irresolutely. Then at last he swung, and taking from his caddie the niblick which the intelligent lad had been holding in readiness from the moment when he had walked onto the tee, trudged wearily off to play his second.

The Oldest Member, who had been observing the scene with a benevolent eye from his favourite chair on the terrace, sighed.

'Poor Jenkinson,' he said, 'does not improve.'

'No,' agreed his companion, a young man with open features and a handicap of six. 'And yet I happen to know that he has been taking lessons all winter at one of those indoor places.'

'Futile, quite futile,' said the Sage with a shake of his snowy head. 'There is no wizard living who could make that man go round in even sevens. I keep advising him to give up the game.'

'You!' cried the young man, raising a shocked and startled face from the driver with which he was toying. '*You* told him to give up golf! Why, I thought—'

'I understand and approve of your horror,' said the Oldest Member gently. 'But you must bear in mind that Jenkinson's is not an ordinary case. You know and I know scores of men who have never broken a hundred and twenty in their lives and yet contrive to be happy, useful members of society. However badly they may play, they are able to forget. But with Jenkinson it is different. He is not one of those who can take it or leave it alone. His only chance of happiness lies in complete abstinence. Jenkinson is a goof.'

'A what?'

'A goof,' repeated the Sage. 'One of those unfortunate beings who have allowed this noblest of sports to get too great a grip upon them, who have permitted it to eat into their souls like some malignant growth. The goof, you must understand, is not like you and me. He broods. He becomes morbid. His goofery unfits him for the battles of life. Jenkinson, for example, was once a man with a glowing future in the hay-corn-and-feed business; but a constant stream of hooks, tops and slices gradually made him so diffident and mistrustful of himself that he let opportunity after opportunity slip, with the result that other, sterner hay-corn-and-feed merchants passed him in the race. Every time he had the chance to put over some big deal in hay, or to execute some flashing *coup* in corn and feed, the fatal diffidence generated by a hundred rotten rounds would undo him. I understand his bankruptcy may be expected at any moment.'

'My golly!' said the young man, deeply impressed. 'I hope I never become a goof. Do you mean to say there is really no cure except giving up the game?'

The Oldest Member was silent for a while.

'It is curious that you should have asked that question,' he said at last, 'for only this morning I was thinking of the one case in my experience where a goof was enabled to overcome his deplorable malady. It was owing to a girl, of course. The longer I live, the more I come to see that most things are. But as you will no doubt wish to hear the story from the beginning—'

The young man rose with the startled haste of some wild creature which, wandering through the undergrowth, perceives the trap in his path.

'I should love to,' he mumbled, 'only I shall be losing my place at the tee—'

'The goof in question,' said the Sage, attaching himself with quiet firmness to the youth's coat-button, 'was a man of about your age, by name Ferdinand Dibble. I knew him well. In fact, it was to me—'

'Some other time, eh?'

'It was to me,' proceeded the Sage placidly, 'that he came for sympathy in the great crisis of his life, and I am not ashamed to say that when he had finished laying bare his soul to me, there were tears in my eyes. My heart bled for the boy.'

'I bet it did. But—'

The Oldest Member pushed him gently back into his seat.

'Golf,' he said, 'is the Great Mystery. Like some capricious goddess—'

The young man, who had been exhibiting symptoms of feverishness, appeared to become resigned. He sighed softly. 'Did you ever read "The Ancient Mariner"?' he asked.

'Many years ago,' said the Oldest Member. 'Why do you ask?'

'Oh, I don't know,' said the young man. 'It just occurred to me.'

Golf (resumed the Oldest Member) is the Great Mystery. Like some capricious goddess, it bestows its favours with what would appear an almost fat-headed lack of method and discrimination. On every side we see big, two-fisted he-men floundering round in three figures, stopping every few minutes to let through little shrimps with knock knees and hollow cheeks who are tearing off snappy seventy-fours. Giants of finance have to accept a stroke per from their junior clerks. Men capable of governing empires fail to control a small white ball which presents no difficulties whatever to others with only one ounce more of brain than a cuckoo-clock. Mysterious, but there it is. There was no apparent reason why Ferdinand Dibble should not have been a competent golfer. He had strong wrists and a good eye. Nevertheless the fact remains that he was a dub. And on a certain evening in June, I realised that he was also a goof. I found it out quite suddenly as the result of a conversation which we had on this very terrace.

I was sitting here that evening, thinking of this and that, when by the corner of the club-house I observed young Dibble in conversation with a girl in white. I could not see who she was, for her back was turned. Presently they parted, and Ferdinand came slowly across to where I sat. His air was dejected. He had had the boots licked off him earlier in the afternoon by Jimmy Fothergill, and it was to this that I attributed his gloom. I was to find out in a few moments that I was partly but not entirely correct in this surmise. He took the next chair to mine and for several minutes sat staring moodily down into the valley.

'I've just been talking to Barbara Medway,' he said, suddenly breaking the silence.

'Indeed?' I said. 'A delightful girl.'

'She's going away for the summer to Marvis Bay.'

'She will take the sunshine with her.'

'You bet she will!' said Ferdinand Dibble with extraordinary warmth, and there was another long silence.

Presently Ferdinand uttered a hollow groan.

'I love her, dammit!' he muttered brokenly. 'Oh, golly, how I love her!'

I was not surprised at his making me the recipient of his confidences like this. Most of the young folk in the place brought their troubles to me sooner or later.

'And does she return your love?'

'I don't know. I haven't asked her.'

'Why not? I should have thought the point not without its interest for you.'

Ferdinand gnawed the handle of his putter distractedly.

'I haven't the nerve,' he burst out at length. 'I simply can't summon up the cold gall to ask a girl, least of all an angel like her, to marry me. You see, it's like this: Every time I work myself up to the point of having a dash at it, I go out and get trimmed by someone giving me a stroke a hole. Every time I feel I've mustered up enough pep to propose, I take a ten on a par three. Every time I think I'm in good midseason form for putting my fate to the test, to win or lose it all, something goes blooey with my swing, and I slice into the rough at every tee. And then my self-confidence leaves me. I become nervous, tongue-tied, diffident. I wish to goodness I knew the man who invented this infernal game; I'd strangle him. But I suppose he's been dead for ages. Still, I could go and jump on his grave.'

It was at this point that I understood all, and the heart within me sank like lead. The truth was out: Ferdinand Dibble was a goof.

'Come, come, my boy,' I said, though feeling the uselessness of any words. 'Master this weakness.'

'I can't.'

'Try!'

'I have tried.'

He gnawed his putter again.

'She was asking me just now if I couldn't manage to come to Marvis Bay too,' he said.

'That surely is encouraging. It suggests that she is not entirely indifferent to your society.'

'Yes, but what's the use? Do you know,' he said, a gleam coming into his eyes for a moment, 'I have a feeling that if I ever could beat some really fairly good player – just once – I could bring the thing off.' The gleam faded. 'But what chance is there of that?'

It was a question which I did not care to answer. I merely patted his shoulder sympathetically, and after a little while he left me and walked away. I was still sitting there, thinking over his hard case, when Barbara Medway came out of the club-house.

She too seemed grave and preoccupied, as if there was something on her mind. She took the chair which Ferdinand had vacated, and sighed wearily.

'Have you ever felt,' she asked, 'that you would like to bang a man on the head with something heavy and hard? With knobs on it?'

I said I had sometimes experienced such a desire, and asked if she had any particular man in mind. She seemed to hesitate for a moment before replying, then apparently made up her mind to confide in me. My advanced years carry with them certain pleasant compensations, one of which is that nice girls often confide in me. I frequently find myself enrolled as a father-confessor on the most intimate matters by beautiful creatures from whom many a younger man would give his eyeteeth to get a friendly word. Besides, I had known Barbara since she was a child. Frequently – though not recently – I had given her her evening bath. These things form a bond.

'Why are men such chumps?' she exclaimed.

'You still have not told me who it is that has caused these harsh words. Do I know him?'

'Of course you do. You've just been talking to him.'

'Ferdinand Dibble? But why should you wish to bang Ferdinand Dibble on the head with something hard and heavy, with knobs on it?'

'Because he's such a goop.'

'You mean a goof?' I queried, wondering how she could have penetrated the unhappy man's secret.

'No, a goop. A goop is a man who's in love with a girl and won't tell her so. I am as certain as I am of anything that Ferdinand is fond of me—'

'Your instinct is unerring. He has just been confiding in me.'

'Well, why doesn't he confide in *me*, the poor fish?' cried the high-spirited girl, petulantly flicking a pebble at a passing grasshopper. 'I can't be expected to fling myself into his arms unless he gives some sort of hint that he's ready to catch me.'

'Would it help if I were to repeat to him the substance of this conversation of ours?'

'If you breathe a word of it, I'll never speak to you again,' she cried. 'I'd rather die an awful death than have any man think I wanted him so badly that I had to send relays of messengers begging him to marry me.'

I saw her point.

'Then I fear,' I said gravely, 'that there is nothing to be done. One can only wait and hope. It may be that in the years to come, Ferdinand Dibble will acquire a nice lissome wristy swing, with the head kept rigid and the right leg firmly braced, and—'

'What are you talking about?'

'I was toying with the hope that some sunny day Ferdinand Dibble would cease to be a goof.'

'You mean a goop?'

'No, a goof. A goof is a man who—' And I went on to explain the peculiar psychological difficulties which lay in the way of any declaration of affection on Ferdinand's part.

'But I never heard of anything so ridiculous in my life,' she ejaculated. 'Do you mean to say that he is waiting till he is good at golf before he asks me to marry him?'

'It is not quite so simple as that,' I said sadly. 'Many bad golfers marry, feeling that a wife's loving solicitude may improve their game. But they are rugged, thick-skinned men, not sensitive and introspective like Ferdinand. Ferdinand has allowed himself to become morbid. It is one of the chief merits of golf that non-success at the game induces a certain decent humility which keeps a man from pluming himself too much on any petty triumphs he may achieve in other walks of life; but in all things there is a happy mean, and with Ferdinand this humility has gone too far. It has taken all the spirit out of him. He feels crushed and worthless. He is grateful to caddies when they accept a tip instead of drawing themselves up to their full height and flinging the money in his face.'

'Then do you mean that things have got to go on like this forever?'

I thought for a moment.

'It is a pity,' I said, 'that you could not have induced Ferdinand to go to Marvis Bay for a month or two.'

'Why?'

'Because it seems to me, thinking the thing over, that it is just possible that Marvis Bay might cure him. At the hotel there he would find collected a mob of golfers – I use the term in its broadest sense, to embrace the paralytics and the men who play left-handed – whom even he would be able to beat. When I was last at Marvis Bay, the hotel links were a sort of Sargasso Sea into which had drifted all the pitiful flotsam and jetsam of golf. I have seen things done on that course at which I shuddered and averted my eyes – and I am not a weak man. If Ferdinand can polish up his game so as to go round in a fairly steady hundred and five, I fancy there is hope. But I understand he is not going to Marvis Bay.'

'Oh, yes, he is,' said the girl.

'Indeed? He did not tell me that, when we were talking just now.'

'He didn't know it then. He will when I have had a few words with him.'

And she walked with firm steps back to the club-house.

It has been well said that there are many kinds of golf, beginning at the top with the golf of professionals and the best amateurs, and working down through the golf of ossified men to that of Scotch university professors. Until recently this last was looked upon as the lowest possible depth; but nowadays, with the growing popularity of summer hotels, we are able to add a brand still lower, the golf you find at places like Marvis Bay.

To Ferdinand Dibble, coming from a club where the standard of play was rather unusually high, Marvis Bay was a revelation, and for some days after his arrival there he went about dazed, like a man who cannot believe it is really true. To go out on the links at this summer resort was like entering a new world. The hotel was full of stout, middle-aged men who, after a misspent youth devoted to making money, had taken to a game at which real proficiency can only be acquired by those who start playing in their cradles and keep their weight down. Out on the course each morning you could see representatives of every nightmare style that was ever invented. There was the man who seemed to be attempting to deceive his ball and lull it into a false security by looking away from it and then making a lightning slash in the apparent hope of catching it off its guard. There was the man who wielded his midiron like one killing snakes. There was the man who addressed his ball as if he were stroking a cat, the man who drove as if he were cracking a whip, the man who brooded over each shot like one whose heart is bowed down by bad news from home, and the man who scooped with his mashie as if he were ladling soup. By the end of the first week Ferdinand Dibble was the acknowledged champion of the place. He had gone through the entire menagerie like a bullet through a cream-puff.

First, scarcely daring to consider the possibility of success, he had taken on the man who tried to catch his ball off its guard, and had beaten him five up and four to play. Then, with gradually growing confidence, he tackled in turn the Cat-stroker, the Whip-cracker, the Heart Bowed Down and the Soup-scooper and walked all over their faces with spiked shoes. And as these were the leading local amateurs, whose prowess the octogenarians and the men who went round in bath-chairs vainly strove to emulate, Ferdinand Dibble was faced on the eighth morning of his visit by the startling fact that he had no more worlds to conquer. He was monarch of all he surveyed, and what is more, had won his first trophy, the prize in the great medal-play handicap tournament, in which he had nosed in ahead of the field by two strokes, edging out his nearest rival, a venerable old gentleman with a handicap of forty-seven, by means of a brilliant and unexpected four on the last hole. The prize was a handsome pewter mug about the size of the old oaken bucket, and Ferdinand used to go to his room immediately after dinner to croon over it like a mother over her child.

You are wondering, no doubt, why, in these circumstances, he did not take advantage of the new spirit of exhilarated pride which had replaced his old humility and instantly propose to Barbara Medway. I will tell you. He did not propose to Barbara because Barbara was not there. At the last moment she had been detained at home to nurse a sick parent, and had been compelled to postpone her visit for a couple of weeks. He could, no doubt, have proposed in one of the daily letters which he wrote to her, but somehow, once he started writing, he found that he used up so much space describing his best shots on the links that day that it was difficult to squeeze in a declaration of undying passion. After all, you can hardly cram that sort of thing into a postscript.

He decided, therefore, to wait till she arrived, and meanwhile pursued his conquering course. The longer he waited, the better in one way, for every morning and afternoon that passed was adding new layers to his self-esteem. Day by day in every way he grew chestier and chestier.

Meanwhile, however, dark clouds were gathering. Sullen mutterings were to be heard in secluded corners of the hotel lounge, and the spirit of revolt was abroad. For Ferdinand's chestiness had not escaped the notice of his defeated rivals. There is nobody so chesty as a normally unchesty man who suddenly becomes chesty, and I am sorry to say that the chestiness which had come to Ferdinand was the aggressive type of chestiness which breeds enemies. He had developed a habit of holding the game up in order to give his opponent advice. The Whip-Cracker had not forgiven, and never would forgive, his well-meant but galling criticism of his back-swing. The Scooper, who had always scooped since the day when at the age of sixty-four he subscribed to the

Correspondence Course which was to teach him golf in twelve lessons, by mail, resented being told by a snip of a boy that the mashie-stroke should be a smooth, unhurried swing. The Snake-Killer— But I need not weary you with a detailed recital of these men's grievances; it is enough to say that they all had it in for Ferdinand; and one night after dinner they met in the lounge to decide what was to be done about it. A nasty spirit was displayed by all.

'A mere lad telling me how to use my mashie!' growled the Scooper. 'Smooth and unhurried, my left eyeball! I get it up, don't I? Well, what more do you want?'

'I keep telling him that mine is the old full St. Andrews swing,' muttered the Whip-Cracker between set teeth, 'but he won't listen to me.'

'He ought to be taken down a peg or two,' hissed the Snake-Killer. It is not easy to hiss a sentence without a single '*s*' in it, and the fact that he succeeded in doing so shows to what a pitch of emotion the man had been goaded by Ferdinand's maddening air of superiority.

'Yes, but what can we do?' queried an octogenarian, when this last remark had been passed on to him down his ear-trumpet.

'That's the trouble,' sighed the Scooper. 'What can we do?'

And there was a sorrowful shaking of heads.

'I know!' exclaimed the Cat-Stroker, who had not hitherto spoken. He was a lawyer and a man of subtle and sinister mind. 'I have it! There's a boy in my office – young Parsloe – who could beat this man Dibble hollow. I'll wire him to come down here, and we'll spring him on this fellow and knock some of the conceit out of him.'

There was a chorus of approval.

'But are you sure he can beat him?' asked the Snake-Killer anxiously. 'It would never do to make a mistake.'

'Of course I'm sure,' said the Cat-Stroker. 'George Parsloe once went round in ninety-four.'

'Many changes there have been since ninety-four,' said the octogenarian, nodding sagely. 'Ah, many, many changes. None of these motor-cars then, tearing about and killing—'

Kindly hands led him off to have an egg-and-milk, and the remaining conspirators returned to the point at issue with bent brows.

'Ninety-four?' said the Scooper incredulously. 'Do you mean counting every stroke?'

'Counting every stroke.'

'Not conceding himself any putts?'

'Not one.'

'Wire him to come at once,' said the meeting with one voice.

That night the Cat-Stroker approached Ferdinand, smooth, subtle, lawyer-like.

'Oh, Dibble,' he said, 'just the man I wanted to see. Dibble, there's a young friend of mine coming down here who goes in for golf a little. George Parsloe is his name. I was wondering if you could spare time to give him a game. He is just a novice, you know.'

'I shall be delighted to play a round with him,' said Ferdinand.

'He might pick up a pointer or two from watching you,' said the Cat-Stroker.

'True, true,' said Ferdinand.

'Then I'll introduce you when he shows up.'

'Delighted,' said Ferdinand.

He was in excellent humour that night, for he had had a letter from Barbara, saying that she was arriving on the next day but one.

It was Ferdinand's healthy custom of a morning to get up in good time and take a dip in the sea before breakfast. On the morning of the day of Barbara's arrival, he arose as usual, donned his flannels, took a good look at the cup and started out. It was a fine, fresh morning and he glowed both externally and internally. As he crossed the links – for the nearest route to the water was through the fairway of the seventh – he was whistling happily and rehearsing in his mind the opening sentences of his proposal. For it was his firm resolve that night after dinner to ask Barbara to marry him. He was proceeding over the smooth turf without a care in the world, when there was a sudden cry of 'Fore!' and the next moment a golf-ball, missing him by inches, sailed up the fairway and came to rest fifty yards from where he stood. He looked round and observed a figure coming toward him from the tee.

The distance from the tee was fully a hundred and thirty yards. Add fifty to that, and you have a hundred and eighty yards. No such drive had been made on the Marvis Bay links since their foundation, and such is the generous spirit of the true golfer, that Ferdinand's first emotion after the not inexcusable spasm of panic caused by the hum of the globule past his ear, was one of cordial admiration. By some kindly miracle, he supposed, one of his hotel acquaintances had been permitted for once in his life to time a drive right. It was only when the other man came up that there began to steal over him a sickening apprehension. The faces of all those who hewed divots on the hotel course were familiar to him, and the fact that this fellow was a stranger seemed to point with dreadful certainty to his being the man he had agreed to play.

'Sorry,' said the man. He was a tall, strikingly handsome youth with brown eyes and a dark moustache.

'Oh, that's all right,' said Ferdinand. 'Er – do you always drive like that?'

'Well, I generally get a bit longer ball, but I'm off my drive this morning. It's lucky I came out and got this practice. I'm playing a match tomorrow with a fellow named Dibble, who's a local champion or something.'

'Me,' said Ferdinand humbly.

'Eh? Oh, you?' Mr Parsloe eyed him appraisingly. 'Well, may the best man win.'

As this was precisely what Ferdinand was afraid was going to happen, he nodded in a sickly manner and tottered off to his bath. The magic had gone out of the morning. The sun still shone, but in a silly, feeble way; and a cold and depressing wind had sprung up. For Ferdinand's inferiority complex, which had seemed cured forever, was back again, doing business at the old stand.

How sad it is in this life that the moments to which we have looked forward with the most glowing anticipation so often turn out on arrival flat, cold and disappointing. For ten days Barbara Medway had been living for that meeting with Ferdinand when, getting out of the train, she would see him popping about on the horizon with the lovelight sparkling in his eyes, and words of devotion trembling on his lips. The poor girl never doubted for an instant that he would unleash his pent-up emotions inside the first five minutes, and her only worry was lest he should give an embarrassing publicity to the sacred scene by falling on his knees on the station platform.

'Well, here I am at last,' she cried gaily.

'Hullo,' said Ferdinand with a twisted smile.

The girl looked at him, chilled. How could she know that his peculiar manner was due entirely to the severe attack of cold feet resulting upon his meeting with George Parsloe that morning? The interpretation which she placed upon it was that he was not glad to see her. If he had behaved like this before, she would of course have put it down to ingrowing goofery, but now she had his written statements to prove that for the last ten days his golf had been one long series of triumphs.

'I got your letters,' she said, persevering bravely.

'I thought you would,' said Ferdinand absently.

'You certainly seem to have been doing wonders.'

'Yes.'

There was a silence.

'Have a nice journey?' said Ferdinand.

'Very,' said Barbara.

She spoke coldly, for she was madder than a wet hen. She saw it all now. In the ten days since they had parted, his love, she realised, had waned. Some other girl, met in the romantic surroundings of this picturesque resort, had supplanted her in his affections. She knew how quickly Cupid gets off the mark at a summer hotel, and for an instant she blamed herself for ever having been so ivory-skulled as to let him come to this place alone. Then regret was swallowed up in wrath, and she became so glacial that Ferdinand, who had been on the point of telling her the secret of his gloom, retired into his shell, and conversation during the drive to the hotel never soared above a certain level. Ferdinand said the sunshine was nice, and Barbara said yes it was nice; and Ferdinand said it looked pretty on the water, and Barbara said yes it did look pretty on the water; and Ferdinand said he hoped it was not going to rain, and Barbara said yes it would be a pity if it rained. And then there was another lengthy silence.

'How is my uncle?' asked Barbara at last.

I omitted to mention that the individual to whom I have referred as the Cat-Stroker was Barbara's mother's brother, and her host at Marvis Bay.

'Your uncle?'

'His name is Tuttle. Have you met him?'

'Oh, yes. I've seen a good deal of him. He has a friend staying with him,' said Ferdinand, his mind returning to the matter nearest his heart, 'a fellow named Parsloe.'

'Oh, is George Parsloe here? How jolly!'

'Do you know him?' barked Ferdinand hollowly. He would not have supposed that anything could add to his existing depression, but he was conscious now of having slipped a few rungs farther down the ladder of gloom. There had been a horribly joyful ring in her voice. Ah, well, he reflected morosely, how like Life it all was. We never know what the morrow may bring forth. We strike a good patch and are beginning to think pretty well of ourselves, and along comes a George Parsloe.

'Of course I do,' said Barbara. 'Why, there he is.'

The cab had drawn up at the door of the hotel, and on the porch George Parsloe was airing his graceful person. To Ferdinand's fevered eye he looked like a Greek god, and Ferdinand's inferiority complex began to exhibit symptoms of giantism. How could he compete at love or golf with a fellow who looked as if he had stepped out of the movies and considered himself off his drive when he did a hundred and eighty yards?

'Geor-gee!' cried Barbara blithely. 'Hullo, George!'

'Why, hullo, Barbara!'

They fell into pleasant conversation, while Ferdinand hung miserably about in the offing. And presently, feeling that his society was not essential to their happiness, he slunk away.

George Parsloe dined at the Cat-Stroker's table that night, and it was with George Parsloe that Barbara roamed in the moonlight after dinner. Ferdinand, after a profitless hour at the billiard-table, went early to his room. But not even the rays of the moon, glinting on his cup, could soothe the fever in his soul. He sombrely practiced putting into his tooth-glass for a while; then, going to bed, fell at last into a troubled sleep.

Barbara slept late the next morning and breakfasted in her room. Coming down toward noon, she found a strange emptiness in the hotel. It was her experience of summer hotels that a really fine day such as this one was the cue for half the inhabitants to collect in the lounge, shut all the windows, and talk about the jute-industry. To her surprise, though the sun was streaming down from a cloudless sky, the only occupant of the lounge was the octogenarian with the ear-trumpet. She observed that he was chuckling to himself in a senile manner.

'Good morning,' she said, politely, for she had made his acquaintance on the previous evening.

'Hey?' said the octogenarian, suspending his chuckling and getting his trumpet into position.

'I said "Good morning!"' roared Barbara into the receiver.

'Hey?'

'Good morning!'

'Ah! Yes, it's a very fine morning, a very fine morning. If it wasn't for missing my bun and glass of milk at twelve sharp,' said the octogenarian, 'I'd be down on the links. That's where I'd be, down on the links. If it wasn't for missing my bun and glass of milk.'

This refreshment arriving at this moment, he began to restore his tissues.

'Watching the match,' he explained, pausing for a moment in his bun-mangling.

'What match?'

The octogenarian sipped his milk.

'What match?' repeated Barbara.

'Hey?'

'What match?'

The octogenarian began to chuckle again and nearly swallowed a crumb the wrong way.

'Take some of the conceit out of him,' he gurgled.

'Out of who?' asked Barbara, knowing perfectly well that she should have said 'whom.'

'Yes,' said the octogenarian.

'Who is conceited?'

'Ah! This young fellow, Dibble. Very conceited. I saw it in his eye from the first, but nobody would listen to me. Mark my words, I said, that boy needs taking down a peg or two. Well, he's going to be this morning. Your uncle wired to young Parsloe to come down, and he's arranged a match between them. Dibble—' Here the octogenarian choked again and had to rinse himself out with milk, 'Dibble doesn't know that Parsloe once went round in ninety-four!'

'What!'

Everything seemed to go black to Barbara. Through a murky mist, she appeared to be looking at a negro octogenarian sipping ink. Then her eyes cleared, and she found herself clutching for support at the back of a chair. She understood now. She realised why Ferdinand had been so distrait, and her whole heart went out to him in a spasm of maternal pity. How she had wronged him!

'Take some of the conceit out of him,' the octogenarian was mumbling, and Barbara felt a sudden sharp loathing for the old man. For two pins she could have dropped a beetle in his milk. Then the need for action roused her. What action? She did not know. All she knew was that she must act.

'Oh!' she cried.

'Hey?' said the octogenarian, bringing his trumpet to the ready. But Barbara had gone.

It was not far to the links, and Barbara covered the distance on flying feet. Looking to left and right, she was presently aware of a group of spectators clustered about a green in the distance. As she hurried toward them, they moved away, and now she could see Ferdinand advancing to the next tee. With a thrill that shook her whole body she realised that he had the honour. So he must have won one hole, at any rate. Then she saw her uncle.

'How are they?' she gasped.

Mr Tuttle seemed moody. It was apparent that things were not going altogether to his liking.

'All square at the fifteenth,' he replied gloomily.

'All square!'

'Yes. Young Parsloe,' said Mr Tuttle with a sour look in the direction of that lissome athlete, 'doesn't seem to be able to do a thing right on the greens. He has been putting like a sheep with the botts.'

From the foregoing remark of Mr Tuttle, you will no doubt have gleaned at least a clue to the mystery of how Ferdinand Dibble had managed to hold his long-driving adversary up to the fifteenth green; but for all that, you will probably consider that some further explanation of this amazing state of affairs is required. Mere bad putting on the part of George Parsloe is not, you feel, sufficient to cover the matter entirely. You are right. There was another very important factor in the situation – to wit, that by some extraordinary chance Ferdinand Dibble had started right off from the first tee playing the game of a lifetime. Never had he made such drives, never chipped his chips so shrewdly.

About Ferdinand's driving there was, as a general thing, a fatal stiffness and over-caution which prevented success. And with his chip-shots he rarely achieved accuracy, owing to his habit of rearing his head like the lion of the jungle just before the club struck the ball. But today he had been swinging with a careless freedom, and his chips had been true and clean. The thing had puzzled him all the way round. It had not elated him, for owing to Barbara's aloofness, and the way in which she had gambolled about George Parsloe like a young lamb in the springtime, he was in too deep a state of dejection to be elated by anything. And now, suddenly, in a flash of clear vision, he perceived the reason why he had been playing so well today. It was just because he was not elated. It was simply because he was so profoundly miserable.

That was what Ferdinand told himself as he stepped off the sixteenth after hitting a screamer down the centre of the fairway, and I am convinced that he was right. Like so many indifferent golfers, Ferdinand Dibble had always made the game hard for himself by thinking too much. He was a deep student of the works of the masters, and whenever he prepared to play a stroke, he had a complete mental list of all the mistakes which it was possible to make. He would remember how Taylor had warned against dipping the right shoulder, how Vardon had inveighed against any movement of the head; he would recall how Ray had mentioned the tendency to snatch back the club, how Braid had spoken sadly of those who sin against their better selves by stiffening the muscles and heaving.

The consequence was that when, after waggling in a frozen manner till mere shame urged him to take some definite course of action, he eventually swung, he invariably proceeded to dip his right shoulder, stiffen his muscles, heave and snatch back the club, at the same time raising his head sharply as in the illustrated plate ('Some Frequent Faults of Beginners – No. 3, Lifting the Bean') facing Page 34 of James Braid's *Golf Without Tears*. Today he had been so preoccupied with his broken heart that he had made his shots absently, almost carelessly, with the result that at least one in every three had been a lallapaloosa.

Meanwhile, George Parsloe had driven off and the match was progressing. George was feeling a little flustered by now. He had been given to understand that this bird Dibble was a hundred-at-his-best man, and all the way round, the fellow had been shooting fives in great profusion, and had once actually got a four. True, there had been an occasional six, and even a seven, but that did not alter the main fact that the man was making the dickens of a game of it. With the haughty spirit of one who had once done a ninety-four, George Parsloe had anticipated being at least three up at the turn. Instead of which, he had been two down and had had to fight strenuously to draw level!

Nevertheless he drove steadily and well, and would certainly have won the hole had it not been for his weak and sinful putting. The same defect caused him to halve the seventeenth after being on in two, with Ferdinand wandering in the desert and only reaching the green with his fourth. There, however, Ferdinand holed out from a distance of seven yards, getting a five which George's three putts just enabled him to equal.

Barbara had been watching the proceedings with a beating heart. At first she had looked on from afar; but now, drawn as by a magnet, she approached the tee. Ferdinand was driving off. She held her breath. Ferdinand held his breath. And all around, one could see their respective breaths being held by George Parsloe, Mr Tuttle and the enthralled crowd of spectators. It was a moment of the acutest tension, and it was broken by the crack of Ferdinand's driver as it met the ball and sent it hopping along the ground for a mere thirty yards. At this supreme crisis in the match Ferdinand Dibble had topped.

George Parsloe teed up his ball. There was a smile of quiet satisfaction on his handsome face. He snuggled the driver in his hands and gave it a preliminary swish. This, felt George Parsloe, was where the happy ending came. He would drive as he had never driven before. He would so drive that it would take his opponent at least three shots to catch up with him. He drew back his club with infinite caution, poised it at the top of the swing –

'I always wonder—' said a clear girlish voice, ripping the silence like the explosion of a bomb.

George Parsloe started. His club wobbled. It descended. The ball trickled into the long grass in front of the tee. There was a grim pause.

'You were saying, Miss Medway?' said George Parsloe in a small, flat voice.

'Oh, I'm so sorry,' said Barbara. 'I'm afraid I put you off.'

'A little, perhaps. Possibly the merest trifle. But you were saying you wondered about something. Can I be of any assistance?'

'I was only saying, that I always wonder why tees are called tees.'

George Parsloe swallowed once or twice. He also blinked a little feverishly. His eyes had a dazed, staring expression.

'I am afraid I cannot tell you off-hand,' he said. 'But I will make a point of consulting some good encyclopaedia at the earliest opportunity.'

'Thank you so much.'

'Not at all. It will be a pleasure. In case you were thinking of inquiring, at the moment when I am putting, why greens are called greens, may I venture the suggestion now that it is because they are green?'

And so saying, George Parsloe stalked to his ball and found it nestling in the heart of some shrub of which, not being a botanist, I cannot give you the name. It was a close-knit, adhesive shrub, and it twined its tentacles so lovingly around George Parsloe's niblick that he missed his first shot altogether. His second made the ball rock, and his third dislodged it.

Playing a full swing with his brassie, and being by now a mere caldron of seething emotions, he missed his fourth. His fifth came to within a few inches of Ferdinand's drive, and he picked it up and hurled it from him into the rough as if it had been something venomous.

'Your hole and match,' said George Parsloe thinly.

Ferdinand Dibble sat beside the glittering ocean. He had hurried off the course with swift strides the moment George Parsloe had spoken those bitter words. He wanted to be alone with his thoughts.

They were mixed thoughts. For a moment joy at the reflection that he had won a tough match came irresistibly to the surface, only to sink again as he remembered that life, whatever its triumphs, could hold nothing for him now that Barbara Medway loved another.

'Mr Dibble?'

He looked up. She was standing at his side. He gulped and rose to his feet.

'Yes?'

There was a silence.

'Doesn't the sun look pretty on the water?' said Barbara.

Ferdinand groaned. This was too much.

'Leave me,' he said hollowly. 'Go back to your Parsloe, the man with whom you walked in the moonlight beside this same water.'

'Well, why shouldn't I walk with Mr Parsloe in the moonlight beside this same water?' demanded Barbara with spirit.

'I never said,' replied Ferdinand, for he was a fair man at heart, 'that you shouldn't walk with Mr Parsloe beside this same water; I simply said you *did* walk with Mr Parsloe beside this same water. And what I mean is, go back to him.'

'I've a perfect right to walk with Mr Parsloe beside this same water,' persisted Barbara. 'He and I are old friends.'

Ferdinand groaned again.

'Exactly! There you are! As I suspected! Old friends! Played together as children and what not, I shouldn't wonder.'

'No, we didn't. I've only known him five years. But he is engaged to be married to my greatest chum, so that draws us together.'

Ferdinand uttered a strangled cry:

'Parsloe engaged to be married!'

'Yes. The wedding takes place next month.'

'But look here,' Ferdinand's forehead was wrinkled. He was thinking tensely. 'Look here,' said Ferdinand, a close reasoner, 'if Parsloe's engaged to your greatest chum, he can't be in love with *you*.'

'No.'

'And you aren't in love with him?'

'No.'

'Then, by gad,' said Ferdinand, 'how about it?'

'What do you mean?'

'Will you marry me?' bellowed Ferdinand.

'Yes.'

'You will?'

'Of course I will.'

'Darling!' cried Ferdinand.

'There is only one thing that bothers me a bit,' said Ferdinand thoughtfully as they strolled together over the scented meadows while in the trees above them a thousand birds trilled Mendelssohn's Wedding March.

'What is that?'

'Well, I'll tell you,' said Ferdinand. 'The fact is, I've just discovered the great secret of golf. You can't play a really hot game unless you're so miserable that you don't worry over your shots. Take the case of a chip-shot, for instance. If you're really wretched, you don't care where the ball is going, and so you don't raise your head to see. Grief automatically prevents pressing and over-swinging. Look at the top-notchers. Have you ever seen a happy pro?'

'No I don't think I have.'

'Well, then!'

'But pros are all Scotchmen,' argued Barbara.

'It doesn't matter. I'm sure I'm right. And the darned thing is that I'm going to be so infernally happy all the rest of my life that I suppose my handicap will go up to thirty or something.'

Barbara squeezed his hand lovingly.

'Don't worry, precious,' she said soothingly. 'It will be all right. I am a woman, and once we are married, I shall be able to think of at least a hundred ways of snootering you to such an extent that you'll be fit to win the Amateur Championship.'

'You will?' said Ferdinand anxiously. 'You're sure?'

'Quite, quite sure, dearest,' said Barbara.

'My angel!' said Ferdinand.

He folded her in his arms, using the interlocking grip.

THE PRIDE OF
BERMONDSEY: 'THE EXIT OF
BATTLING BILLSON'

After Sheen of The White Feather, *perhaps the most memorable fist-fighter in the Plum oeuvre is Wilberforce 'Battling' Billson, hinge figure in a trio of stories Wodehouse published in 1923, a fourth arriving belatedly in 1935.*

Picture, if you will, a 'strong, silent' and 'enormous red-headed man' of 'formidable physique' with 'the jaw of a Wild West motion-picture star registering Determination'. Imagine him, further, 'stripped to a breath-taking semi-nudity … Muscles resembling the hawsers of an Atlantic liner coiled down his arms and rippled along his massive shoulders'. Thus Billson, or 'The Battler'.

And yet, on the face of it, Billson is really only the catspaw of Stanley Featherstonehaugh Ukridge, Wodehouse's irrepressible ducker-and-diver and scam-merchant, forever seeking to get-rich-quick. The premise of the four Billson stories (narrated by Ukridge's old school chum Corky Corcoran) is that Ukridge has come to believe that managing a boxer in the fight game is a sure-fire earner. 'That bloke's going to make my everlasting fortune,' Ukridge asserts to Corky. 'The man's a champion, laddie, nothing less. You couldn't hurt him with a hatchet, and every time he hits anyone all the undertakers in the place jump up and make bids for the body.'

Moreover: Ukridge sees Billson not merely as a means to trouser fifty per cent of legitimate winnings from the ring but, further, to manipulate the betting odds and the possible outcomes of a fight in his financial favour.

So Ukridge can't lose? Of course he can. The man–mountain Billson is also soft–hearted, firmly principled, and quite easily conned, especially in any business touching upon his fiancée Flossie, barmaid at the Crown in Kennington. 'Who ever heard of a mushy pugilist?' Ukridge comes to lament. 'It's the wrong spirit. It doesn't make for success.' But it does, of course, make for comedy.

This, the third of the four Billson stories, appeared in Cosmopolitan *in December 1923.*

The Theatre Royal, Llunindnno, is in the middle of the principal thoroughfare of that repellent town, and immediately opposite its grubby main entrance there is a lamp-post. Under this lamp-post, as I approached, a man was standing. He was a large man, and his air was that of one who has recently passed through some trying experience. There was dust on his person, and he had lost his hat. At the sound of my footsteps he turned, and the rays of the lamp revealed the familiar features of my old friend Stanley Featherstonehaugh Ukridge.

'Great Scott!' I ejaculated. 'What are you doing here?'

There was no possibility of hallucination. It was the man himself in the flesh. And what Ukridge, a free agent, could be doing in Llunindnno was more than I could imagine. Situated, as its name implies, in Wales, it is a dark, dingy, dishevelled spot, inhabited by tough and sinister men with suspicious eyes and three-day beards; and to me, after a mere forty minutes' sojourn in the place, it was incredible that anyone should be there except on compulsion.

Ukridge gaped at me incredulously. 'Corky, old horse,' he said, 'this is, upon my Sam, without exception the most amazing event in the world's history. The last bloke I expected to see.'

'Same here. Is anything the matter?' I asked, eying his bedraggled appearance.

'Matter? I should say something was the matter!' snorted Ukridge, astonishment giving way to righteous indignation. 'They chucked me out!'

'Chucked you out? Who? Where from?'

'This infernal theatre, laddie. After taking my good money, dash it! At least, I got in on my face, but that has nothing to do with the principle of the thing. Corky, my boy, don't you ever go about this world seeking for justice, because there's no such thing under the broad vault of Heaven. I had just gone out for a breather after the first act, and when I came back I found some fiend in human shape had pinched my seat. And just because I tried to lift the fellow out by the ears, a dozen hired assassins swooped down and shot me out. Me, I'll trouble you! The injured party! Upon my Sam,' he said heatedly, with a longing look at the door, 'I've a dashed good mind to—'

'I shouldn't,' I said soothingly. 'After all, what does it matter? It's just one of those things that are bound to happen from time to time. The man of affairs passes them off with a light laugh.'

'Yes, but—'

'Come and have a drink.'

The suggestion made him waver. The light of battle died down in his eyes. He stood for a moment in thought.

'You wouldn't bung a brick through the window?' he queried doubtfully.

'No, no.'

'Perhaps you're right.'

He linked his arm in mine and we crossed the road to where the lights of a public house shone like heartening beacons. The crisis was over.

'Corky,' said Ukridge, warily laying down his mug of beer a few minutes later lest emotion should cause him to spill any of its precious contents, 'I can't get over, I simply cannot get over the astounding fact of your being in this blighted town.'

I explained my position. My presence in Llunindnno was due to the fact that the paper which occasionally made use of my services as a special writer had sent me to compose a fuller and more scholarly report than its local correspondent seemed capable of concocting of the activities of one Evan Jones, the latest of those revivalists who periodically convulse the emotions of the Welsh mining population. His last and biggest meeting was to take place next morning at eleven o'clock.

'But what are you doing here?' I asked.

'What am I doing here?' said Ukridge. 'Who, me? Why, where else would you expect me to be? Haven't you heard? Haven't you seen the posters?'

'What posters? I only arrived an hour ago.'

'My dear old horse! Then naturally you aren't abreast of local affairs.' He drained his mug, breathed contentedly and led me out into the street. 'Look!'

He was pointing at a poster, boldly lettered in red and black, which decorated the side wall of the Bon Ton Millinery Emporium. The street-lighting system of Llunindnno is defective, but I was able to read what it said.

ODDFELLOWS HALL
Special Ten-Round Contest
LLOYD THOMAS
(Llunindnno)

v.

BATTLING BILLSON
(Bermondsey)

'Comes off tomorrow night,' said Ukridge. 'And I don't mind telling you, laddie, that I expect to make a colossal fortune.'

'Are you still managing the Battler?' I said, surprised at this dogged perseverance. 'I should have thought that after your last two experiences you would have had about enough of it.'

'Oh, he means business this time! I've been talking to him like a father.'

'How much does he get?'

'Twenty quid.'

'Twenty quid? Well, where we does the colossal fortune come in? Your share will only be a tenner.'

'No, my boy. You haven't got on to my devilish shrewdness. I'm not in on the purse at all this time. I'm the management.'

'The management?'

'Well, part of it. You remember Isaac O'Brien, the bookie I was partner with till that chump Looney Coote smashed the business? Izzy Previn is his real name. We've gone shares in this thing. Izzy came down a week ago, hired the hall and looked after the advertising and so on; and I arrived with good old Billson this afternoon. We're giving him twenty quid, and the other fellow's getting another twenty; and all the rest of the cash Izzy and I split on a fifty-fifty basis. Affluence, laddie! That's what it means. Affluence beyond the dreams of a Monte Cristo. Owing to this Jones fellow the place is crowded, and every sports-man for miles around will be there tomorrow at five bob a head, cheaper seats two-and-six, and standing room one shilling. Add lemonade and fried fish privileges, and you have a proposition almost without parallel in the annals of commerce. I couldn't be more on velvet if they gave me a sack and a shovel and let me loose in the Mint.'

I congratulated him in suitable terms.

'How is the Battler?' I asked.

'Trained to an ounce. Come see him tomorrow morning.'

'I can't. I've got to go to this Jones meeting.'

'Oh, yes. Well, make it early in the afternoon, then. Don't come later than three, because he will be resting. We're at Number Seven Caerleon Street. Ask for the Cap and Feathers public house and turn sharp to the left.'

*

I was in a curiously uplifted mood on the following afternoon as I set out to pay my respects to Mr Billson. This was the first time I had had occasion to attend one of these revival meetings, and the effect it had had on me was to make me feel as if I had been imbibing large quantities of champagne to the accompaniment of a very loud orchestra. Even before the revivalist rose to speak, the proceedings had had an effervescent quality singularly unsettling to the sober mind, for the vast gathering had begun to sing hymns directly they took their seats; and while the opinion I had formed of the inhabitants of Llunindnno was not high, there was no denying their vocal powers.

There is something about a Welsh voice when raised in song that no other voice seems to possess – a creepy, heart-searching quality that gets right into a man's inner consciousness and stirs it up with a pole. And on top of this had come Evan Jones's address.

It did not take me long to understand why this man had gone through the countryside like a flame. He had magnetism, intense earnestness and the voice of a prophet crying in the wilderness. His fiery eyes seemed to single out each individual in the hall, and every time he paused, sighings and wailings went up like the smoke of a furnace. And then, after speaking for what I discovered with amazement on consulting my watch was considerably over an hour, he stopped. And I blinked like an aroused somnambulist, shook myself to make sure I was still there, and came away.

And now, as I walked in search of the Cap and Feathers, I was, as I say, oddly exhilarated; and I was strolling along in a sort of trance when a sudden uproar jerked me from my thoughts. I looked about me and saw the sign of the Cap and Feathers over a building across the street.

It was a dubious looking hostelry in a dubious neighbourhood; and the sounds proceeding from its interior were not reassuring to a peace-loving pedestrian. There was a good deal of shouting going on and much smashing of glass, and as I stood there the door flew open and a familiar figure emerged rather hastily. A moment later there appeared in the doorway a woman.

She was a small woman, but she carried the largest and most intimidating mop I had ever seen. It dripped dirty water as she brandished it; and the man, glancing apprehensively over his shoulder, proceeded rapidly on his way.

'Hullo, Mr Billson,' I said as he shot by me.

It was not perhaps the best chosen moment for endeavouring to engage him in light conversation. He showed no disposition whatever to linger. He vanished round the corner, and the woman, with a few winged words, gave her mop a victorious flourish and re-entered the public house. I walked on, and a little later a huge figure stepped cautiously out of an alleyway and fell into step at my side.

'Didn't recognise you, mister,' said Mr Billson apologetically.

'You seemed in rather a hurry,' I agreed.

'R!' said Mr Billson, and a thoughtful silence descended upon him for a space.

'Who,' I asked, tactlessly perhaps, 'was your lady friend?'

Mr Billson looked a trifle sheepish. Unnecessarily, in my opinion. Even heroes may legitimately quail before a mop wielded by an angry woman.

'She come out of a back room,' he said with embarrassment. 'Started makin' a fuss when she saw what I'd done. So I come away. You can't dot a woman,' he argued chivalrously.

'Certainly not,' I agreed. 'But what was the trouble?'

'I been doin' good,' said Mr Billson virtuously.

'Doing good?'

'Spillin' their beers.'

'Whose beers?'

'All of their beers. I went in, and there was a lot of sinful fellers drinkin' beers. So I spilled 'em. All of 'em. Walked round and spilled all of them beers, one after the other. Not 'arf surprised, them pore sinners wasn't,' said Mr Billson with what sounded to me not unlike a worldly chuckle.

'I can readily imagine it.'

'Huh?'

'I say, I bet they were.'

'R!' said Mr Billson. He frowned. 'Beer,' he proceeded with cold austerity, 'ain't right. Sinful, that's what beer is. It stingeth like a serpent and biteth like a ruddy adder.'

My mouth watered a little. Beer like that was what I had been scouring the country for for years. I thought it imprudent, however, to say so.

For some reason which I could not fathom my companion, one as fond of his half-pint as the next man, seemed to have conceived a puritanical hostility to the beverage. I decided to change the subject.

'I'm looking forward to seeing you fight tonight,' I said.

He eyed me woodenly. 'Me?'

'Yes. At the Oddfellows Hall, you know.'

He shook his head. 'I ain't fighting at no Oddfellows Hall,' he replied. 'Not at no Oddfellows Hall nor nowhere else I'm not fighting, not tonight nor no night.' He pondered stolidly, and then, as if coming to the conclusion that his last sentence could be improved by the addition of a negative, added 'No!'

And having said this, he suddenly stopped and stiffened like a pointing dog; and, looking up to see what interesting object by the wayside had attracted his notice, I perceived that we were standing beneath another public house sign, that of the Blue Boar. Its windows were hospitably open, and through them came a musical clinking of glasses. Mr Billson licked his lips with a quiet relish.

'Scuse me, mister,' he said, and left me abruptly.

My one thought now was to reach Ukridge as quickly as possible in order to acquaint him with these sinister developments. For I was startled. More, I was alarmed and uneasy. In one of the star performers at a special ten-round contest, scheduled to take place that evening, Mr Bilison's attitude seemed to me peculiar, not to say disquieting. So, even though a sudden crash and uproar from the interior of the Blue Boar called invitingly to me to linger, I hurried on and neither stopped, looked nor listened until I stood on the steps of Number Seven Caerleon Street. And eventually, after my prolonged ringing and knocking had finally induced a female of advanced years to come up and open the door, I found Ukridge lying on a horsehair sofa in the far corner of the sitting room.

I unloaded my grave news. It was wasting time to try to break it gently.

'I've just seen Billson,' I said, 'and he seems to be in rather a strange mood. In fact, I'm sorry to say, old man, he rather gave me the impression—'

'That he wasn't going to fight tonight?' said Ukridge with a strange calm. 'Quite correct. He isn't. He's just been in here to tell me so. What I like about the man is his consideration for all concerned. He doesn't want to upset anybody's arrangements.'

'But what's the trouble? Is he kicking about only getting twenty pounds?'

'No. He's got religion.'

'What!'

'Nothing more nor less, Corky, my boy. Like chumps, we took our eyes off him for half a second this morning, and he sneaked off to that revival meeting. Went out shortly after a light and wholesome breakfast for what he called a bit of a mooch round, and came in half an hour ago a changed man. Full of loving kindness, curse him. Nasty, shifty gleam in his eye. Told us he thought fighting sinful and it was all off, and then buzzed out to spread the Word.'

I was shaken to the core. Wilberforce Billson, the peerless but temperamental Battler, had never been an ideal pugilist to manage, but hitherto he had drawn the line at anything like this. Other problems which he might have brought up for his manager to solve might have been overcome by patience and tact, but not this one. The psychology of Mr Billson was as an open book to me. He possessed one of those single-track minds capable of accommodating but one idea at a time, and he had the tenacity of the simple soul. Argument would leave him unshaken. On that bone-like head reason would beat in vain. And, these things being so, I was at a loss to account for Ukridge's extraordinary calm. His fortitude in the hour of ruin amazed me. His next remark, however, offered an explanation.

'We're putting on a substitute,' he said.

I was relieved. 'Oh, you've got a substitute? That's a bit of luck. Where did you find him?'

'As a matter of fact, laddie, I've decided to go on myself.'

'What! You!'

'Only way out, my boy. No other solution.'

I stared at the man. Years of the closest acquaintance with S. F. Ukridge had rendered me almost surprise-proof at anything he might do, but this was too much.

'Do you mean to tell me that you seriously intend to go out there tonight and appear in the ring?' I cried.

'Perfectly straightforward business-like proposition, old man,' said Ukridge stoutly. 'I'm in excellent shape. I sparred with Billson every day while he was training.'

'Yes, but—'

'The fact is, laddie, you don't realise my potentialities. Recently, it's true, I've allowed myself to become slack and what you might call enervated, but, damme, when I was on that trip in that tramp steamer scarcely a week used to go by without my having a good earnest scrap with somebody. Nothing barred,' said Ukridge, musing lovingly on the carefree past, 'except biting and bottles.'

'Yes, but, hang it – a professional pugilist!'

'Well, to be absolutely accurate, laddie,' said Ukridge, suddenly dropping the heroic manner and becoming confidential, 'the thing's going to be fixed. Izzy Previn has seen the bloke Thomas's manager and has arranged a gentleman's agreement. The manager, a Class A bloodsucker, insists on us giving his man another twenty pounds after the fight, but that can't be helped. In return, the Thomas bloke consents to play light for three rounds, at the end of which period, laddie, he will tap me on the side of the head and I shall go down and out, a popular loser. What's more, I'm allowed to hit him hard – once – just so long as it isn't on the nose. So you see – a little tact, a little diplomacy, and the whole thing fixed up as satisfactorily as anyone could wish.'

'But suppose the audience demands its money back when they find they're going to see a substitute?'

'My dear old horse,' protested Ukridge, 'surely you don't imagine that a man with a business head like mine overlooked that? Naturally I'm going to fight as Battling Billson. Nobody knows him in this town. I'm a good big chap, just as much a heavyweight as he is. No, laddie, pick how you will, you can't pick a flaw in this.'

'Why mayn't you hit him on the nose?'

'I don't know. People have these strange whims. And now, Corky, my boy, I think you had better leave me. I ought to relax.'

The Oddfellows Hall was certainly filling up nicely when I arrived that night. Indeed, it seemed as though Llunindnno's devotees of sport would cram it to the roof. I took my place in the line before the pay window, and, having completed the business end of the transaction, went in and inquired my way to the dressing rooms. And presently, after wandering through divers passages, I came upon Ukridge, clad for the ring and swathed in his familiar yellow mackintosh.

'You're going to have a wonderful house,' I said. 'The populace is rolling up in shoals.'

He received the information with a strange lack of enthusiasm. I looked at him in concern and was disquieted by his forlorn appearance. That face, which had beamed so triumphantly at our last meeting, was pale and set. Those eyes, which normally shone with the flame of an unquenchable optimism, seemed dull and careworn. And even as I looked at him he seemed to rouse himself from a stupor and, reaching out for his shirt, which hung on a near-by peg, proceeded to pull it over his head.

'What's the matter?' I asked.

His head popped out of the shirt, and he eyed me wanly.

'I'm off,' he announced briefly.

'Off? How do you mean, off?' I tried to soothe what I took to be an eleventh hour attack of stage fright. 'You'll be all right.' Ukridge laughed hollowly. 'Once the gong goes, you'll forget the crowd.'

'It isn't the crowd,' said Ukridge in a pale voice, climbing into his trousers. 'Corky, old man, if ever you feel your angry passions rising to the point where you want to swat a stranger, restrain yourself. This bloke Thomas was in here a moment ago with his manager to settle the final details. He's the fellow I had the trouble with at the theatre last night!'

'The man you pulled out of the seat by his ears?' I gasped.

Ukridge nodded. 'Recognised me at once, confound him, and it was all his manager, a thoroughly decent cove, whom I liked, could do to prevent him getting at me there and then.'

'Good Lord!' I said, aghast at this grim development, yet thinking how thoroughly characteristic it was of Ukridge, when he had a whole townful of people to quarrel with, to pick the one professional pugilist.

At this moment, when Ukridge was lacing his left shoe, the door opened and a man came in.

The newcomer was small, dark and beady-eyed, and from his manner of easy comradeship and the fact that, when he spoke, he supplemented words with the language of the waving palm, I deduced that this must be Mr Izzy Previn, recently trading as Isaac O'Brien. He was cheeriness itself.

'Vell,' he said with ill-timed exuberance, 'how'th the boy?' The boy cast a sour look at him. 'The house,' proceeded Mr Previn with an almost lyrical enthusiasm, 'is abtholutely full. Crammed, jammed and packed. They're hanging from the roof by their eyelids. It'th goin' to be a knockout.'

The expression, considering the circumstances, could hardly have been less happily chosen. Ukridge winced painfully, then spoke in no uncertain voice.

'I'm not going to fight!'

Mr Previn's exuberance fell from him like a garment. His cigar dropped from his mouth, and his beady eyes glittered with sudden consternation.

'What do you mean?'

'Rather an unfortunate thing has happened,' I explained. 'It seems that this man Thomas is a fellow Ukridge had trouble with at the theatre last night ... '

'What do you mean, Ukridge?' broke in Mr Previn. 'This is Battling Billson.'

'I've told Corky all about it,' said Ukridge over his shoulder as he laced his right shoe. 'Old pal of mine.'

'Oh!' said Mr Previn, relieved. 'Of course, if Mr Corky is a friend of yours and quite understands that all this is quite private among ourselves and don't want talking about outside, all right. But what were you thayin'? I can't make head or tail of it. How do you mean you're not goin' to fight? Of course you're goin' to fight.'

'Thomas was in here just now,' I said. 'Ukridge and he had a row at the theatre last night, and naturally Ukridge is afraid he will go back on the agreement.'

'Nonthense,' said Mr Previn, and his manner was that of one soothing a refractory child. 'He won't go back on the agreement. He promised he'd play light and he will play light. Gave me his word as a gentleman.'

'He isn't a gentleman,' Ukridge pointed out moodily.

'But lithen!'

'I'm going to get out of here as quick as I dashed well can!'

'Conthider!' pleaded Mr Previn, clawing great chunks out of the air. Ukridge began to button his collar. 'Reflect!' moaned Mr Previn. 'There's that lovely audience all sitting out there, jammed like thardines, waiting for the thing to start. Do you expect me to go and tell 'em there ain't goin' to be no fight? I'm thurprised at you,' said Mr Previn, trying an appeal to his pride. 'Where's your manly spirit? A big, husky feller like you, that's done all sorts of scrappin' in your time—'

'Not,' Ukridge pointed out coldly, 'with any professional pugilists who've got a grievance against me.'

'He won't hurt you.'

'He won't get the chance.'

'You'll be as safe and cozy in that ring with him as if you was playing ball with your little thister.'

Ukridge said he didn't have a little sister.

'But think!' implored Mr Previn, flapping like a seal. 'Think of the money! Do you realise we'll have to return it all, every penny of it?'

A spasm of pain passed over Ukridge's face, but he continued buttoning his collar.

'And not only that,' said Mr Previn, 'but, if you ask me, they'll be so mad when they hear there ain't goin' to be no fight they'll lynch me' – Ukridge seemed to regard this possibility with calm – 'and you, too,' added Mr Previn.

Ukridge started. It was a plausible theory, and one that had not occurred to him before.

He paused irresolutely.

And at this moment a man came hurrying in.

'What's the matter?' he demanded fussily. 'Thomas has been in the ring for five minutes. Isn't your man ready?'

'In one-half tick,' said Mr Previn. He turned meaningly to Ukridge. 'That's right, ain't it? You'll be ready in half a tick?'

Ukridge nodded wanly. In silence he shed shirt, trousers, shoes and collar, parting from them as if they were old friends whom he never expected to see again. One wistful glance he cast at his mackintosh, lying forlornly across a chair, and then, with more than a suggestion of a funeral procession, we started down the corridor that led to the main hall. The hum of many voices came to us; there was a sudden blaze of light; and we were there.

I must say for the sport-loving citizens of Llunindnno that they appeared to be fair-minded men. Stranger in their midst though he was, they gave Ukridge an excellent reception as he climbed into the ring; and for a moment, such is the tonic effect of applause on a large scale, his depression seemed to lift. A faint, gratified smile played about his drawn mouth, and I think it would have developed into a bashful grin had he not at this instant caught sight of the redoubtable Mr Thomas towering massively across the way. I saw him blink as one who, thinking absently of this and that, walks suddenly into a lamp-post; and his look of unhappiness returned.

My heart bled for him. If the offer of my little savings in the bank could have transported him there and then to the safety of his London lodgings, I would have made it unreservedly. Mr Previn had disappeared, leaving me standing at the ring-side, and as nobody seemed to object I remained there, thus getting an excellent view of the mass of bone and sinew that made up Lloyd Thomas. And there was certainly plenty of him to see.

Mr Thomas was, I should imagine, one of those men who do not look their most formidable in mufti, for otherwise I could not conceive how even the fact that he had stolen his seat could have led Ukridge to lay the hand of violence upon him. In the exiguous costume of the ring he looked a person from whom the sensible man would suffer almost any affront with meekness. He was about six feet in height, and wherever a man could bulge with muscle he bulged. For a moment my anxiety for Ukridge was tinged with a wistful regret that I should never see this sinewy citizen in action with Mr Billson. It would, I mused, have been a battle worth coming even to Llunindnno to see.

The referee, meanwhile, had been introducing the principals in the curt, impressive fashion of referees. He now retired, and with a strange, foreboding note a gong sounded on the farther side of the ring. The seconds scuttled under the ropes. The man Thomas, struggling – it seemed to me – with powerful emotions, came ponderously out of his corner.

In these reminiscences of a vivid and varied career, it is as a profound thinker that I have for the most part had occasion to portray Stanley Featherstonehaugh Ukridge. I was now to be reminded that he also had it in him to be a doer. Even as Mr Thomas shuffled toward him, his left fist shot out and thudded against the other's ribs. In short, in a delicate and difficult situation Ukridge was comporting himself with an adequacy that surprised me. However great might have been his reluctance to embark on this contest, once in he was doing well.

And then, halfway through the first round, the truth dawned upon me. Injured though Mr Thomas had been, the gentleman's agreement still held. The word of a Thomas was as good as his bond. Poignant though his dislike of Ukridge might be, nevertheless, having pledged himself to mildness and self-restraint for the first three rounds, he intended to abide by the contract. Probably, in the interval between his visit to Ukridge's dressing room and his appearance in the ring, his manager had been talking earnestly to him. At any rate, whether it was managerial authority or his own sheer nobility of character that influenced him, the fact remains that he treated Ukridge with a quite remarkable forbearance, and the latter reached his corner at the end of round one practically intact.

And it was this that undid him. No sooner had the gong sounded for round two than out he pranced from his corner, thoroughly above himself. He bounded at Mr Thomas like a dervish.

I could read his thoughts as if he had spoken them. Nothing could be clearer than that he had altogether failed to grasp the true position of affairs. Instead of recognising his adversary's for-bearance for what it was and being decently grateful for it, he was filled with a sinful pride. Here, he told himself, was a man who had a solid grievance against him, and, dash it, the fellow couldn't hurt him a bit. What the whole thing boiled down to, he felt, was that he, Ukridge, was better than he had expected, a man to be reckoned with, and one who could show a distinguished gathering of patrons of sport something worth looking at. The consequence was that, where any sensible person would have grasped the situation at once and endeavoured to show his appre-ciation by toying with Mr Thomas in gingerly fashion, whispering soothing compliments into his ear during the clinches and gener-ally trying to lay the foundations of a beautiful friendship against the moment when the gentleman's agreement should lapse, Ukridge committed the one unforgivable act. There was a brief moment of fiddling and feinting in the centre of the ring, then a sharp smacking sound, a startled yelp, and Mr Thomas, with gradually reddening eye, leaning against the ropes muttering to himself in Welsh.

Ukridge had hit him on the nose.

Once more I must pay a tribute to the fair-mindedness of the sportsmen of Llunindnno. The stricken man was one of them – possibly Llunindnno's favourite son; yet nothing could have exceeded the heartiness with which they greeted the visitor's achievement. A shout went up as if Ukridge had done each indi-vidual present a personal favour. It continued as he advanced buoyantly upon his antagonist, and – to show how entirely Llun-indnno audiences render themselves impartial and free from any personal bias – it became redoubled as Mr Thomas, swinging a fist like a ham, knocked Ukridge flat on his back. Whatever happened, so long as it was sufficiently violent, seemed to be all right with that broad-minded audience.

Ukridge heaved himself laboriously to one knee. His sensibilities had been ruffled by this unexpected blow about fifteen times as hard as the others he had received since the beginning of the affray, but he was a man of mettle and determination. He struggled painfully to his feet, while Mr Thomas, now definitely abandoning the gentleman's agreement, hovered about him with ready fists, only restrained by the fact that one of Ukridge's gloves still touched the floor.

It was at this tensest of moments that a voice spoke in my ear. 'Alf a mo', mister!'

A hand pushed me gently aside. Something large obscured the lights. And Wilberforce Billson, squeezing under the ropes, clambered into the ring.

For the purposes of the historian it was a good thing that for the first few moments after this astounding occurrence a dazed silence held the audience in its grip. Otherwise, it might have been difficult to probe motives and explain underlying causes. I think the spectators were either too surprised to shout, or else they entertained for a few brief seconds the idea that Mr Billson was the forerunner of a posse of plain-clothes police about to raid the place. At any rate, for a space they were silent, and he was enabled to say his say.

'Fightin',' bellowed Mr Billson, 'ain't right!'

There was an uneasy rustle in the audience. The voice of the referee came thinly, saying 'Here! Hi!'

'Sinful,' explained Mr Billson in a voice like a fog-horn.

His oration was interrupted by Mr Thomas, who was endeavoring to get round him and attack Ukridge. The Battler pushed him gently back.

'Gents,' he roared, 'I, too, have been a man of voylence! I 'ave struck men in anger. R. Yes! But I 'ave seen the light. Oh, my brothers ... '

The rest of his remarks were lost. With a startling suddenness the frozen silence melted. In every part of the hall indignant seat-holders were rising to state their views.

But it is doubtful whether, even if he had been granted a continuance of their attention, Mr Billson would have spoken to much greater length, for at this moment Lloyd Thomas, who had been gnawing at the strings of his gloves with the air of a man who is able to stand just so much and whose limit has been exceeded, now suddenly shed these obstacles to the freer expression of self and, advancing bare-handed, smote Mr Billson violently on the jaw.

Mr Billson turned. He was pained, one could see that, but more spiritually than physically. For a moment he seemed uncertain how to proceed. Then he turned the other cheek. The fermenting Mr Thomas smote that too.

There was no vacillation or uncertainty now about Wilberforce Billson. He plainly considered that he had done all that could reasonably be expected of any pacifist. A man has only two cheeks. He flung up a mast-like arm to block a third blow, countered with an accuracy and spirit which sent his aggressor reeling to the ropes; and then, swiftly removing his coat, went into action with the unregenerate zeal that had made him the petted hero of a hundred water-fronts. And I, tenderly scooping Ukridge up as he dropped from the ring, hurried him away along the corridor to his dressing room. I would have given much to remain and witness a mix-up which, if the police did not interfere, promised to be the battle of the ages, but the claims of friendship are paramount.

Ten minutes later, however, when Ukridge, washed, clothed, and restored as near to the normal as a man may be who has received the full weight of a Lloyd Thomas on a vital spot, was reaching for his mackintosh, there filtered through the intervening doors and passageways a sudden roar so compelling that my sporting spirit declined to ignore it.

'Back in a minute, old man,' I said.

And, urged by that ever swelling roar, I cantered back to the hall.

In the interval during which I had been ministering to my stricken friend a certain decorum seemed to have been restored to the proceedings. The conflict had lost its first riotous abandon. Upholders of the decencies of debate had induced Mr Thomas to resume his gloves, and a pair had also been thrust upon the Battler. Moreover, it was apparent that the etiquette of the tourney now governed the conflict, for rounds had been introduced, and one had just finished as I came in view of the ring. Mr Billson was leaning back in a chair in one corner, undergoing treatment by his seconds, and in the opposite corner loomed Mr Thomas; and one sight of the two men was enough to tell me what had caused that sudden tremendous outburst of enthusiasm among the patriots of Llunindnno.

In the last stages of the round which had just concluded the native son must have forged ahead in no uncertain manner. Perhaps some chance blow had found its way through the Battler's guard, laying him open and defenceless to the final attack. For his attitude, as he sagged in his corner, was that of one whose moments are numbered. His eyes were closed, his mouth hung open and exhaustion was writ large upon him. Mr Thomas, on the contrary, leaned forward with hands on knees, wearing an impatient look, as if this formality of a rest between rounds irked his imperious spirit.

The gong sounded and he sprang from his seat.

'Laddie,' breathed an anguished voice, and a hand clutched my arm.

I was dimly aware of Ukridge standing beside me. I shook him off. This was no moment for conversation. My whole attention was concentrated on what was happening in the ring.

'I say, laddie!'

Matters in there had reached that tense stage when audiences lose their self-control – when strong men stand on seats and weak men cry 'Siddown!' The air was full of that electrical thrill that precedes the knock-out.

And the next moment it came. But it was not Lloyd Thomas who delivered it. From some mysterious reservoir of vitality Wilberforce Billson, the pride of Bermondsey, who an instant before had been reeling under his antagonist's blows like a stricken hulk before a hurricane, produced that one last punch that wins battles. Up it came, whizzing straight to its mark, a stupendous, miraculous uppercut which caught Mr Thomas on the angle of the jaw just as he lurched forward to complete his task. It was the last word. Anything milder Llunindnno's favourite son might have borne with fortitude, for his was a teak-like frame impervious to most things short of dynamite; but this was final. It left no avenue for argument or evasion. Lloyd Thomas spun around once in a complete circle, dropped his hands and sank slowly to the ground.

There was one wild shout from the audience, and then a solemn hush fell. And in this hush Ukridge's voice spoke once more in my ear.

'I say, laddie, that blighter Previn has bolted with every penny of the receipts!'

The little sitting room of Number Seven Caerleon Street was very quiet and gave the impression of being dark. This was because there is so much of Ukridge and he takes fate's blows so hardly that, when anything goes wrong, his gloom seems to fill a room like a fog. For some minutes after our return from the Oddfellows Hall a gruesome silence had prevailed. Ukridge had exhausted his vocabulary on the subject of Mr Previn; and as for me, the disaster seemed so tremendous as to render words of sympathy a mere mockery.

'And there's another thing I've just remembered,' said Ukridge hollowly, stirring on his sofa.

'What's that?' I inquired in a bedside voice.

'The bloke Thomas. He was to have got another twenty pounds.'

'He'll hardly claim it, surely?'

'He'll claim it, all right,' said Ukridge moodily. 'Except, by Jove,' he went on, a sudden note of optimism in his voice, 'that he doesn't know where I am. I was forgetting that. Lucky we legged it away from the hall before he could grab me.'

'You don't think that Previn, when he was making the arrangements with Thomas's manager, may have mentioned where you were staying?'

'Not likely. Why should he? What reason would he have?'

'Gentleman to see you, sir,' crooned the aged female at the door.

The gentleman walked in. It was the man who had come to the dressing room to announce that Thomas was in the ring; and though on that occasion we had not been formally introduced I did not need Ukridge's faint groan to tell me who he was.

'Mr Previn?' he said. He was a brisk man, direct in manner and speech.

'He's not here,' said Ukridge.

'You'll do. You're his partner. I've come for that twenty pounds.'

There was a painful silence.

'It's gone,' said Ukridge.

'What's gone?'

'The money, dash it. And Previn too. He's bolted.'

A hard look came into the other's eyes. Dim as the light was, it was strong enough to show his expression, and that expression was not an agreeable one.

'That won't do,' he said in a metallic voice.

'Now, my dear old horse—'

'It's no good trying anything like that on me. I want my money or I'm going to call a policeman. Now then!'

'But, laddie, be reasonable—'

'Made a mistake in not getting it in advance. But now'll do. Out with it!'

'But I keep telling you Previn's bolted!'

'He's certainly bolted,' I put in, trying to be helpful.

'That's right, mister,' said a voice at the door. 'I met 'im sneakin' away.'

It was Wilberforce Billson. He stood in the doorway diffidently, as one not sure of his welcome. His whole bearing was apologetic. He had a nasty bruise on his left cheek and one of his eyes was closed, but he bore no other signs of his recent conflict.

Ukridge was gazing upon him with bulging eyes. 'You met him!' he moaned. 'You actually met him?'

'R,' said Mr Billson. 'When I was comin' to the 'all. I seen 'im puttin' all that money into a liddle bag, and then 'e 'urried off.'

'Good Lord!' I cried. 'Didn't you suspect what he was up to?'

'R,' agreed Mr Billson. 'I always knew 'e was a wrong 'un.'

'Then why, you poor woollen-headed fish,' bellowed Ukridge, exploding, 'why on earth didn't you stop him?'

'I never thought of that,' admitted Mr Billson apologetically. Ukridge laughed a hideous laugh. 'I just pushed 'im in the face,' proceeded Mr Billson, 'and took the liddle bag away from 'im.'

He placed on the table a small, weather-worn suitcase that jingled musically as he moved it; then, with the air of one who dismisses some triviality from his mind, moved to the door.

'"Scuse me, gents,' said Battling Billson deprecatingly. 'Can't stop. I've got to go and spread the light.'

'PROSPECTS
FOR WAMBLEDON'

Aspiring writers are often advised to 'kill their darlings', a brutal way of saying that story ideas at first unsuccessful ought then to be discarded, at once and forever. Wilier professionals tend to advise that nothing even vaguely presentable should ever be thrown away but, rather, kept in a refrigerated state that could yet be reheated for consumption under the right circumstances. Wodehouse, of course, didn't write very many outright duffers; but he sometimes found that the first published version of a story or skit could be even better done with suitable changes a second time round.

Such is the following piece on a tennis theme, which has its origins in something American-set that he penned for Vanity Fair *in 1916, entitled 'A Great Coming Tennis Match: A Little Amateur Affair Soon to be Settled on Long Island'. But this iteration, revised for inclusion in the collection* Louder and Funnier, *refurbishes some of the original gags within a far funnier comic concept related to the All England Tennis Club of Wodehouse's homeland, and its immortal grass-court championship, traditionally settled in July.*

*

When I received a letter from a prominent editor asking me to write a crisp, chatty article on the form of the more generally fancied contestants for the forthcoming Lawn Tennis Championships at Wambledon, I confess I was a little surprised. As one who goes to that bracing seaside resort every summer to recuperate from the fatigues of the London Season, I naturally felt a patriotic thrill; but at the same time I was, as I say, somewhat puzzled. We who love Wambledon-on-Sea yield to none in our appreciation of its ozone-filled breezes, its water-supply, its Esplanade, and the inspiring architecture of its new Assembly Hall, but I should have thought myself that its tennis was scarcely of a calibre to excite nationwide interest.

However, editors know what they are doing. If the public wishes to hear all about Wambledon tennis, it simply shows – well, I cannot at the moment think just what it does show, but it obviously has a significance of some sort.

Tennis at Wambledon is confined mostly to the residents. Owing to the fact that the words 'On Sea' are really justified only twice a day, and that at other times all that meets the pleasure-seeker's eye is a waste of grey mud picked out with broken bottles and dead starfish, we get few visitors. And our isolation is increased by the supine policy of the railway company, which refuses to bring the branch line any nearer than Gluebury Mortimer. It is among the native sons and daughters, then, that we must seek for the winners of the handsome pewter cups so generously presented by Squire Bloomenstein of Wambledon Hall.

Of the Ladies' Singles there is little that one can say. It is always an open event. Matilda Jervis has outgeneralled her rivals by securing a Helen Wills' eyeshade. Jane Willoughby, on the other hand, has a larger collection of autographs of tennis celebrities. Muriel Debenham's aunt met Borotra last winter in the South of

France. In these circumstances, form is hard to estimate, and I should prefer not to commit myself, but to hasten on to the *bonne-bouche* of the day,

THE MEN'S SINGLES,

which, in the general consensus of Wambledon opinion, lies this year between four men. I allude to George Murgatroyd, Arthur ('Grandpop') Binns, Archibald Twirling, and John Jasper Jones – the last-named our courteous and popular undertaker.

In every event of a sporting nature there is, of course, always the possibility of a dark horse coming along at the last moment to upset the form-book; but to me – and I am supported in the view by the knowledgeable editor of *The Wambledon and West Worsley Intelligencer and Farmer's Gazette* – it seems that when, as Kipling finely says, the tumult and the shouting have died – and I hope those boys will try to be a little quieter this year, especially during the rallies, and, more particularly will refrain from throwing portions of fish at the players – when, I say, the tumult and the shouting have died and the captains and the kings have departed, the handsome pewter cup will be found on one of these four mantelpieces. Let us, then, concentrate upon this quartette and endeavour, by a minute examination of their methods when in action, to find the answer to the question,

WHO WILL THE VICTOR BE?

A few weeks ago, had I been asked to prognosticate, I should doubtless have confined my observations entirely to the first-named. And this though I am fully alive to the many merits of the other three. Like everybody else in Wambledon, I was dazzled, and I am man enough to admit it. It was early in June that

GEORGE WINSTANLEY MURGATROYD

made his initial appearance on our tennis-court. A graduate of Cambridge University, he had been engaged by Squire Bloomenstein to act as tutor to his son Oscar, a charming but somewhat backward boy; and it is not too much to say that he caused a veritable sensation. I was standing chatting when he arrived, I remember, with little Euphrosyne Burwash, daughter of the well-known contractor and surveyor, and I can testify that she shook like a jelly. At the moment she had been speaking with a good deal of enthusiasm of Ronald Colman; but at the sight of George Murgatroyd the words died on her lips, a strange light came into her eyes, and a bag of pear-drops fell from her nerveless fingers. She was discovered at a late hour that night, seated on the breakwater, reading Elinor Glyn and at intervals uttering little moans.

And I, for one, cannot blame her. No such magnificent vision had ever been seen before in the Wambledon area. About George's well-modelled shoulders there hung the prismatic scarf of his old college, loosely draped over the throat and blending subtly with the green, orange, and purple blazer of a dining-club to which he had belonged when at the University. He had a lovely tan, and on his snowy trousers and gleaming shoes there was no spot or blemish. Add to this the fact that he carried his racket in a case, and it will readily be seen that here was no ordinary man.

But now, as far as his actual tennis is concerned, the impression created by George Murgatroyd's advent has to a certain extent been blunted by familiarity and the passage of time. That was June. This is July. And in the intervening weeks we have seen George do his stuff, and the scales have fallen from our eyes.

For some days it seemed as though no opposition could live against George Murgatroyd. Nothing like his first serve, the fast one, had ever been seen at Wambledon. It astounded all beholders, dismayed all adversaries. And then, little by little, critics arose to point out that this serve, superb though it was in conception and magnificent as a mere spectacle, had never yet succeeded in getting over the net.

It was a serve that relied entirely on moral suasion. It was a sort of frightfulness. Leaping some feet into the air, George would hurl the ball to the clouds, strike it with hideous violence, and return to earth with a loud grunt. And his pallid opponent, cowering on the other side of the net, was invariably so unnerved by these phenomena that he nearly always failed to return the second serve, which was of a milder nature and more semicircular, reminiscent rather of the gentle rain after a thunderstorm.

But now, as I say, criticism has done its deadly work. His antagonists of late have been plucking up heart. They cower as before, but rally more swiftly, and recently the second serve has generally been killed. Nevertheless, there always remains the possibility of something practical developing from that first terrific slosh, and it is still felt that George Murgatroyd is a man to be reckoned with. He has the Law of Averages on his side. In the ten years that have passed since he first took up the game he has never yet got that first serve over the net. It may – nay, must – happen soon, and who knows but that it will happen during our annual tournament? Certainly, therefore, we must include George Murgatroyd in our list of Possibles.

We come next to

J. ARTHUR BINNS.

In Arthur Binns we find a player of a very different order. 'Grandpop', as he is called – affectionately and at a safe distance – by Wambledon's younger set, is a man of maturer years. Nobody, in fact, knows exactly how old he is. George Murgatroyd's statement that when Julius Caesar landed in England the first thing he saw was Grandpop Binns dancing about on the foreshore, painted bright blue and dressed in a wolf-skin, is, of course, pure persiflage. Personally, I should put Arthur Binns in the early seventies.

His years tell both for and against him. They have of necessity diminished the boyish sprightliness of his nonage, but on the other hand they have given him a wonderful steadiness and poise. He is not a remorseless machine like Archibald Twirling (with whom I shall deal presently), but nothing upsets him. He serves underhand, and has only once been known to volley – in June of the year 1910. His principal asset is his extraordinary knowledge of the ground. And in Wambledon tournaments to have a familiarity with the terrain is half the battle.

The tennis-court at Wambledon adjoins the Sea-View Hotel, and in his capacity of proprietor of that establishment it falls to Grandpop Binns to look after it and prepare it for the annual Championships. No one, therefore, knows better than he the exact position of the many bumps and hollows which punctuate the smoothness of its surface. Try as we may to prevent them, the village children will play rowdy games all over the court, and it is consequently full of heel-marks. These are thinly filled with loose sand, and a ball which strikes one of them sometimes stops dead and tries to bury itself, sometimes trickles off at a sharp angle. A man who knows the topography of the arena as well as does Arthur Binns must have more than a sporting chance of victory. Local opinion, it is true, is to some extent prejudiced against Grandpop, because he plays in his Sunday trousers and a stiff shirt, and rarely removes the top-hat which is his inseparable companion in his walks abroad: but looks are not everything in tennis, or who could compete with George Murgatroyd?

Let us not, then, dismiss Arthur Binns hastily. He is a distinct possibility. Indeed I, personally, would rank him a shade higher than the third player on my list, his friendly rival,

ARCHIBALD TWIRLING.

Archibald Twirling is a man of method. I have called him a remorseless machine, and that is what he is. In this restless age it is rarely that we find a man who takes one definite line and sticks to it. Archibald Twirling is one of the exceptions. A builder by profession, he builds nothing but bungalows, and each Twirling bungalow is precisely the same as every other Twirling bungalow, even down to the horse-shoe nailed over the front door. He rises at the same hour every day, retires to rest at the same hour every night. He eats one lightly boiled egg every morning for breakfast, and winds the clock up every evening at precisely ten. And so with his tennis. Right from the beginning, Archibald Twirling made up his mind how he proposed to play tennis, and he has never deviated from his chosen course. Whether his opponent be a George Murgatroyd or a Grandpop Binns, his method never varies.

It is Archibald's custom to stand at the back of the court and lob. If his adversary smashes, Archibald lobs. If he tries placing, Archibald still lobs. The longer the game goes on, the higher he lobs, until his antagonist, losing patience or, it may be, forgetting during the long wait for the ball to descend that he is engaged in a game of tennis, omits to return the stroke. Then Archibald shifts his chewing-gum from left to right, or vice versa, calls out the score in a rather melancholy voice, and goes on lobbing.

But Achilles had his heel, and so has Archibald Twirling. For a while, Archibald's progress was one of unalloyed triumph. All Wambledon's best and bravest fell before him. And then one day some shrewd student of the game discovered that he was physically and mentally unable to deal with a back-hand stroke, and now his rivals play sedulously on that fatal weakness.

It is an interesting and a pitiful sight to see Archibald Twirling when a crisis arrives which can only be met by a judicious application of the back-hand. There was a time when he would dive at the ball and try to lob it in the constrained attitude which had been forced upon him. But after lobbing perhaps a hundred balls into the sea, directly at right-angles to the spot where they should have gone, a frozen calm, a sort of dull resignation, seemed to descend on the unhappy man. He has now decided to treat such crises as Acts of God. There is something of the defeatist Russian philosophy in his attitude, a kind of crushed refusal to battle with Fate. Today, when a ball comes at his back-hand, Archibald just stands and looks at it sadly, in his eye something of that mild reproach which a hat-check boy bestows on a client who tips him with an aspirin tablet.

The vital flaw in his game of necessity diminishes his chances for the Championship, and if it were not for the peculiarly maddening nature of his methods one might rule him out of the race. Persistent lobbing, however, has worn down many a fine player, and we must accord Archibald Twirling at least an outside chance.

We now come to the last name on the list, and it is the name of a dangerous man. There is, indeed, a strong school of thought in the village whose members refuse to hear of anybody but

JOHN JASPER JONES

as the next Wambledon champion. I happen to know that down at the Fisherman and Mackerel odds are being offered on his success which would stun the public.

This Jones has practically everything. As regards service, he is undoubtedly the superior of any of the other entrants. True, he lacks George Murgatroyd's cavalier-like dash and fire, but on the other hand he has frequently been known to get his first serve over the net and on several occasions to place the ball in the right section of his opponent's territory. He does not slash at the ball like George, preferring to throw it a few inches in front of him and then give a sort of stabbing lunge at it. No one who has not played at Wambledon can understand the moral effect of a first serve that gets over the net. One might almost say that it is etiquette not to return it. And, while Jones does not intentionally put any spin on the ball, the irregularities of the ground frequently co-operate with him so happily that he becomes unplayable.

In addition to this, he is, if given plenty of time, a master of the back-hand. I speak a little loosely, perhaps. To be perfectly accurate, John Jasper Jones has never brought off a back-hand shot in his life, and never expects to. But Nature having made him ambidextrous, he has found a way of meeting the situation. Where Archibald Twirling merely stands and sighs, John Jasper Jones acts. If the ball comes to his left, he rapidly shifts the racket to the other hand, and before his startled adversary can brace himself to cope with this new development the sphere is on its way back over the net. I have seen strong men positively paralysed by the manoeuvre.

The only flaw in Jones's game is that he serves nothing but foot-faults. This might at first sight seem to reduce his chances of the handsome pewter cup to nil; but the resourceful man has found a way of overcoming this difficulty, too. Only a week ago he became engaged to the elderly sister of Bernard Thistleby, our sexton, who is to act as umpire in the tournament: and few of the cognoscenti doubt that, when it comes to the acid test, blood will prove thicker than water. Let me, therefore, come boldly out and state that, after weighing all the pros and cons, my money is on

JOHN JASPER JONES

for the big event.

There is just one other small point to be considered. Old Colonel Warburton will be a spectator, as usual, and something must undoubtedly depend on whether his vocal cords are in shape again or not. At the moment of writing, he is suffering from Clergyman's Sore Throat, induced by a lengthy argument with the driver of a lorry who backed into the left mud-guard of his car last Tuesday, and, when last seen, was virtually speechless. If he is still in this condition when the tournament opens, his influence on the fortunes of the contestants will, of course, be neutralised. If, on the other hand, he is in good voice, one cannot say what will happen. It is the Colonel's practice, when watching tennis, to throw his head back from time to time and emit sudden, sharp, hunting noises by way of encouraging the players. You never know when these will occur, and the effect of the suspense on a highly strung performer is frequently to put him right off his stroke. George Murgatroyd is particularly susceptible to them, and has been known in the hour of defeat to draw comparisons between the Colonel and the laughing hyena of the Indian jungle. They also affect John Jasper Jones and Archibald Twirling. Should the Colonel have recovered his full voltage by the great day, I should be inclined to transfer my support to Grandpop Binns, whom nothing can disturb. It was Grandpop Binns who, on the famous occasion in 1923 when the soap-boxes which form the foundation of the Grand Stand collapsed, injuring dozens of Wambledon's smartest residents, merely looked over his shoulder with a lack-lustre eye and, observing 'Forty-fifteen', proceeded to serve one right over the net into a hole left by Farmer Wilberforce's cow when that animal was pasturing on the court. One cannot afford to ignore nerve like that, for it is nerve that wins championships.

To sum up, let me conclude with those splendid words which are the bed-rock of that love of sport which makes us Englishmen what we are – May the best man win. That the contests will be conducted in the true spirit of British sportsmanship goes without saying. Tea will be provided on the ground and will be followed by a short address from the Vicar in aid of the Church Organ Fund. Should it rain, the Championship will be postponed until next August and a Shove-Ha'penny Tournament in the saloon bar of the Fisherman and Mackerel substituted. As this scarcely comes within the scope of my present article, I will not deal with the prospects for this event, merely contenting myself with recommending as a Safety Bet William Anstruther Simpson, the son and heir of Simpson's Bon Ton Drapery Stores, who, I am told, shoves a superb ha'penny.

NOTE – I find, on re-reading the Editor's letter, that it was the Wimbledon, not the Wambledon, Lawn Tennis Championships with which he wished me to deal; and, strictly speaking, I suppose, I ought to write this article all over again. I am informed, however, that by the time these lines are in print this other meeting will have been concluded; so I will leave things as they stand, merely mentioning that the date of the Wambledon Tournament is August the First and that any of my readers who care to be present will be assured of a warm welcome and hearty English fare. The station bus meets all trains at Gluebury Mortimer, unless it happens to slip the driver's mind, in which case there is a five-miles' walk through delightful scenery. Come one, come all.

WODEHOUSE & CRICKET:
INTERREGNUM YEARS

Back in London in August of 1923 for the rehearsals of a stage show, Wodehouse wrote to William Townend with less than his usual brio: '... there seems something dead and depressing about London. I don't know what it is. I've suddenly discovered that I don't care any more for watching first-class cricket, and of course that knocks the scheme of things endways, as last year I used to spend all my spare time at the Oval. Oh well, there it is, anyway.'

Such periodic low points aside, it would be quite wrong to imagine that English cricket ever really lost its place in the heart of the mainly expatriate Wodehouse. However unpropitious to the game his later domiciles might have appeared, he found ways to keep following cricket. For instance, during a stint in Hollywood as a not especially productive screenwriter, he took on the role of secretary for the Hollywood Cricket Club, an outfit founded by other homesick Anglo-exiles in Tinseltown, chief among these the former test cricketer turned actor C. Aubrey Smith.

Come the mid-1930s, Wodehouse had made his home at Le Touquet, the opulent French seaside town just south of Calais, blessed with its own golf course, racecourse, sea-front pool and (yes) cricket ground.

Living near Calais also allowed Wodehouse – as he confided in a letter of 1936 to his brother Armine – to get back to England 'for any cricket match I want to see'. He had, in other words, regained the savour for taking in the first-class game.

It was at Le Touquet that Wodehouse resided when war broke out in 1939. At first, such was his faith in the Allied Forces that he felt no great need to move. But the rapid German advance into France of May 1940 changed everything; and just as Wodehouse was making concerted efforts to flee, the occupying forces closed in. In July the 58-year-old Wodehouse was taken away to internment, first at Loos Prison, then Liege Barracks, then the Citadel of Huy, and finally a former asylum in Tost, Upper Silesia.

Conditions in those first three camps were a severe test of Wodehouse's resilience and geniality; yet he found the atmosphere of Tost a shade more conducive. The internees even passed the time with a little improvised cricket, and so Wodehouse had his first semi-serious game in twenty-seven years. 'We used to play with a string ball (string wound round a nut) which our sailors manufactured,' he would recall. Always abler with ball than bat, he remembered having 'played havoc with the opposition with slow leg-breaks'. In time the Germans would permit their prisoners a weekly excursion to the institution's sports field, where they had use of a proper ball. Wodehouse found he 'could still skittle the rabble out, but was helpless when I came up against a decent bat'.

On the evening of 21 June 1941 Wodehouse was playing with his fellow inmates – 'in the middle of an over', even – when Gestapo officers arrived to inform him he was being sent to Berlin. His internment was concluded, but the war, of course, still had immeasurable misery to inflict – a story far too big for these pages. Eventually, in 1947, Wodehouse and his wife returned to the US, and this time they never left.

*

In 1975 Wodehouse told a BBC interviewer: 'My game now is baseball. Oh I am crazy about it. I'd much rather watch a baseball game than a cricket match. I think what's wrong with cricket, if you are keen on one team – I was very keen on Surrey ... well, I'd go to see Surrey play, say, Lancashire, and I'd find Lancashire has won the toss, and they'd bat all day, whereas with baseball, the other side only bats about ten minutes at the most.'

How perfectly foul, one might say, if one is of a traditionalist bent. But something about the special rhythms of America's great sports had got Wodehouse hooked. C.L.R. James once imagined that an ancient Athenian transported through time to study a modern cricket match might suppose that 'the white-flannelled actors moving so sedately from place to place were performing the funeral rites over the corpse of a hero buried between the wickets'. Such is the special atmosphere of cricket, and Wodehouse was divorced from it for the last three decades of his life. But he managed one more treatment of the game – a tad sardonic, but set most fittingly at 'The Home of Cricket' – in his 1950 collection Nothing Serious.

'HOW'S THAT, UMPIRE?'

The story of Conky Biddle's great love begins at about six-forty-five on an evening in June in the Marylebone district of London. He had spent the day at Lord's cricket ground watching a cricket match, and driving away at close of play had been held up in a traffic jam. And held up alongside his taxi was a car with a girl at the wheel. And he had just lit a cigarette and was thinking of this and that, when he heard her say:

'Cricket is not a game. It is a mere shallow excuse for walking in your sleep.'

It was at this point that love wound its silken fetters about Conky. He leaped like a jumping bean and the cigarette fell from his nerveless fingers. If a girl who talked like that was not his dream girl, he didn't know a dream girl when he heard one.

You couldn't exactly say that he fell in love at first sight, for owing to the fact that in between him and her, obscuring the visibility, there was sitting a robust blighter in blue flannel with a pin stripe, he couldn't see her. All he had to go on was her voice, but that was ample. It was a charming voice with an American intonation. She was probably, he thought, an American angel who had stepped down from Heaven for a short breather in London.

'If I see another cricket game five thousand years from now,' she said, 'that'll be soon enough.'

Her companion plainly disapproved of these cracks. He said in a stiff, sniffy sort of way that she had not seen cricket at its best that afternoon, play having been greatly interfered with by rain.

'A merciful dispensation,' said the girl. 'Cricket with hardly any cricket going on is a lot better than cricket where the nuisance persists uninterrupted. In my opinion the ideal contest would be one where it rained all day and the rival teams stayed home doing their crossword puzzles.'

The traffic jam then broke up and the car shot forward like a B.29, leaving the taxi nowhere.

The reason why this girl's words had made so deep an impression on the young Biddle was that of all things in existence, with the possible exception of slugs and his uncle Everard, Lord Plumpton, he disliked cricket most. As a boy he had been compelled to play it, and grown to man's estate he was compelled to watch it. And if there was one spectacle that saddened him more than another in a world where the man of sensibility is always being saddened by spectacles, it was that of human beings, the heirs of the ages, waddling about in pads and shouting 'How's that, umpire?'

He had to watch cricket because Lord Plumpton told him to, and he was dependent on the other for his three squares a day. Lord Plumpton was a man who knew the batting averages of every first-class cricketer back to the days when they used to play in top hats and whiskers, and recited them to Conky after dinner. He liked to show Conky with the assistance of an apple (or, in winter, of an orange) how Bodger of Kent got the fingerspin which enabled him to make the ball dip and turn late on a sticky wicket. And frequently when Conky was walking along the street with him and working up to touching him for a tenner, he would break off the conversation at its most crucial point in order to demonstrate with his umbrella how Codger of Sussex made his late cut through the slips.

It was to the home of this outstanding louse, where he had a small bedroom on an upper floor, that Conky was now on his way. Arriving at journey's end, he found a good deal of stir and bustle going on, with doctors coming downstairs with black bags and parlourmaids going upstairs with basins of gruel, and learned from the butler that Lord Plumpton had sprained his ankle.

'No, really?' said Conky, well pleased, for if his uncle had possessed as many ankles as a centipede he would thoroughly have approved of him spraining them all. 'I suppose I had better go up and view the remains.'

He proceeded to the star bedroom and found his uncle propped up with pillows, throwing gruel at the parlourmaid. It was plain that he was in no elfin mood. He was looking like a mass murderer, though his face lacked the genial expression which you often see in mass murderers, and he glared at Conky with the sort of wild regret which sweeps over an irritable man when he sees a loved one approaching his sick bed and realises that he has used up all the gruel.

'What ho, Uncle Everard,' said Conky. 'The story going the round of the clubs is that you have bust a joint of sorts. What happened?'

Lord Plumpton scowled darkly. He looked now like a mass murderer whose stomach ulcers are paining him.

'I'll tell you what happened. You remember I had to leave you at Lord's to attend a committee meeting at my club. Well, as I was walking back from the club, there were some children playing cricket in the street and one of them skied the ball towards extra-cover, so naturally I ran out into the road to catch it. I judged it to a nicety and had just caught it when a homicidal lunatic of a girl came blinding along at ninety miles an hour in her car and knocked me base over apex. One of these days,' said Lord Plumpton, licking his lips, 'I hope to meet that girl again, preferably down a dark alley. I shall skin her very slowly with a blunt knife, dip her in boiling oil, sever her limb from limb, assemble those limbs on the pavement and dance on them.'

'And rightly,' said Conky. 'These girls who bust your ankles and prevent you going to Lord's tomorrow need a sharp lesson.'

'What do you mean, prevent me going to Lord's tomorrow? Do you think a mere sprained ankle will stop me going to a cricket match? I shall be there, with you at my side. And now,' said Lord Plumpton, wearying of these exchanges, 'go to hell!'

Conky did not go to hell, but he went downstairs and out on to the front steps to get a breath of air. He was feeling low and depressed. He had been so certain that he would be able to get tomorrow off. He had turned to go in again when he heard a noise of brakes as a car drew up behind him.

'Excuse me,' said a voice. 'Could I see Lord Plumpton?'

Simple words, but their effect on Conky as he recognised that silvery voice was to make him quiver from stay-combed hair to shoe sole. He uttered a whinnying cry which, as he swivelled round and for the first time was privileged to see her face, became a gasp. The voice had been the voice of an angel. The face measured up to the voice.

Seeing him, she too gasped. This was apt to be the reaction of the other sex on first beholding Conky Biddle, for though his I.Q. was low his outer crust was rather sensational. He was, indeed, a dazzlingly good-looking young man, who out-Caryed Grant and began where Gregory Peck left off.

'I say,' he said, going to the car and placing a foot on the running-board, 'Don't look now, but did I by chance hear you expressing a wish to meet my uncle, Lord Plumpton?'

'That's right. I recently flattened him out with my car, and I was planning to give him some flowers.'

'I wouldn't,' said Conky. 'I really wouldn't. I say this as a friend. Time, the great healer, will have to pull up its socks and spit on its hands quite a bit before it becomes safe for you to enter the presence.'

'I see. Then I'll take the blooms around the corner and have them delivered by a messenger boy. How's that, umpire?'

Conky winced. It was as though he had heard this divine creature sully her lips with something out of a modern historical novel.

'Good God!' he said. 'Where did you pick up that obscene expression?'

'From your uncle. He was chanting it at the top of his voice when I rammed him. A mental case, I imagine. What does it mean?'

'It's what you say at cricket.'

'Cricket!' The girl shuddered strongly. 'Shall I tell you what I think of cricket?'

'I have already heard your views. Your car got stuck abaft my taxi in a traffic block this evening. I was here, if you follow what I mean, and you were there, a few feet to the nor'-nor'-east, so I was able to drink in what you were saying about cricket. Would you mind if I thanked you with tears in my eyes?'

'Not at all. But don't you like cricket? I thought all Englishmen loved it.'

'Not this Englishman. It gives me the pip.'

'Me, too. I ought never to have gone near that Lord's place. But in a moment of weakness I let myself be talked into it by my fiancé.'

Conky reeled.

'Oh, my sainted aunt! Have you got a fiancé?'

'Not now.'

Conky stopped reeling.

'Was he the bloke you were talking to in the car?'

'That's right. Eustace Davenport-Simms. I think he plays for Essex or Sussex or somewhere. My views were too subversive for him, so after kidding back and forth for a while we decided to cancel the order for the wedding cake.'

'I thought he seemed a bit sniffy.'

'He got sniffier.'

'Very sensible of you not to marry a cricketer.'

'So I felt.'

'The upshot, then, when all the smoke has blown away, is that you are once more in circulation?'

'Yes.'

'Well, that's fine,' said Conky. A sudden thought struck him. 'I say, would you object if I pressed your little hand?'

'Some other time, I think.'

'Any time that suits you.'

'You see, I have to hie me back to my hotel and dress. I'm late already, and my father screams like a famished hyæna if he's kept waiting for his rations.'

And with a rapid thrust of her shapely foot she set the machinery in motion and vanished round the corner on two wheels, leaving Conky staring after her with a growing feeling of desolation. He had just realised that he was unaware of her name, address and telephone number and had had what was probably his last glimpse of her. If the expression 'Ships that pass in the night' had been familiar to him, he would certainly have uttered it, using clenched teeth for the purpose.

It was a Conky with heart bowed down and a general feeling of having been passed through the wringer who accompanied his uncle to Lord's next morning. The thought that a Grade A soulmate had come into his life and buzzed out again, leaving no clue to her identity or whereabouts, was a singularly bitter one. Lord

Plumpton on the journey to the Mecca of cricket spoke well and easily of the visit of the Australian team of 1921, but Conky proved a distrait listener; so distrait that Lord Plumpton prodded him irascibly in the ribs and called him an infernal goggle-eyed fathead, which of course he was.

He was still in a sort of trance when they took their seats in the pavilion, but here it was less noticeable, for everybody else was in a sort of trance. The somnambulists out in the field tottered to and fro, and the spectators lay back and let their eyes go glassy. For perhaps an hour nothing happened except that Hedger of Middlesex, waking like Abou ben Adhem from a deep dream of peace, flicked his bat at a rising ball and edged it into the hands of a sleeper dozing in what is technically known as the gully. Then Lord Plumpton, who had been silent except for an occasional 'Nice! Nice!' sat up with a sudden jerk and an explosive 'Well, I'm dashed!' and glared sideways at the three shilling seats which adjoined the pavilion. And Conky, following his gaze, felt his heart execute four separate buck and wing steps and come to rest quivering like a jelly in a high wind.

'Well, I'm dashed!' said Lord Plumpton, continuing to direct at the three shilling seats the kind of look usually associated with human fiends in mystery stories. 'There's that blasted girl!'

It was not a description which Conky himself would have applied to the divinest of her sex, nor one which he enjoyed hearing applied to her, and for a moment he was in two minds as to whether to haul off and sock his relative on the beezer. Wiser counsels prevailed, and he said:

'Yes, there she spouts.'

Lord Plumpton seemed surprised.

'You know her?'

'Just slightly. She ran into me last night.'

'Into you, too? Good gad, the female's a public menace. If she's allowed to remain at large, the population of London will be decimated. I've a good mind to go over and tell her what I think of her.'

'But your uncle, ankle.'

'What the devil are you gibbering about?'

'I mean your ankle, uncle. You mustn't walk about on it. How would it be if I popped over and acquainted her with your displeasure?'

Lord Plumpton considered.

'Yes, that's not a bad idea. A surprisingly good idea, in fact, considering what a nitwit you are. But pitch it strong.'

'Oh, I will,' said Conky.

He rose and hurried off, and Lord Plumpton fell into conversation with the barely animate spectator on his left. They were soon deep in an argument as to whether it was at square leg or at extra-cover that D. C. L. Wodger of Gloucestershire had fielded in 1904.

If the girl had looked like the better class of angel in the uncertain light of last night, she looked more than ever so in the reasonably bright sunshine of today. She was one of those lissom girls of medium height. Her eyes and hair were a browny hazel. The general effect was of a seraph who ate lots of yeast.

'Oh, hullo,' said Conky, lowering himself into a seat beside her. 'We meet again, what?'

She seemed surprised and startled. In her manner, as she gazed at his clean-cut face and then into his frank blue eyes, there was something that might almost be described as fluttering.

'You!' she cried. 'What are you doing here?'

'Just watching cricket.'

'But you told me last night that cricket gave you the pip, which I imagine is something roughly equivalent to the megrims or the heeby-jeebies.'

'Quite. But, you see, it's like this. My uncle is crazy about the ghastly game and I'm dependent on him, so when he says "Come along and watch cricket", I have to come along and watch it like a lynx.'

The girl frowned. It was as if she had been hurt and disappointed.

'Why are you dependent on your uncle? Why don't you get a job?'

Conky hastened to defend himself.

'I do get a job. I get dozens of jobs. But I lose them all. The trouble is, you see, that I'm not very bright.'

'No?'

'Not very. That's why they call me Conky.'

'Do they call you Conky?'

'Invariably. What started it was an observation one of the masters at school happened to drop one day. He said, addressing me— "To attempt to drive information into your head, Biddle, is no easy task, for Providence, mysterious in its workings has, given you instead of the more customary human brain a skull full of concrete." So after that everyone called me Conky.'

'I see. What sort of jobs have you tried?'

'Practically everything except Chancellor of the Duchy of Lancaster.'

'And you get fired every time?'

'Every time.'

'I'm sorry.'

'It's dashed white of you to be sorry, but as a matter of fact it's all right.'

'How do you mean it's all right?'

Conky hesitated. Then he reflected that if you couldn't confide in an angel in human shape, who could you confide in? He glanced about him. Except for themselves, the three shilling tier of seats was almost empty.

'Well, you'll keep it under your hat, won't you, because it's supposed to be very hush-hush at the moment. I am on the eve of making a stupendous fortune. You know sea water?'

'The stuff that props the ship up when you come over from New York?'

'That's right. Well, you probably aren't aware of it, but it's full of gold, and I'm in with a fellow who's got a secret process for scooping it out. I saw his advertisement in the paper saying that if you dashed along and brassed up quick you could get in on an invention of vast possibilities, so I dashed along and brassed up. He was a nice chap and let me into the thing without a murmur. Bloke of the name of MacSporran. I happened to have scraped up ten quid, so I put that in and he tells me that at a conservative estimate I shall get back about two hundred and fifty thousand. I call that a nice profit.'

'Very nice.'

'Yes, it's all very convenient. And when I say that, I'm not thinking so much of the jolliness of having all that splosh in the old sock, I am alluding more to the difference this has made in what you might call my matrimonial plans. If I want to get married, I mean. What I'm driving at,' said Conky, giving her a melting look, 'is that I am now in a position, when I meet the girl I love, to put the binge on a practical basis.'

'I see.'

'In fact,' said Conky, edging a little closer, 'I might almost start making my plans at once.'

'That's the spirit. Father's slogan is "Do it now", and he's a tycoon.'

'I thought a tycoon was a sort of storm.'

'No, a millionaire.'

'Is your father a millionaire?'

'Yes, and more pouring in all the time.'

'Oh?'

A sudden chill had come over Conky's dashing mood. The one thing he had always vowed he would never do was marry for money. For years his six uncles and seven aunts had been urging him to cash in on his looks and grab something opulent. They had paraded heiresses before him in droves, but he had been firm. He had his principles.

Of course, in the present case it was different. He loved this girl with every fibre of his being. But all the same ... No, he told himself, better wait till his bank balance was actually bulging.

With a strong effort he changed the conversation.

'Well, as I was saying,' he said, 'I hope to clean up shortly on an impressive scale, and when I do I'll never watch another cricket match as long as I live. Arising from which, what on earth are you doing here, holding the views on cricket which you do?'

A slight shadow of disappointment seemed to pass over the girl's face. It was as if she had been expecting the talk to develop along different lines.

'Oh, I came for a purpose.'

'Eh? What purpose?'

She directed his attention to the rows of living corpses in the pavilion. Lord Plumpton and his friend, having settled the Wodger question, were leaning back with their hats over their eyes. It was difficult to realise that life still animated those rigid limbs.

'When I was here yesterday, I was greatly struck by the spectacle of those stiffs over there. I wondered if it was possible to stir them up into some sort of activity.'

'I doubt it.'

'I'm a little dubious myself. They're like fish on a slab or a Wednesday matinee audience. Still, I thought I would try. Yesterday, of course I hadn't elastic and ammo with me.'

'Elastic? Ammo?'

Conky stared. From the recesses of her costume she had produced a piece of stout elastic and a wad of tin foil. She placed the tin foil on the elastic and then between her teeth. Then, turning, she took careful aim at Lord Plumpton.

For a sighting shot it was an admirable effort. Conky, following the projectile with a rapt gaze, saw his uncle start and put a hand to his ear. There seemed little reason to doubt that he had caught it amidships.

'Good Lord!' he cried. 'Here, after you with that elastic. I used to do that at school, and many was the fine head I secured. I wonder if the old skill still lingers.'

It was some minutes later that Lord Plumpton turned to the friend beside him.

'Wasps very plentiful this year,' he said.

The friend blinked drowsily.

'Watts?'

'Wasps.'

'There was A. R. K. Watts who used to play for Sussex. Ark we used to call him.'

'Not Watts. Wasps.'

'Wasps?'

'Wasps.'

'What about them?'

'They seem very plentiful. One stung me in the ear just now. And now one of them has knocked off my hat. Most extraordinary.'

A man in a walrus moustache who had played for Surrey in 1911 came along, and Lord Plumpton greeted him cordially.

'Hullo, Freddie.'

'Hullo.'

'Good game.'

'Very. Exciting.'

'Wasps are a nuisance, though.'

'Wasps?'

'Wasps.'

'What Wasps?'

'I don't know their names. The wasps around here.'

'No wasps around here.'

'Yes.'

'Not in the pavilion at Lord's. You can't get in unless you're a member.'

'Well, one has just knocked off my hat. And look, there goes Jimmy's hat.'

The walrus shook his head. He stooped and picked up a piece of tin foil.

'Someone's shooting this stuff at you. Used to do it myself a long time ago. Ah yes,' he said, peering about him, 'I see where the stuff's coming from. That girl over there in the three shilling seats with your nephew. If you look closely, you'll see she's drawing a bead on you now.'

Lord Plumpton looked, started and stiffened.

'That girl again! Is one to be beset by her through all eternity? Send for the attendants! Rouse the attendants and give them their divisional orders. Instruct the attendants to arrest her immediately and bring her to the committee room.'

And so it came about that just as Conky was adjusting the elastic to his lips a short while later and preparing to loose off, a heavy hand fell on his shoulder, and there was a stern-faced man in the uniform of a Marylebone Cricket Club attendant. And simultaneously another heavy hand fell on the girl's shoulder, and there was another stern-faced man in the uniform of another Marylebone Cricket Club attendant.

It was a fair cop.

The committee room of the Marylebone Cricket Club is a sombre and impressive apartment. Photographs of bygone cricketers, many of them with long beards, gaze down from the walls – accusingly, or so it seems to the man whose conscience is not as clear as it might be. Only a man with an exceptionally clear conscience can enter this holy of holies without feeling that he is about to be stripped of his M.C.C. tie and formally ticketed as a social leper.

This is particularly so when, as in the present instance the President himself is seated at his desk. It was at Lord Plumpton's request that he was there now. It had seemed to Lord Plumpton that a case of this magnitude could be dealt with adequately only at the very highest levels.

He mentioned this in his opening speech for the prosecution. 'I demand,' said Lord Plumpton, 'the most exemplary punishment for an outrage unparalleled in the annals of the Marylebone Cricket Club, the dear old club we all love so well, if you know what I mean.' Here he paused as if intending to bare his head, but realising that he had not got his hat on continued, 'I mean to say, taking pot-shots at members with a series of slabs of tin foil, dash it! If that isn't a nice bit of box fruit, what is? Bad enough, if you see what I'm driving at, to take pot-shots at even the canaille, as they call them in France, who squash in in the free seats, but when it comes to pot-shotting members in the pavilion, I mean where are we? Personally I would advocate skinning the girl, but if you consider that too extreme I am prepared to settle for twenty years in solitary confinement. A menace to the community, that's what this girl is. Busting about in her car and knocking people endways with one hand and flicking their hats off with the other, if you follow my drift. She reminds me of ... who was that woman in the Bible whose work was always so raw? ... Delilah? ... No ... It's on the tip of my tongue ... Ah yes, Jezebel. She's a modern streamlined Jezebel, dash her insides.'

'Uncle Everard,' said Conky, 'you are speaking of the woman I love.'

The girl gave a little gasp.

'No, really?' she said.

'Absolutely,' said Conky. 'I had intended to mention it earlier. I don't know your name ...

'Clarissa. Clarissa Binstead.'

'How many s's?'

'Three, if you count the Binstead.'

'Clarissa, I love you. Will you be my wife?'

'Sure,' said the girl. 'I was hoping you'd suggest it. And what all the fuss is about is more than I can understand. Why when we go to a ball-game in America, we throw pop bottles.'

There was a silence.

'Are you an American, madam?' said the President.

'One hundred per cent. Oh, say, can you see ... No, I never can remember how it goes after that. I could whistle it for you.'

The President had drawn Lord Plumpton aside. His face was grave and anxious.

'My dear Everard,' he said in an urgent undertone, 'we must proceed carefully here, very carefully. I had no notion this girl was American. Somebody should have informed me. The last thing we want is an international incident, particularly at a moment when we are hoping, if all goes well, to get into America's ribs for a bit of the stuff. I can fully appreciate your wounded feelings ...'

'And how about my wounded topper?'

'The club will buy you a new hat, and then, my dear fellow, I would strongly urge that we consider the matter closed.'

'You mean not skin her?'

'No.'

'Not slap her into the cooler for twenty years?'

'No. There might be very unfortunate repercussions.'

'Oh, all right,' said Lord Plumpton sullenly. 'Oh, very well. But,' he proceeded on a brighter note, 'there is one thing I can do, and that is disinherit this frightful object here. Hoy!' he said to Conky.

'Hullo?' said Conky.

'You are no longer a nephew of mine.'

'Well, that's a bit of goose,' said Conky.

As he came out of the committee room, he was informed by an attendant that a gentleman wished to speak to him on the telephone. Excusing himself to Clarissa and bidding her wait for him downstairs Conky went to the instrument, listened for a few moments, then reeled away, his eyes bulging and his jaw a-droop. He found Clarissa at the spot agreed upon.

'Hullo, there,' said Conky. 'I say, you remember me asking you to be my wife?'

'Yes.'

'You said you would.'

'Yes.'

'Well, the words that spring to the lips are "Will you?" Because I'm afraid the whole thing's off. That was MacSporran on the 'phone. He said he'd made a miscalculation, and my tenner won't be enough to start that sea water scheme going. He said he would need another thirty thousand pounds and could I raise it? I said No, and he said "Too bad, too bad". And I said: "Do I get my tenner back?" and he said: "No, you don't get your tenner back." So there you are. I can't marry you.'

Clarissa wrinkled her forehead.

'I don't see it. Father's got it in gobs. He will provide.'

'Not for me, he won't. I always swore I'd never marry a girl for her money.'

'You aren't marrying me for my money. You're marrying me because we're soulmates.'

'That's true. Still, you appear to have a most ghastly lot of the stuff, and I haven't a bean.'

'Suppose you had a job?'

'Oh, if I had a job.'

'That's all right, then. Father runs a gigantic business and he can always find room for another Vice-President.'

'Vice-President?'

'Yes.'

'But I don't know enough to be a Vice-President.'

'It's practically impossible not to know enough to be a Vice-President. All you would have to do would be to attend conferences and say "Yes" when Father made a suggestion.'

'What in front of a whole lot of people?'

'Well, at least you could nod.'

'Oh yes, I could nod.'

'Then that's settled. Kiss me.'

Their lips met long and lingeringly. Conky came out of the clinch with sparkling eyes and a heightened colour. He raised a hand to heaven.

'How's that, umpire?' he cried.

'Jolly good show, sir,' said Clarissa.

THE PREFACE TO
THE GOLF OMNIBUS

From July 1952 until his death in 1975, Wodehouse lived in Remsenburg, New York, close to the fine golf course of Shinnecock Hills, with its Stanford White-designed clubhouse. Shinnecock was not yet the prestigious major championship venue it would become; but, in any case, Wodehouse never became a member. To all intents and purposes he was done roaming the fairways.

The final accomplishment of his golfing career, rather, was the 1973 Golf Omnibus *which collected his stories from tee to green in a substantive, indeed near-cuboid, volume. The lines with which he introduced the* Omnibus *are as well-minted as ever, and an elegant gathering together of all the themes that golf had gifted to him.*

As I start to write this Preface, I am brooding a bit. My brow is furrowed, sort of, and I can't help sighing a good deal.

The trouble about reaching the age of ninety-two, which I did last October, is that regrets for a misspent life are bound to creep in, and whenever you see me with a furrowed brow you can be sure that what is on my mind is the thought that if only I had taken up golf earlier and devoted my whole time to it instead of fooling about writing stories and things, I might have got my handicap down to under eighteen. If only they had put a putter in my hands when I was four and taught me the use of the various clubs, who knows what heights I might not have reached. It is this reflection that has always made my writing so sombre, its whole aroma like that of muddy shoes in a Russian locker room.

And yet I may have managed to get a few rays of sunshine into the stories which follow. If so, this is due to the fact that while I was writing them I won my first and only trophy, a striped umbrella in a hotel tournament at Aiken, South Carolina, where, hitting them squarely on the meat for once, I went through a field of some of the fattest retired businessmen in America like a devouring flame.

I was never much of a golfer. Except for that glorious day at Aiken I was always one of the dregs, the sort of man whose tee shots, designed to go due north, invariably went nor-nor-east or in a westerly direction. But how I loved the game. I have sometimes wondered if we of the canaille don't get more pleasure out of it than the top-notchers. For an untouchable like myself two perfect drives in a round would wipe out all memory of sliced approach shots and foozled putts, whereas if Jack Nicklaus does a sixty-four he goes home and thinks morosely that if he had not just missed that eagle on the seventh, he would have had a sixty-three.

I have made no attempt to bring this book up to date, and many changes have taken place since I wrote 'The Clicking of Cuthbert' in 1916. Time like an ever-rolling stream bears all its sons away, and with them have gone the names of most of the golf clubs so dear to me. I believe one still drives with a driver nowadays, though at any moment we may have to start calling it the Number One wood, but where is the mashie now, where the cleek, the spoon and the baffy?

All Scottish names, those, dating back to the days (1593 A.D.) when we are told that John Henrie and Pat Rogie were imprisoned for 'playing of the Gowff' on the links of Leith every Sabbath the time of the sermonises'. It is very sad, the way the Scottish atmosphere has gone out of the game. In my youth, when the Badminton book was a comparatively new publication, one took it for granted that to be a good golfer you had to be Scottish, preferably with a name like Sandy McHoots or Jock Auchtermuchty. And how we reverenced them. 'These,' we said, 'are the men whose drives fly far, like bullets from a rifle, who when they do a hole in par regard it as a trifle. Of such as these the bard has said, 'Hech thrawfu' raltie rorkie, wi' thecht ta' croonie clapperhead and fash wi' unco' pawkie'.' And where are they now? How long is it since a native Scot won an Open? All Americans these days, except for an occasional Mexican.

No stopping Progress, of course, but I do think it a pity to cast away lovely names like mashie and baffy in favour of numbers. I like to think that when I got into a bunker (isn't it called a trap now?) I got out of it, if I ever did, with a niblick and not a wedge. I wonder what Tommy Morris, winner of the British Open four years in succession, would have had to say to all this number six iron, number twelve iron, number twenty-eight iron stuff. Probably he wouldn't have said anything, just made one of those strange Scottish noises at the back of his throat like someone gargling.

A FOOTNOTE. In one of these little opuses I allude to Stout Cortez staring at the Pacific. Shortly after the appearance of this narrative in the Saturday Evening Post I received a letter from a usually well-informed source which began

Dear Sir, *you big stiff:*

Where do you get that Cortez stuff? It was Balboa.

This, I believe, is historically accurate. On the other hand, if Cortez was good enough for Keats, he is good enough for me. Besides, even if it was Balboa, the Pacific was open for being stared at about that time, and I see no reason why Cortez should not have had a look at it as well.

P.G. WODEHOUSE.

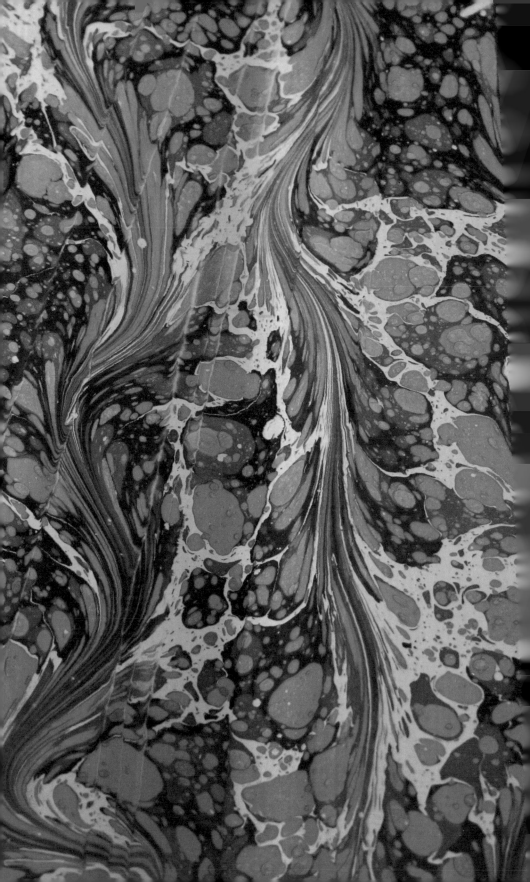